Life After Bankruptcy

The Complete, Do-It-Yourself Guide to Surviving and Prospering After Personal Bankruptcy

By Charles Price
Attorney at Law

Practical Publications, Inc.,
Tallahassee, Florida

Life After Bankruptcy: The Complete
Do-It-Yourself Guide to Surviving and
Prospering After Personal Bankruptcy

Published by
Practical Publications, Inc.
P.O. Box 1244
Tallahassee, FL 32302
(904) 877-2095

Printed and bound in the United States of America
by McNaughton & Gunn, Inc. of Saline, Michigan

Cover design by Gallery Graphics of Tallahassee, Florida

NOTE: This publication is designed to provide accurate and authoritative information in regard to the subject matter covered. It is sold with the understanding that the publisher is not engaged in rendering legal, accounting or other professional service. If legal advice or other expert assistance is required, the services of a competent professional person should be sought.

Library of Congress Catalog Card Number: 93-83404
ISBN 1-882784-13-8

Acknowledgements

The author gratefully acknowledges the following people for their support and creative contributions:

My wife, Lonnie, who endured many hardships while I wrote this book. Without her continuing support and assistance, this book would still be just a few pages on my office floor. She was my editor, advisor, and critic—all jobs for which I rarely thanked her.

My Mother, who was always there to catch me when I fell. She sacrificed her entire life to ensure that my brother and I would excel in all of life's pursuits. Without her unwavering emotional devotion—and financial support—I would never have made it.

My brother Walter, and sister-in-law, Barb, for helping me to research many areas of the book. Additionally, I'd like to thank Walter for meticulously reviewing and editing several early versions of the book. He is truly the most meticulous person I know.

My Father, for his continuing financial support and for providing many useful comments on earlier versions of the book. He finally persuaded me to stop writing like a lawyer.

My aunt and uncle, June and Buddy, for their valuable comments and continuing moral and financial support.

My brother-in-law, Tommy Iamaio, who provided invaluable information about current trends in automobile financing.

My good friend Joe Hope, who constantly badgered me until I completed the book. His enthusiasm for the project kept me going when I stalled.

Everyone at RAM Research Corporation, for allowing me to quote their excellent materials on catalog credit cards, and for providing useful information about secured credit cards. Their many publications have helped me personally and professionally.

My good friend Bob Bivins, who guided my professional career, and fine-tuned my writing abilities. He has always been the voice of reason and logic that argues against my wildest dreams—but never fails to finance them. I am forever indebted to him—literally.

Dedication

I dedicate this book to all who endure the pain and agony of bankruptcy, but have the strength and courage to rise from the ashes.

Contents

1. Beginning the Quest

2. Reviewing Your Bankruptcy File

3. Learning the Law

4. Reviewing Your Credit File

5. Your Equifax Credit Report

6. Your Trans Union Credit Report

7. Your TRW Credit Report

8. Finding the Mistakes

9. Repairing Your Credit

10. Complaining About Credit Bureaus

11. Rebuilding Your Credit

12. Transportation

13. Housing

14. Employment

15. Education & Discrimination

16. Avoiding Credit Scams

17. Starting a New Life

A1. Bankruptcy Courts

A2. State Consumer Protection Agencies

A3. Banks Offering Secured Bankcards

A4. Restrictions on Credit Repair Companies

A5. Additional Resources

Chapter 1

Beginning the Quest

You gain strength, courage and confidence by every experience in which you really stop to look fear in the face. You are able to say to yourself, "I lived through this horror. I can take the next thing that comes along." ... You must do the next thing you think you cannot do.

Anna Eleanor Roosevelt

O.K. You did it. You filed for BANKRUPTCY. You wiped out most or all of your debts, and you probably got to keep most of your property too. Most people probably think you got a good deal.

But, I know better. I know that your bankruptcy haunts you every day. I know that you suffer from guilt and feelings of inadequacy, and cringe every time you think someone might find out about your "dark" secret. I know that you'd like to get on with your life, but your bankruptcy keeps getting in your way. I know that you wish your lawyer had told you what your life would be like after bankruptcy. And, I know that you wish that you'd never filed for bankruptcy—believe me, I know.

I know because I've felt all these feelings—the shame, the guilt, and the low self-esteem. That's right. I declared personal bankruptcy too. And although it's been more than seven years now, I still feel its effects. Believe me—I know what you're feeling and what you're up against.

Fortunately, my bankruptcy was the BEGINNING of my success. Sure, I've had many setbacks along the way. But, I didn't let these setbacks stop my quest for success. I kept pushing forward, and turned my life around. After all, that's what bankruptcy is all about.

And, you can turn your life around too! My goal is to help in your quest. During the last seven years, I've learned everything I can about bankruptcy and consumer credit laws. I studied diligently in law school for three years, and practiced bankruptcy law after that. This book is the result of those years of study and research, and many hours spent interviewing experts in finance, real estate, banking, and consumer credit. Now all this information is yours!

Over the course of this book, I will share with you everything you need to know about surviving the effects of your bankruptcy. You'll learn how to read your credit report, repair any bad credit information, and gain new credit. But that's not enough. I want you to do more than just survive. I want you to prosper as well.

Therefore, I'll also tell you about strategies that you can use to get ahead in life—how to buy a car or house, how to avoid discrimination and credit scams, and how to continue your education. But ... I can only present the information to you. YOU have to make the commitment to succeed after bankruptcy. It's your life, and it's up to you to make the most of it. Are you ready? Then let's go!

Success Stories

I want to show you just how much you can achieve after your bankruptcy. And, what better way to do that than with a good story?

Frank and Ethel fought hard to keep their Seattle candy business. Although they made some of the best candy around, nothing ever seemed to go right. Twice they tried, and twice they failed. Finally, they faced the inevitable and filed for bankruptcy.

Most people would probably say they were failures. After two failed business efforts, they should have given up. That's what most people would do. After all, how many times do you need to fail before you realize you're a failure?

Well, fortunately for all of us, Frank and Ethel didn't give up. They knew they were winners and were determined to be successful. So they moved to Minnesota and tried again.

This time, they were successful. After three years, they finally came up with the winning combination—the Milky Way candy bar. Yes, that's right. Frank and Ethel were Frank and Ethel Mars, the original founders of the Mars, Inc. empire. With their candy fortune, Frank and Ethel financed their son's British candy company. The rest is history. Today, Mars, Inc. is one of the world's largest companies. And to think—it all started with bankruptcy, and a determination to be successful.

Your Own Success Story

I could tell you thousands of bankruptcy success stories. The people behind these stories are ordinary people—just like you and me—but with a true desire to succeed and prosper. And you can succeed and prosper too. You may not create a candy empire, but you CAN succeed in whatever you WANT to do. But ... you MUST believe in yourself.

Unfortunately, bankruptcy has a way of preventing this. You see, "bankruptcy" isn't just a word, it's also an emotion. Think about your bankruptcy. How does it make you feel? sad? ... angry? ... frustrated? If you're like most people, your bankruptcy has probably caused you to feel one or more of these emotions.

Unfortunately, these feelings probably reflect how you feel about yourself, and probably how you think other people feel about you. O.K. Let's try a test. How do you think other people feel about bankruptcy? Or more precisely, how do you think other people feel about YOUR bankruptcy? I'm not talking about people that have filed for bankruptcy. I'm talking about all of the OTHER people—the people that have never personally experienced bankruptcy.

I've asked hundreds of bankrupts this same question. And unfortunately, the answer has always been remarkably similar. The OTHER people think that bankrupts are deadbeats, cheaters, and spenders. THEY think that bankrupts are responsible for higher consumer prices, higher interest rates, world turbulence, earthquakes, and other forms of man-made and natural disasters. And maybe some of that is true. But it doesn't matter. You know the special circumstances that forced you into bankruptcy.

That's right ... FORCED you into bankruptcy! If you're like most people, the last thing in the world that you wanted to do was to file for bankruptcy. I understand this completely. With your back against the wall and creditors unwilling to compromise—bankruptcy seemed like the only way out. In fact, at least one study suggests that many consumers resist the bankruptcy court for too long.

In 1989, the Oxford University Press published the results of an extensive survey of personal bankruptcies in a book titled "As We Forgive Our Debtors: Bankruptcy and Consumer Credit in America." In this survey, called the Consumer Bankruptcy Project, several researchers analyzed 1547 bankruptcy cases filed in 1981. These researchers found that most people DO NOT want to file for bankruptcy, and that many people wait too long to do so.

Although the creditor lobby tries to depict bankrupts as criminals, the Consumer Bankruptcy Project proved that this just isn't true. Most people that end up in the bankruptcy court are honest, decent, and honorable people. Most bankruptcies are caused by uncontrollable events like unemployment and unexpected emergencies. THIS is what all the OTHER people fail to realize. Without experiencing the pain and frustration of bankruptcy, the other people will never understand.

Therefore, YOU must understand them. When people discover your "deep" secret, try your best to make them understand the circumstances behind your decision. And if they can't, or won't, accept your reasoning, then let it go at that. THEY may not understand now. But someday they might be in the same situation. Then they'll understand!

In any case, you MUST accept that it happened. For whatever reason, you are now one of the MILLIONS of people that have filed for bankruptcy protection in the last few years. Most of these consumers are honest and law-abiding citizens. You are too! There is NOTHING wrong with you.

However, you may encounter some people who believe that bankruptcy is illegal and immoral. If you do encounter this type of ignorance, it might help you to remember that bankruptcy has been an accepted institution since early times. Civilized cultures have long recognized that bankruptcy is morally and legally necessary to the smooth functioning of society.

For example, the Bible describes an early form of bankruptcy, where debtors were forgiven of their debts and given a "fresh start." Additionally, the Framers of the United States Constitution recognized the importance and necessity of bankruptcy in society, and required that Congress create and administer bankruptcy laws.

So what's the lesson here? Don't be afraid of your bankruptcy. Don't let it handicap you or prevent you from moving forward in life. Bankruptcy isn't illegal or immoral. It's an unfortunate occurrence that happens to good people with bad luck. So don't despair, lift up your head and ...
GET ON WITH YOUR LIFE! Are you ready? O.K. LET'S DO IT!

Miscellaneous Bankruptcy Facts

Did You Know That ...

Over the last 10 years, there has been one bankruptcy filing for every 16 households in the United States.

Approximately 35% of bankruptcy filings are joint filings involving a husband and wife.

On a per capita basis, bankruptcy filings during the 1980's were about double the level of the 1970's, and nearly ten times as high as during the 1940's.

Filings so far in the 1990's are at nearly double the average rate for the 1980's.

Year Ended June 30	Total Filings	Chapter 7	Chapter 11	Chapter 12	Chapter 13	Other Cases
1983	374,734	251,319	21,206	N/A	102,201	8
1984	344,275	232,991	19,913	N/A	91,358	13
1985	364,536	244,647	21,420	N/A	98,452	17
1986	477,856	332,675	24,442	N/A	120,726	13
1987	561,278	397,548	22,564	4,824	136,300	42
1988	594,567	423,789	18,889	3,099	148,771	19
1989	642,993	457,234	17,447	1,717	166,539	56
1990	725,484	505,332	19,591	1,351	199,186	24
1991	880,399	612,324	22,493	1,358	244,192	32
1992	972,490	679,662	24,029	1,634	267,121	44
Totals	5,938,61	4,137,52	211,994	13,983	1,574,84	268

Source: Administrative Office of the U.S. Courts

Chapter 2

Reviewing Your Bankruptcy File

If a little knowledge is dangerous, where is the man who has so much as to be out of danger?

Thomas Henry Huxley

How much do you really know about your bankruptcy? I know that sounds like a strange question. You're probably saying, "I know everything about my bankruptcy. I lived it!"

O.K. You lived it. But, how much do you know about it? Do you know about all the papers you signed and that your attorney prepared? Do you know about all the papers that the judge prepared? Do you know why you still need to pay some creditors, or why you don't need to pay any creditors?

If you don't know the answers, don't worry. I didn't either. I didn't learn what everything meant until I studied bankruptcy in law school. And, I didn't really understand what everything meant until I became a practicing bankruptcy attorney.

Fortunately, you don't need to go to law school or practice law to understand bankruptcy. However, you DO need to understand YOUR bankruptcy and the many papers in your bankruptcy file. Why? Because your bankruptcy file contains some important keys to your future prosperity.

Therefore, in this chapter, I'll give you a very quick summary of the bankruptcy process and tell you about the various papers in your bankruptcy file. And if you don't already have your bankruptcy file, I'll tell you how to get it. Then, in later chapters, I'll show you how to use the information in these bankruptcy papers in your quest for prosperity. So, if you're ready, let's go!

Why do we have bankruptcy laws anyway?

So why do we have bankruptcy laws? You can probably think of the first reason. We have bankruptcy laws because stuff happens. For one reason or another, people get into a position where they can't pay their bills. Then, the creditors start writing, then calling, then visiting, then suing, etc. In the old days, creditors could send you to jail at this point—debtor's prison.

Fortunately, our society has progressed beyond debtor's prison. We now understand that sometimes people just need to call it quits and start over. Therefore, Congress created the bankruptcy laws to give all Americans this opportunity. This is what bankruptcy does. It allows you the opportunity to just call it quits and start over—to give you a "fresh start" in life.

The Automatic Stay

To give you this fresh start, Congress designed the bankruptcy laws to stop creditors from harassing you during, and after, your bankruptcy. To stop creditors from harassing you during your bankruptcy, Congress created the "automatic stay." (If you're interested, you can find the automatic stay provision in Section 362 of the Bankruptcy Code. For you legal buffs, the exact citation is 28 U.S.C. § 362.)

The automatic stay prevents creditors from making ANY collection efforts against you once you file your petition with the bankruptcy court. This allows you to "take a breather" and concentrate on your financial problems without constant harassment.

This meant that your creditors had to stop calling you at home and work, stop sending you threatening letters, and stop any efforts to repossess your property. The "automatic stay" also prevented the electric company from turning off your power, and prevented your landlord from evicting you.

The automatic stay, then, was the first protection you received from the bankruptcy laws. Unfortunately, this protection was only temporary. Once the bankruptcy judge closed your case, the automatic stay stopped protecting you. Without some additional protection, your creditors would have eventually resumed their collection efforts, and you would never have made your fresh start. Therefore, the bankruptcy laws also provided a permanent solution.

Discharged Debts

At the end of your bankruptcy case, the bankruptcy judge probably said that most of your debts were "discharged." This meant that you were no longer personally responsible for repaying them. Therefore, any of your creditors that held these "discharged debts" can NEVER force you to repay them—or even TRY to make you repay them. This gave you the opportunity to make your fresh start in life without the constant fear of harassment from your creditors.

(The bankruptcy judge may not have discharged all of your debts. Certain types of debts are "nondischargeable." Congress believed that certain types of debts, such as alimony, student loans, and tax obligations, are sacred and shouldn't be wiped away with bankruptcy. Therefore, you may still be responsible for repaying some of your debts.)

Exempt Property

By discharging your debts, the bankruptcy court protected you from future harassment. However, if the bankruptcy laws allowed your creditors to take ALL of your belongings, then you'd still be in bad shape. Fortunately, Congress understood that you could only get a fresh start if you had enough assets to begin a new and financially stable life. Therefore, Congress and several state legislatures identified a variety of assets that creditors could not take from you. Federal and state laws call these assets "exempt assets" because they are "exempt" from seizure.

The type and quantity of exempt assets vary from state to state. However, most states generally allow you to exempt some or all of the equity in your house, your work tools and supplies, and your personal articles. A typical exempt property provision would allow you to keep the equity in your home and $1,000 of personal property.

I know that doesn't sound like very much property. However, the bankruptcy court will value your assets at their current value. As you probably know, most of your personal property isn't worth very much after you've used it. Therefore, you can "exempt" a lot more property than you might first imagine. In fact, most debtors can often keep most or all of their assets.

If you were able to exempt most of your assets, the bankruptcy judge probably said that you had a "no asset" bankruptcy. You could have a "no asset" bankruptcy even if you technically had assets—if they were exempt assets. This is because your creditors received "no assets" in repayment of their loans.

Organized Distribution of Your Assets

O.K. So the first goal of the bankruptcy laws is to protect you from creditors and to give you a fresh start. But you're not the only person that the bankruptcy laws try to protect. They also try to protect your creditors—from you and from each other.

To do this, the bankruptcy laws give your creditors an organized method for dividing your nonexempt assets. Without this organized method, your creditors would start a "feeding frenzy" for your assets. Some would get everything, and others would get nothing. However, by providing specific rules for dividing your assets among your various creditors, Congress has created fair and logical distribution schemes.

The bankruptcy code divides these distribution schemes into various "types" of bankruptcy. Each type provides specific protections for your creditors and specific relief for you. For example, if you filed a Chapter 7 bankruptcy, you probably wiped out most of your debts. However, you probably also lost all of your nonexempt assets. That's the trade-off. Each bankruptcy type, or Chapter, has certain advantages and disadvantages—the trade-offs. (Bankruptcy attorneys refer to the type of bankruptcy as "Chapter" because they are literally "chapters" in the bankruptcy code.)

Let's take a moment now to review the three most common types of bankruptcy—Chapter 7, 11, and 13. Because you probably filed one of these types, it's important that you understand the trade-offs. Then, you'll know what you're likely to face in the future.

Chapter 7, the "Liquidation Bankruptcy"

Most people think of Chapter 7 when you mention bankruptcy. If you filed a Chapter 7 bankruptcy, the bankruptcy judge probably eliminated most of your debts. However, you may have paid a high price for this freedom.

Under the Chapter 7 rules, the bankruptcy court takes possession of all your nonexempt assets and liquidates (sells) them to repay your creditors. This is why the bankruptcy code refers to a Chapter 7 bankruptcy as a "liquidation" bankruptcy.

In reality, however, most people who file a Chapter 7 bankruptcy lose few, if any, assets to creditors. As we've already seen, this is because your personal property isn't worth very much after you've used it. You were probably amazed when your attorney valued the total of all your personal property at less than the personal property exemption—perhaps less than $1,000. Suddenly, thanks to depreciation and the creative appraisals of your attorney, you had a no asset bankruptcy case. If so, you were able to walk away from the bankruptcy court with all your assets and without your dischargeable debts. They were gone forever—just bad memories and worthless plastic.

However, Chapter 7 bankruptcies aren't always this painless. If you had substantial assets and filed a Chapter 7 bankruptcy, you probably weren't able to shield many of those assets under the exempt property laws. Therefore, you probably lost these assets to your creditors. Under Chapter 7, you lose ALL of your nonexempt assets to creditors. That's the trade-off. (If you had substantial nonexempt assets, I hope your attorney advised you against filing a Chapter 7 bankruptcy.)

Another disadvantage of filing a Chapter 7 bankruptcy is that it stirs up the most negative feelings in creditors and average individuals who have never faced financial disaster. Why? Because, other than nonexempt assets, a Chapter 7 filer doesn't pay ANYTHING back, unlike the Chapter 11 and Chapter 13 bankruptcies.

Chapters 11 and 13, the "Rehabilitation Bankruptcies"

There are two other types of bankruptcies that consumers may use. The first type is the Chapter 11 bankruptcy. The bankruptcy code calls this type of bankruptcy the "reorganization bankruptcy" because it provides a method for reorganizing, or rearranging, your debts and assets. Unlike the Chapter 7 bankruptcy, the Chapter 11 bankruptcy doesn't force you to liquidate your assets, nor does it automatically eliminate your debts. Instead, it allows you the opportunity to refinance and rearrange your debts under more favorable terms. If all goes as planned, you get to keep your assets, and your creditors get all of their money.

The second type of bankruptcy is the Chapter 13 bankruptcy. The bankruptcy code calls this type of bankruptcy the "Adjustment of Debts of an Individual With Regular Income" bankruptcy. The Chapter 13 bankruptcy is similar in many ways to the Chapter 11 bankruptcy. The main differences between the two involve the total dollar amount of assets and debts. Generally, the Chapter 13 bankruptcy is for average consumers, whereas the Chapter 11 bankruptcy is for those with more assets and greater debt.

Bankruptcy attorneys refer to Chapter 11 and Chapter 13 as the "rehabilitation" bankruptcies. This is probably because under both types, you work with your creditors to repay some or all of your outstanding debts, and in the process are somehow "rehabilitated."

Why would you have filed one of these rehabilitation bankruptcies, instead of the Chapter 7 liquidation bankruptcy? There are two reasons. First, you may have wanted to keep your nonexempt assets. Under a Chapter 7 bankruptcy, you would have lost all of your nonexempt assets to your creditors. Under a Chapter 11 or 13 bankruptcy, however, you were probably able to keep most of your nonexempt assets.

Second, you may have felt a moral responsibility to repay your creditors. Under a Chapter 11 or 13 bankruptcy, you generally repay at least some of your debts. Many people feel better about themselves with the knowledge that they tried to repay some of their debts.

O.K. Let me tell you how these rehabilitation bankruptcies work. The rehabilitation bankruptcies both operate under a "Plan." Generally, your attorney creates the plan and your creditors and the court must agree to it.

If you filed a rehabilitation bankruptcy, your Plan listed your debts and assets, and proposed a timetable for you to repay your creditors—probably over several years. During this time, you repaid some percentage of your total debts and you probably kept your personal assets. In return, the bankruptcy court maintained a constant watch on your financial affairs and the bankruptcy judge expected you to live a frugal life. This was the trade-off.

Then, when you had successfully completed all payments under the Plan, the bankruptcy court probably discharged most of your remaining debts. From that point on, you were free to begin your new financial life with a "fresh start."

Your creditors, of course, were probably happy if you did file a rehabilitation bankruptcy. (Well, maybe not happy, but happier than they could have been.) Creditors generally receive more money from you under the rehabilitation bankruptcies than if they received the proceeds from your liquidated assets.

Therefore, many creditors and credit bureaus are more lenient with people that file a rehabilitation bankruptcy instead of the liquidation bankruptcy. Unfortunately, many other creditors view all bankruptcies with equal contempt, and give little thought to the distinctions between bankruptcy types. Therefore, I hope you chose your bankruptcy with care.

Getting Copies of Your Bankruptcy File

Your bankruptcy file contains most of the information you'll need to start your new life. Therefore, you'll need to become familiar with its various forms and papers. Throughout the rest of this book, we'll look to your bankruptcy file for information about your bankruptcy, your former creditors, and your former debts.

You should have complete records of your bankruptcy file. If you filed the bankruptcy petition yourself, you should have retained copies of everything. If an attorney filed the bankruptcy petition for you, your attorney should have provided you with copies of everything submitted to the bankruptcy court.

Unfortunately, attorneys sometimes fail to keep their clients fully informed. If you didn't receive a complete copy of all records relating to your bankruptcy petition, you should contact your attorney. However, you can also get your bankruptcy records from the Clerk of the Bankruptcy Court.

To help you with this, I've included a nationwide list of Bankruptcy Court Clerks in Appendix 1. To use this list, find the city and state in which you filed your bankruptcy petition. This should be the city and state you lived in when you filed the bankruptcy petition. If Appendix 1 doesn't list your city, look for the nearest city that the appendix does list. This should be the court where you filed your petition.

Once you've located the proper court, call or write the Clerk of the Bankruptcy Court for your records. If it's been some time since you received your discharge, the Clerk may have to retrieve your file from an archive. If so, you may have to pay a small fee, and it may take several weeks to get your file.

Look at Your File

Once you have a copy of your bankruptcy file, it's time to take a close look at it. Although you probably provided the information to your attorney, you may not be familiar with the contents and structure of all the forms and papers contained in your file. It's important, however, that you become familiar with some of these forms and papers, because they contain the information you'll need to correct and repair your credit report.

The Voluntary Petition

The first paper you or your attorney filed with the Bankruptcy Court was probably the Voluntary Petition. Take a moment to look at the sample Voluntary Petitions in Diagrams 2-1 and 2-2. Diagram 2-1 is a copy of Form B1, Form 1. Voluntary Petition. If you filed for bankruptcy after August 1, 1991, your Voluntary Petition will probably resemble Diagram 2-1. If you filed for bankruptcy before August 1, 1991, then your Voluntary Petition will probably resemble Diagram 2-2. (Don't worry if your Voluntary Petition doesn't look like either Diagram. Some attorneys use different forms.)

It's important that you become familiar with the Voluntary Petition, because it starts the bankruptcy process and provides some useful information. Locate your Voluntary Petition from your bankruptcy case file, and then compare it to either Diagram 2-1 or 2-2. Continue reading when you've found the correct diagram.

Case Number

First locate your case number. You should find the case number on the second page of Form 1, or on the first page of the "old" Voluntary Petition form. For either form, you'll probably notice that the type style of the case number looks different from the type style in the rest of the form. This is because the bankruptcy court imprints the number on the form after you hand it to the court's employees. (You may also notice a time and date stamp. This starts the automatic stay and keeps creditors from pursuing collection efforts against you after this time and date.)

Look at Diagrams 2-1 and 2-2. In Diagram 2-1, the case number for our example case is "86-00258." You'll also find this number in Diagram 2-2, the "old" Voluntary Petition form, at the top right of the page. The example case number tells us something about the bankruptcy. We know from looking at the case number that John Consumer filed this case in 1986—from the "86" at the beginning of the case number. We also know that this was the 258th case filed with this bankruptcy court in 1986—this comes from the "00258" at the end of the case number. (You may find more numbers and letters on your case number. Some courts add additional information to the case number, such as the type of bankruptcy you filed or the particular bankruptcy judge that heard your case.)

Now compare your case number with the case number in Diagram 2-1 or 2-2. You should be able to tell the same information about your case number, as we did with the example. For instance, you may have 91-01218. This number shows that you filed your bankruptcy petition in 1991, and that your case was the 1218th case filed in 1991 with this bankruptcy court.

The case number will be very important in all of our upcoming efforts to repair and rebuild your credit history. The bankruptcy court uses the case number to keep track of your case while it's "open" and after it's "closed." The credit reporting agencies and individual creditors will also keep track of your case with this number. That's why it's important that you can find and identify the case number. Once you find the case number, keep track of it for our future discussions on credit repair and rebuilding.

Bankruptcy Court

The next bit of information on the Voluntary Petition is the name and location of the bankruptcy court that handled your bankruptcy case. Look at Diagrams 2-1 and 2-2. For Diagram 2-1, you'll find the name of the bankruptcy court in the first box on the form. The box has the permanent inscription "United States Bankruptcy Court" followed by a blank line. Examine the blank line in 2-1. In our sample Voluntary Petition, the bankruptcy court that handled John Consumer's bankruptcy case is the "Middle District of Florida, Colonia Division."

For Diagram 2-2, you'll find the name of the bankruptcy court at the top of the page, and in the center. The bankruptcy court may have preprinted this information, or you or your attorney may have typed it on the form. In either case, the information will be identical to the information in 2-1. Note for comparison purposes that the bankruptcy court in 2-2 is also called the "United States Bankruptcy Court for the Middle District of Florida, Colonia Division."

The name of the court describes the court's "jurisdiction." A court's jurisdiction tells what types of cases the court hears and what its physical boundaries are. In our case, the subject matter that the court deals with is federal bankruptcy law. That's why the first part of the court's name is "United States Bankruptcy Court."

The name of the court also tells what the court's physical boundaries are. Congress has divided the bankruptcy courts into various "districts" throughout the nation. Each of these districts falls within the physical boundaries of some state. Additionally, some of these districts have so many bankruptcy cases that Congress has further subdivided them into divisions. In our example, the bankruptcy court hears cases filed by persons in the Middle District of Florida, and more specifically in the imaginary Colonia Division.

Now look at your Voluntary Petition. Find the name of the court in the first box for Form 1 (Diagram 2-1) or at the top and center of page one on the "old" Voluntary Petition form (Diagram to 2-2.) Make sure that this information corresponds to what you remember about your bankruptcy, and note the name for our upcoming discussions. The name of the court will also be important to our efforts to repair and rebuild your credit report, and for discussions with your creditors.

Your Name

Next, find your name on the form. You'll find this information in the second box on Form 1, and at the top left of the old Form. Make sure that the information is correct in every detail, including middle name, and any Junior, Senior, III, etc. designation. If there are any mistakes, record the information for later use.

Social Security Number

Now look for your Social Security number. You'll find this number in the fourth box down in Form 1, and after the designation for the Social Security number on the old Form. Make sure that the listed number is correct, and remember the number for our upcoming efforts. Yes, that's right, this is important too!

Mailing Address

Examine the form again to make sure that it correctly lists your address at the time you filed your petition. Take particular note of street numbers, apartment numbers, and "Street," "Avenue," "Way," etc. designations. This is an area where typographical errors may pop up. As always, note any problems, and remember for future reference.

Joint Debtor Information

If you filed with a joint debtor—your spouse—make sure that all of the information above is correct for that person too. Go through each item and record any problems for future reference.

Type of Bankruptcy

Finally, find the section of the Voluntary Petition that lists the type of bankruptcy that you filed. Remember, the type of bankruptcy comes from a particular chapter in the Bankruptcy Code. For most individual debtors, this is either Chapter 7 or 13. However, you may have filed under Chapter 9 or 11 as well.

You'll find the type of bankruptcy that you filed on the Voluntary Petition. For Form 1 (Diagram 2-1), you'll find this information in the 10th right box from the top. Form 1 labels this box "Chapter or Section of the Bankruptcy Code under which the Petition is Filed." For the old Voluntary Petition (Diagram 2-2), you should find this information in the top right corner of the form.

Look at Diagrams 2-1 and 2-2. Notice that our imaginary debtor filed for bankruptcy under Chapter 7 of the Bankruptcy Code. Therefore, this is a Chapter 7, or liquidation bankruptcy.

Now look at your Voluntary Petition. Find the information regarding the type of bankruptcy you filed. Make sure that this information is correct, and file your thoughts away for future reference.

As a final check, review the entire Voluntary Petition form. Make sure that you understand each entry in the form, and that all information is correct. If not, record any errors, and remember them for our upcoming credit repair and rebuilding efforts.

The Schedules

As you look through your bankruptcy file, you'll probably also notice several other papers. These papers show your income and expenses at the time of your bankruptcy, identify all your creditors and liabilities, and list your assets. The bankruptcy code calls these papers "schedules." Although there are many schedules, we'll only review the ones that will help you in your quest. In the next several sections, we'll examine the schedules that list (1) creditors holding secured claims, (2) creditors holding unsecured priority claims, and (3) creditors holding unsecured nonpriority claims. We'll also talk about what those things mean.

Types of Creditors

Perhaps the best way to begin this section is to quickly discuss the different types of creditors. Under the bankruptcy laws, there are four major types of creditors. Creditors are either "secured" or "unsecured" and either "have priority" or are "without priority."

Secured Creditors

"Secured" or "unsecured" refers to whether your debt is "backed up" by one of your assets. You probably know this as collateral. A creditor is "secured" if it asked you to pledge your asset as collateral for the loan. If you don't repay the secured creditor, then the creditor may seize the asset that you pledged. This gives the creditor some security for the loan, other than your golden word. Hence, the term "secured" creditor. A secured creditor is a creditor that has a legal right to some asset of yours if you fail to repay the obligation.

The most common secured creditor is your mortgage company. Your mortgage company lends you money to purchase your house. In return, you pledge your house as collateral for the loan. If you don't repay the loan, then the mortgage company can take your house in payment.

Another example of a secured creditor is the bank or other financial institution that lends you money to finance the purchase of your new car. You pledge the car as collateral for the money they lend you. (Just a bit of legal trivia, attorneys call this a "purchase money mortgage" because you used the money the bank lent you to purchase the collateral.) If you fail to repay the car loan, then the bank will repossess the car and try to sell it to recoup the amount they lent to you.

Finally, perhaps the earliest form of secured creditor, and one that persists to this day, is the pawnbroker. The pawnbroker is the ultimate secured creditor. Unlike other secured creditors, the pawnbroker doesn't just get some legal right to your collateral. The pawnbroker actually GETS your asset. If you don't repay the loan, then the pawnbroker just keeps and sells your asset—at virtually no risk to the pawnbroker.

Unsecured Creditors

As you might have guessed, an unsecured creditor is a creditor that does NOT have the safety of collateral backing up the loan. Therefore, if you fail to repay the loan, an unsecured creditor can only proceed against your nonexempt assets. To do this, an unsecured creditor must generally get a judgment against you in court, and then try to seize one of your nonexempt assets.

The unsecured creditors with which you are probably most familiar include those that issued you bank cards like VISA and MasterCard, and department stores which issue their own credit cards. Other unsecured creditors may include your landlord and your local utility, cable, and telephone companies. However, there are many types of unsecured creditors. In fact, most creditors are unsecured creditors.

Unsecured creditors are at greater risk than secured creditors. If you fail to repay a loan, your unsecured creditors are usually out of luck. Without a specific asset to seize, your unsecured creditors must first get a court judgment, and then hope that you have other assets. Unfortunately for your creditors, you may be "judgment proof" if you don't have any assets that the creditors can seize. For many unsecured creditors, a court judgment is a worthless piece of paper. This can be particularly so if you file for bankruptcy.

Unsecured creditors generally lose out in bankruptcy. This is because of the way the bankruptcy laws divide your assets among creditors in bankruptcy. Secured creditors can usually seize their collateral from you, and recoup some or all of their loan amount. Everyone else has to "line up" for the handouts.

At the head of the line are "creditors with priority." These are unsecured creditors that hold "priority" claims against your estate. (We'll talk about these creditors in a moment.) Everyone else goes behind. And guess where most creditors go? That's right, most creditors go to the end of the line. Therefore, even if you had assets when you filed your bankruptcy, they were probably gone before your unsecured creditors got any of them.

If you filed a "no asset" bankruptcy, then the situation for the unsecured creditor was even worse. As we discussed earlier, you filed a no asset bankruptcy if you only had exempt assets. If so, the exemption statutes protected the few assets you owned, and your unsecured creditors walked away from your bankruptcy without any of your assets. (There's a lesson in this. If you ever lend money to someone, make sure you secure the loan with collateral.)

Creditors with Priority

The next general classification for creditors depends on whether they have priority claims against you. A priority claim is a creation of the bankruptcy laws, and allows some creditors to get paid ahead of other creditors, hence the name "priority." The bankruptcy laws specify several creditors that have priority claims. Among the creditors entitled to priority claims are: (1) your employees, (2) financial institutions that lent you money after you filed the bankruptcy petition, (3) your employees or others entitled to employee benefit plan contributions, and (4) governmental entities to which you owe taxes, penalties, etc.

As you can see, most individual debtors will have very few, if any, creditors that have priority claims. Probably the most common creditor in this area that an individual debtor would face is the Internal Revenue Service. The I.R.S. gets paid before any of your other unsecured creditors that don't have priority claims.

Creditors Without Priority

So now we're down to everyone else. This is the category where most of your creditors will fall—unsecured creditors without any priority claims against your estate. In theory, this means that most of your creditors will have equal claims to your estate. In practice, this means that most of your creditors will walk away empty-handed from the bankruptcy court.

Specific Schedules

Now that we've reviewed the different types of creditors, we can put our knowledge to use and examine the specific schedules in your bankruptcy file. We'll go through them one at a time, and compare the sample schedules in the book with your actual schedules.

Creditors Holding Secured Claims

Look at Diagrams 2-3 and 2-4. Diagram 2-3 is an example of Schedule D—Creditors Holding Secured Claims. Your secured creditor schedule should look like Schedule D if you filed your bankruptcy petition after August 1, 1991. Diagram 2-4 is an example of Schedule A-2, the form that you probably used if you filed your bankruptcy petition before August 1, 1991. In either case, this schedule should list all claims against you that you secured with some asset.

Compare your secured claim schedule with the samples in Diagrams 2-3 and 2-4. Now decide which Diagram looks like your secured creditor schedule, and then return to the Diagrams.

In each of our examples, John Consumer has listed two secured claims on the schedule. The first claim is for a car loan. In this case, GMAK lent John money to purchase a car, and he still owed GMAK $15,000 at the time of his bankruptcy. Notice that the listed "value" of the claim is only $8,000. This amount represents the "market value" of the collateral. Under the Bankruptcy Code, the secured creditor can only secure the market value of the asset. (That makes sense, though, because the creditor could only sell the asset for its market value.)

In this example, then, GMAK is only secured up to the $8,000 value of the car. The remaining $7,000 claim is unsecured. Therefore, GMAK would have to stand in line with all the other unsecured creditors for that amount—and would probably come away from the bankruptcy court without the $7,000.

The second claim is for $1,500 and represents money that Househeld Finance lent to John Consumer to purchase furniture. As above, Househeld Finance's secured claim is limited to the present market value of the furniture—or $300. The remaining $1,200 is unsecured.

Now find the schedule in your bankruptcy file that lists secured claims. This should be Schedule D if you filed your petition after August 1, 1991. If you filed before August 1, 1991, this should be Schedule A-2.

Carefully review each piece of information on the schedule. Make sure that the claim amounts are correct. If not, record any problems and remember for future reference. You should pay the most attention to the actual value of the claim, but you should also review the total claim amounts and unsecured portions as well.

The information you collect in this section, and in the next several sections, will help you to repair and rebuild your credit. But let me tell you where we're going with all of this. Over the next several chapters, we're going to get your credit reports and carefully review them. And, if you're like most people, your credit reports will probably contain many mistakes.

Then, we're going to use your bankruptcy papers to find and correct the mistakes in your credit reports. But that's just a taste of where we're going. I didn't want you to think that you were doing all of this checking for nothing!

Creditors Holding Unsecured Priority Claims

The next schedule lists any creditors that held unsecured priority claims against you. You'll remember from our earlier discussion that the bankruptcy code gives a special status to these creditors. You'll also remember that you probably have very few, if any, of these creditors. Probably the only creditor in this category will be the I.R.S.. However, if you had a complicated financial situation at the time of your bankruptcy filing, then you may have had other creditors with priority as well.

If you filed your bankruptcy petition after August 1, 1991, and you had creditors holding unsecured priority claims, you'll find a list of these creditors in Schedule E—Creditors Holding Unsecured Priority Claims. Diagram 2-5 corresponds to this schedule. If you filed your bankruptcy petition before August 1, 1991, then you'll find a list of your unsecured creditors holding priority claims in Schedule A-1. Diagram 2-6 corresponds to this schedule. Compare your schedule with Diagrams 2-5 and 2-6, and decide which Diagram looks the most like your schedule.

Now look at the sample schedules for John Consumer. Notice that the only creditor holding a priority claim in these examples is the I.R.S.. The I.R.S. has a claim against John Consumer for $1,800. Under bankruptcy law, John's bankruptcy will probably not discharge this debt. Therefore, John will still owe the I.R.S. for back taxes even after his bankruptcy.

Now look at your schedule. If it lists any creditors, make sure that all of the information is correct. If there are any mistakes, record them for future use. Also, keep this schedule handy for our upcoming credit repair efforts.

Creditors Holding Unsecured Nonpriority Claims

The final schedule lists all of your creditors that held unsecured nonpriority claims. As you'll remember from our earlier discussions, this probably includes most of your creditors.

If you filed your bankruptcy petition after August 1, 1991, you'll find a list of these creditors in "Schedule F—Creditors Holding Unsecured Nonpriority Claims." Diagram 2-7 corresponds to this schedule. If you filed your bankruptcy petition before August 1, 1991, you'll find these creditors in "Schedule A-3—Creditors Having Unsecured Claims Without Priority." Diagram 2-8 corresponds to this schedule. Compare your schedule with Diagrams 2-7 and 2-8. Then, follow along with the example after you've decided which schedule you have.

Our example schedules, Diagrams 2-7 and 2-8, list eight creditors. All of these creditors held unsecured nonpriority claims against John's estate. You can see that there are many types of creditors in this category—everything from clothing to hospital bills. (It looks like high and unexpected medical bills may have caused John's bankruptcy.)

Notice that the schedules list all of the claims at their full amount. They don't divide the claims into initial and market value amounts. This is because there is no corresponding asset to value at market value. The claims here stand alone.

There are several important pieces of information in this schedule. Notice that Diagrams 2-7 and 2-8 differ in the information they include in this section. The new Schedule F, as shown in Diagram 2-7, requires the account numbers for each creditor. This information will be very helpful in tracking down your accounts when you receive your credit report. Notice that the old schedule does not include this information, as shown in Diagram 2-8. Schedule A-3 may or may not have included this account information, depending upon the thoroughness of your attorney.

Other important information in this schedule includes the amount of each claim, and the date that you became responsible for each debt. We'll review each of these items with great care when we start reviewing your credit report. For now, just get a sense for the schedule and the information that it contains.

Why have we examined your bankruptcy file so carefully?

As I said before, it's very important that you really understand the information contained within your bankruptcy file. Now let me give you some specific reasons.

To Prevent Harassing Phone Calls After You File

The first reason that you should become familiar with your bankruptcy file is that many of your creditors may not realize that you've filed for bankruptcy and received a discharge of your debts. Although your creditors probably received notification of the entire process, the collection people may not have received the word. This is fairly common given the size and bureaucracy of many creditors. Therefore, although bankruptcy law prevents creditors from seeking to collect their debts from you, you'll probably receive many calls even after you receive your discharge.

So what should you do if you receive a call from one of your creditors after you've filed your bankruptcy petition? The answer depends on whether the bankruptcy judge has discharged your case. If you have not already received your discharge, tell the creditor that you've filed for bankruptcy, and give him the name and number of your attorney. If you're representing yourself, give the creditor the case number that the Clerk of the Bankruptcy Court assigned to your case.

If the bankruptcy judge has discharged your debts, and your attorney is out of the picture, tell the creditor that you filed for bankruptcy and received a discharge. The creditor will probably want to know the case number and date of filing. (Remember, you'll find this information on the Voluntary Petition.)

By knowing the date of your petition and its assigned case number, you can quickly satisfy your creditors and prevent further communication. Most creditors are very professional and courteous once you tell them you've filed for bankruptcy. They know that they can't threaten you once you've filed for bankruptcy. This would be in direct violation of bankruptcy law and could result in a contempt order. Therefore, you'll probably find that most creditors will be very polite and businesslike during these conversations.

To Help You Repair and Rebuild Your Credit

You'll also want to become familiar with your bankruptcy file because we're going to use it's information to repair and rebuild your credit. Although we're going to discuss this in great detail in the coming chapters, let's take a quick look at the process.

By comparing your Voluntary Petition and the various schedules contained in your bankruptcy file with your credit report, you can locate any discrepancies between them. This will help you in two ways. First, as we've discussed, many creditors will not "get the word" on your bankruptcy and will continue to list your account as active and delinquent. This will prevent you from getting a new start and from rebuilding a "good" credit record. Second, you can use the discrepancies to help you repair your credit report. Sound interesting? Read on!

Diagram 2-1

FORM B1
(6/90)

FORM 1. VOLUNTARY PETITION

United States Bankruptcy Court
Middle District of **Florida, Colonia Division**

VOLUNTARY PETITION

IN RE (Name of debtor-If individual, enter Last, First, Middle)
Consumer, John Joe

NAME OF JOINT DEBTOR (Spouse) (Last, First, Middle)
N/A

ALL OTHER NAMES used by the debtor in the last 6 years
(Include married, maiden, and trade names)
N/A

ALL OTHER NAMES used by the debtor in the last 6 years
(Include married, maiden, and trade names)
N/A

SOC. SEC./TAX I.D. NO. (If more than one, state all)
123-45-6789

SOC. SEC./TAX I.D. NO. (If more than one, state all)

STREET ADDRESS OF DEBTOR (No. and street, city, state, and zip code)
5825 Red Wood Dr.
Colonia, FL 32331

COUNTY OF RESIDENCE OR PRINCIPAL PLACE OF BUSINESS
Colonia

STREET ADDRESS OF DEBTOR (No. and street, city, state, and zip code)
N/A

COUNTY OF RESIDENCE OR PRINCIPAL PLACE OF BUSINESS

MAILING ADDRESS OF DEBTOR (If different from street address)
N/A

MAILING ADDRESS OF DEBTOR (If different from street address)
N/A

LOCATION OF PRINCIPAL ASSETS OF BUSINESS DEBTOR
(If different from addresses listed above)
N/A

VENUE (Check one box)

[X] Debtor has been domiciled or has a residence, principal place of business, or principal assets in this District for 180 days immediately preceding the date of this petition or a longer part of such 180 days than in any other District.
☐ There is a bankruptcy case concerning debtor's affiliate, general partner, or partnership pending in this District.

INFORMATION REGARDING DEBTOR (Check applicable boxes)

TYPE OF DEBTOR
[X] Individual
☐ Joint (Husband & Wife)
☐ Partnership
☐ Other:
☐ Corporation Publicly Held
☐ Corporation Not Publicly Held
☐ Municipality

NATURE OF DEBT
[X] Non-Business/Consumer
☐ Business-Complete A&B below

A. TYPE OF BUSINESS (Check one box)
☐ Farming
☐ Professional
☐ Retail/Wholesale
☐ Railroad
☐ Transportation
☐ Manufacturing/ Mining
☐ Stockbroker
☐ Commodity Broker
☐ Construction
☐ Real Estate
☐ Other Business

B. BRIEFLY DESCRIBE NATURE OF BUSINESS

CHAPTER OR SECTION OF BANKRUPTCY CODE UNDER WHICH THE PETITION IS FILED (Check one box)
[X] Chapter 7
☐ Chapter 9
☐ Chapter 11
☐ Chapter 12
☐ Chapter 13
☐ Sec. 304-Case Ancillary to Foreign Proceeding

FILING FEE (Check one box)
[X] Filing fee attached
☐ Filing fee to be paid in installments. (Applicable to individuals only). Must attach signed application to the court's consideration certifying that the debtor is unable to pay fee except in installments. Rule 1006(b) Form No. 3

NAME AND ADDRESS OF LAW FIRM OR ATTORNEY
Joe Lawyer, P.O. Box 1234, Colonia, FL 33672

NAME OF ATTORNEY(S) DESIGNATED TO REPRESENT THE DEBTOR
Same

☐ Debtor is not represented by an attorney.

STATISTICAL/ADMINISTRATIVE INFORMATION (28 U.S.C. §604)
(Estimates only) (Check applicable boxes)

☐ Debtor estimates that funds will be available for distribution to unsecured creditors.
[X] Debtor estimates that after any exempt property is excluded and administrative expenses paid, there will be no funds available for distribution to unsecured creditors.

THIS SPACE FOR COURT USE ONLY

ESTIMATED NUMBER OF CREDITORS

1-15	16-49	50-99	100-199	200-999	1,000-over
[X]	☐	☐	☐	☐	☐

ESTIMATED ASSETS (In thousands of dollars)

Under 50	50-99	100-499	500-999	1,000-9,999	10,000-99,999	100,000-over
[X]	☐	☐	☐	☐	☐	

ESTIMATED LIABILITIES (In thousands of dollars)

Under 50	50-99	100-499	500-999	1,000-9,999	10,000-99,999	100,000-over
[X]	☐	☐	☐	☐	☐	

ESTIMATED NUMBER OF EMPLOYEES CH. 11 & 12 ONLY

0	1-19	20-99	100-999	1,000-over	
☐	☐	☐	☐	☐	☐

EST. NO. OF EQUITY SECURITY HOLDERS-CH.11 & 12 ONLY

0	1-19	20-99	100-499	500-over
☐	☐	☐	☐	☐

FORM B1-Cont.
(6/90)

Name of Debtor Consumer, John Joe

Case No. 86 00258
(Court use only)

FILING OF PLAN N/A

For Chapter 9, 11, 12 and 13 cases only. Check appropriate box.

☐ A copy of debtor's proposed plan dated is attached.

☐ Debtor intends to file a plan within the time allowed by statute, rule, or order of the court.

PRIOR BANKRUPTCY CASE FILED WITHIN LAST 6 YEARS (If more than one, attach additional sheet)

Location where filed	Case Number	Date Filed
N/A	N/A	N/A

PENDING BANKRUPTCY CASE FILED BY ANY SPOUSE, PARTNER, OR AFFILIATE OF THIS DEBTOR (If more than one, attach additional sheet)

Name of Debtor	Case Number	Date
N/A	N/A	N/A
Relationship	**District**	**Judge**
N/A	N/A	N/A

REQUEST FOR RELIEF

Debtor requests relief in accordance with the chapter of title 11, United States Code, specified in his petition.

SIGNATURES

ATTORNEY

X ______________________ 5/14/86
Signature Date

____
Attorney I.D. Number

INDIVIDUAL/JOINT DEBTOR(S)

I declare under penalty of perjury that the information provided in this petition is true and correct.

X ______________________
Signature of Debtor

Date 5/14/86

Signature of Joint Debtor

Date

CORPORATE OR PARTNERSHIP DEBTOR

I declare under penalty of perjury that the information provided in this petition is true and correct, and that the filing of this petition on behalf of the debtor has been authorized.

X ______________________
Signature of Authorized Individual

Print or Type Name of Authorized Individual

Title of Individual Authorized by Debtor to File This Petition

Date

EXHIBIT "A" (To be completed if debtor is a corporation requesting relief under Chapter 11.)

☐ Exhibit "A" is attached and made part of this petition.

TO BE COMPLETED BY INDIVIDUAL CHAPTER 7 DEBTOR WITH PRIMARILY CONSUMER DEBTS (See P.L. 96-353 §322)

I am aware that I may proceed under Chapter 7, 11, or 12, or 13 of title 11, United States Code, understand the relief available under each such chapter, and choose to proceed under Chapter 7 of such title.

If I am represented by an attorney, Exhibit "B" has been completed. 5/14/86

X ______________________ Date
Signature of Debtor

X ______________________ Date
Signature of Joint Debtor

EXHIBIT "B" (To be completed by attorney for individual Chapter 7 debtor(s) with primarily consumer debts.)

I, the attorney for the debtor(s) named in the foregoing petition, declare that I have informed the debtor(s) that (he, she, or they) may proceed under Chapter 7, 11, 12, or 13 of title 11, United States Code, and have explained the relief available under each such chapter. 5/14/86

X ______________________ Date
Signature of Attorney

Diagram 2-2

UNITED STATES BANKRUPTCY COURT
MIDDLE DISTRICT OF FLORIDA
COLONIA DIVISION

IN RE:

Case No. **86 00258**

JOHN JOE CONSUMER,

Chapter 7

Debtor (set forth here all names including trade names used by the Debtor within the last 6 years).
Social Security No. 123-45-6789
and Debtor's Employer's Tax I.D.
Number________________________

VOLUNTARY PETITION

1. Petitioner's mailing address, including county, is 5825 Red Wood Dr., Colonia, Colonia County, Florida 32331

2. Petitioner has resided (or has had his principal place of business or has had his principal assets) within this district for the preceding 180 days (or for a longer portion of the preceding 180 days than in any other district).

3. Petitioner is qualified to file this petition and is entitled to the benefits of title 11, United States Code, as a voluntary debtor.

4. (If appropriate) A copy of petitioner's proposed plan, dated __________________ is attached (or petitioner intends to file a plan pursuant to chapter 11 (or chapter 13) of title 11, United States Code).

5. (If petitioner is a corporation) Exhibit "A" is attached to and made a part of this petition.

6. (If petitioner is an individual whose debts are primarily consumers debts) Petitioner is aware that (he or she) may proceed under chapter 7 or 13 of title 11, United States Code, understands the relief available under each such chapter, and chooses to proceed under chapter 7 of such title.

7. (If petitioner is an individual whose debts are primarily consumer debts and such petitioner is represented by an attorney) A declaration or an affidavit in the form of Exhibit "B" is attached to and made a part of this petition.

WHEREFORE, petitioner prays for relief in accordance with [X] chapter 7, [ ] chapter 11, [ ] chapter 13 of title 11, United States Code.

LAW OFFICES OF JOE LAWYER
P.O BOX 1234
COLONIA, FL 33672

BY: ______________________________
Joe Lawyer, Attorney at Law

DECLARATION

INDIVIDUAL: I, **JOHN JOE CONSUMER**, the petitioner named in the foregoing petition, declare under penalty of perjury under the laws of the United States that the foregoing is true and correct.

JOINT INDIVIDUALS: We, and , the petitioners named in the foregoing petition, declare under penalty of perjury under the laws of the United States that the foregoing is true and correct.

CORPORATION: I, the of the corporation named as petitioner in the foregoing petition, declare under penalty of perjury under the laws of the United States that the foregoing is true and correct, and that the filing of this petition on behalf of the corporation has been authorized.

PARTNERSHIP: I, , a member - an authorized agent - of the partnership named as petitioner in the foregoing petition, declare under penalty of perjury under the laws of the United States that the foregoing is true and correct, and that the filing of this petition on behalf of the partnership has been authorized.

Executed on :**5/14/86**

______________________ Petitioner ______________________ Petitioner

EXHIBIT "B"

I, Joe Lawyer, the attorney for the petitioner named in the foregoing petition, declare that I have informed the petitioner that he or she may proceed under chapter 7 or 13 of title 11, United States Code, and have explained the relief available under each such chapter.

Executed on:**5/14/86**

____
Attorney for Petitioner

Diagram 2-3

FORM B6D
(6/90)

In re **Consumer, John Joe**, Case No. ______
Debtor (If known)

SCHEDULE D-CREDITORS HOLDING SECURED CLAIMS

State the name, mailing address, including zip code, and account number, if any, of all entities holding claims secured by property of the debtor as of the date of filing of the petition. List creditors holding all types of secured interest such as judgment liens, garnishments, statutory liens, mortgages, deeds of trust, and other security interests. List creditors in alphabetical order to the extent practicable. If all secured creditors will not fit on this page, use the continuation sheet provided.

If any entity other than a spouse in a joint case may be jointly liable on a claim, place an "X" in the column labeled "Codebtor," include the entity on the appropriate schedule of creditors, and complete Schedule H-Codebtors. If a joint petition is filed, state whether husband, wife, both of them, or the marital community may be liable on each claim by placing an "H," "W," "J," or "C" in the column labeled "Husband, Wife, Joint, or Community."

If the claim is contingent, place an "X" in the column labeled "Contingent." If the claim is unliquidated, place an "X" in the column labeled "Unliquidated." If the claim is disputed, place an "X" in the column labeled "Disputed." (You may need to place an "X" in more than one of these three columns.)

Report the total of all claims listed on this schedule in the box labeled "Total" on the last sheet of the completed schedule. Report this total also on the Summary of Schedules.

☐ Check this box if debtor has no creditors holding secured claims to report on this Schedule D.

CREDITOR'S NAME AND MAILING ADDRESS INCLUDING ZIP CODE	CODEBTOR	HUSBAND, WIFE, JOINT OR COMMUNITY	DATE CLAIM WAS INCURRED, NATURE OF LIEN, AND DESCRIPTION	CONTINGENT	UNLIQUIDATED	DISPUTED	AMOUNT OF CLAIM WITHOUT DEDUCTING VALUE OF COLLATERAL	UNSECURED PORTION, IF ANY
ACCOUNT NO. **20043748** **GMAK** **P.O. Box 8795** **Motor City, MI 37992**			**4/13/85, Purchase money secured debt; auto** VALUE $**8,000**				**15,000**	**7,000**
ACCOUNT NO. **25-2872-34572** **Househeld Finance** **P.O. Box 1404** **Atlee, GA 10527**			**5/15/83, Purchase money secured debt; furniture** VALUE $ **300**				**1,500**	**1,200**
ACCOUNT NO.			VALUE $					
ACCOUNT NO.			VALUE $					

0 continuation sheets attached

Subtotal (Total of this page)	**16,500**
Total (Use only on last page)	**16,500**

Diagram 2-4

Schedule A-2 - Creditors Holding Security

Name of creditor and complete mailing address including zip code (if unknown, so state)	Description of security and date when obtained by creditor	Specify when claim was incurred and the consideration therefor, when claim is contingent, unliquidated, disputed, or subject to setoff, evidenced by a judgment, so indicate	Indicate if claim is contingent, unliquidated or disputed	Market value		Amount of claim without deduction of value of security	
				$		$	
GMAK P.O. Box 8795 Motor City, Mi. 37992	1985 Oldsmobile			8,000	00	15,000	00
Househeld Finance P.O. Box 1404 Atlee, Ga. 10527	furniture			300	00	1,500	00
				8,300	00	16,500	00

Diagram 2-5

FORM B6E
(6/90)

In re Consumer, John Joe, Debtor

Case No. ______ (If known)

SCHEDULE E-CREDITORS HOLDING UNSECURED PRIORITY CLAIMS
(Continuation Sheet)

TYPE OF PRIORITY

CREDITOR'S NAME AND MAILING ADDRESS INCLUDING ZIP CODE	CODEBTOR	HUSBAND, WIFE, JOINT, OR COMMUNITY	DATE CLAIM WAS INCURRED, AND CONSIDERATION FOR CLAIM	CONTINGENT	UNLIQUIDATED	DISPUTED	TOTAL AMOUNT OF CLAIM	AMOUNT ENTITLED TO PRIORITY
ACCOUNT NO. **N/A** **I.R.S.** **Atlanta, GA 33901**			**April 15, 1985** **Tax Liability**				**1,800**	**1,800**
ACCOUNT NO								
ACCOUNT NO								
ACCOUNT NO								
ACCOUNT NO								
						Subtotal (Total of this page)	$ **1,800**	
						Total (Use only on last page)	$ **1,800**	

Sheet no. 1 of 1 sheets attached to Schedule of Creditors Holding Unsecured Priority Claims

Diagram 2-6

UNITED STATES BANKRUPTCY COURT FOR THE **MIDDLE** DISTRICT OF **FLORIDA**

In re **John Joe Debtor**

CASE NO.

Include here all names used by debtor within last 6 years. DEBTOR

Schedule A - STATEMENT OF ALL LIABILITIES OF DEBTOR

Schedules A-1, A-2, and A-3 must include all the claims against the debtor or his property as of the date of filing of the petition by or against him.

SCHEDULE A-1 - CREDITORS HAVING PRIORITY

Nature of claim		Name of creditor and complete mailing address including zip code (If unknown, so state)	Specify when claim was incurred and the consideration therefore, when claim is contingent, unliquidated, disputed, or subject to setoff, evidenced by a judgment, negotiable instrument, or other writing, or incurred as partner or joint contractor, so indicate, specify name of any partner or joint contractor	Indicate if claim is contingent, unliquidated or disputed	Amount of claim
(a) Wages, salary, and commissions, including vacation, severance and sick leave pay owing to workmen, servants, clerks, or traveling salesmen on salary or commission basis, whole or part time, whether or not selling exclusively for the debtor not exceeding $2,000 to each, earned within 90 days before filing of petition or cessation of business, if earlier (specify date).					$
(b) Contributions to employee benefit plans for services rendered within 180 days before filing of petition or cessation of business, if earlier (specify date).					
(c) Deposits by individuals, not exceeding $900 for each for purchase, lease, or rental of property or services for personal, family, or household use that were not delivered or provided.					
(d) Taxes owing (itemize by type of tax and taxing authority.) (1) To the United States (2) To any state (3) To any other taxing authority	**1.**	**I.R.S. Atlanta, GA 33901**	**April 15, 1985 Tax Liability**		**1,800**

Diagram 2-7

FORM B6F
(6/90)

In re **Consumer, John Joe**, Debtor

Case No. ____________ (If known)

SCHEDULE F-CREDITORS HOLDING UNSECURED NONPRIORITY CLAIMS

State the name, mailing address, including zip code, and account number, if any, of all entities holding unsecured claims without priority against the debtor or the property of the debtor as of the date of filing of the petition. Do not include claims listed in Schedules D and E. If all secured creditors will not fit on this page, use the continuation sheet provided.

If any entity other than a spouse in a joint case may be jointly liable on a claim, place an "X" in the column labeled "Codebtor," include the entity on the appropriate schedule of creditors, and complete Schedule H-Codebtors. If a joint petition is filed, state whether husband, wife, both of them, or the marital community may be liable on each claim by placing an "H," "W," "J," or "C" in the column labeled "Husband, Wife, Joint, or Community."

If the claim is contingent, place an "X" in the column labeled "Contingent." If the claim is unliquidated, place an "X" in the column labeled "Unliquidated." If the claim is disputed, place an "X" in the column labeled "Disputed." (You may need to place an "X" in more than one of these three columns.)

Report the total of all claims listed on this schedule in the box labeled "Total" on the last sheet of the completed schedule. Report this total also on the Summary of Schedules.

☐ Check this box if debtor has no creditors holding unsecured nonpriority claims to report on this Schedule F.

CREDITOR'S NAME AND MAILING ADDRESS INCLUDING ZIP CODE	CODEBTOR	HUSBAND, WIFE, JOINT, OR COMMUNITY	DATE CLAIM WAS INCURRED AND CONSIDERATION FOR CLAIM. IF CLAIM IS SUBJECT TO SETOFF, SO STATE	CONTINGENT	UNLIQUIDATED	DISPUTED	AMOUNT OF CLAIM
ACCOUNT NO. **2178319** **Candlelight Hospital** **1385 N.E. First St.** **Colonia, FL 32331**			**12/17/85, hospital charges**				**14,822**
ACCOUNT NO. **792783-1452** **Colonia Cable** **C/O Accounts Mgmt. Corp.** **P.O. Box 6350, Colonia, FL 32332**			**4/1/86, cable television charges**				**69**
ACCOUNT NO. **17579234-1987** **Colonia Power, Light & Water** **C/O Accounts Mgmt. Corp.** **P.O. Box 6350, Colonia, FL 32332**			**2/31/86 - 4/31/86, electric service**				**218**
ACCOUNT NO. **56568966674** **American Axpress** **P.O. Box 1340** **Newark, NJ 07102**			**1/3/86 - 4/31/86, credit card charges**				**1,258**
						Subtotal (Total of this page)	**16,367**
						Total (Use only on last page)	

1 continuation sheets attached

FORM B6F-Cont.
(6/90)

In re **Consumer, John Joe**, Debtor — Case No. ______ (If known)

SCHEDULE F-CREDITORS HOLDING UNSECURED NONPRIORITY CLAIMS
(Continuation Sheet)

CREDITOR'S NAME AND MAILING ADDRESS INCLUDING ZIP CODE	CODEBTOR	HUSBAND, WIFE, JOINT, OR COMMUNITY	DATE CLAIM WAS INCURRED AND CONSIDERATION FOR CLAIM. IF CLAIM IS SUBJECT TO SETOFF, SO STATE	CONTINGENT	UNLIQUIDATED	DISPUTED	AMOUNT OF CLAIM
ACCOUNT NO. **P-3852-19** **Forest Glenn Apt.** **12303 33rd St. South** **Colonia, FL** **32330**			**12/1/85 - 1/31/86, apartment lease payments**				**1,305**
ACCOUNT NO. **4357701104136** **Freedman Card Center** **P.O. Box 470911** **Orlando, FL** **33857**			**12/2/85 - 3/31/86, VISA credit card charges**				**1,800**
ACCOUNT NO. **427138254914** **Sitibank** **P.O. Box 1492** **Dallas, TX** **75343**			**1985-86, credit card charges**				**4,985**
ACCOUNT NO. **17492732** **Tirby's** **909 N. Manhattan** **Colonia, FL** **32331**			**12/20/85, clothing**				**545**
ACCOUNT NO.							
						Subtotal (Total of this page)	**8,635**
						Total (Use only on last page)	**25,002**

Sheet no. 1 of 1 continuation sheets attached to Schedule of Creditors Holding Unsecured Nonpriority Claims

Diagram 2-8

Schedule A-3 - Creditors Having Unsecured Claims Without Priority

Name of creditor (including last known holder of any negotiable instrument) and complete mailing address inc zip code	Specify when claim was incurred and the consideration therefor when claim is contingent, unliquidated, disputed, subject to setoff, evidenced by a judgment, so indicate. Specify name of any partner on any debt	Indicate if claim is contingent, unliquidated or disputed	Amount of claim	
Freedman Card Center P.O. Box 470911 Orlando, FL 33857			$ 1,800	00
Sitibank P.O. Box 1492 Dallas, TX 75343			4,985	00
Colonia Power, Light & Water c/o Accounts Mgmt. Corp. P.O. Box 6350 Colonia, FL 32332			217	58
Tirby's 909 N. Manhattan Colonia, FL 32331			544	92
American Axpress P.O. Box 1340 Newark, NJ 07102			1,257	59
Colonia Cable c/o Accounts Mgmt. Corp. P.O. Box 6350 Colonia, FL 32332			68	91
Forest Glen Apt. 12303 33rd St. South Colonia, FL 32330			1,305	00
Candlelight Hospital 1385 N.E. First Street Colonia, FL 32331			14,822	75
			25,001	75

Chapter 3

Learning the Law

Knowledge is power [Nam et ipsa scientia potestas est].

Francis Bacon

There's really only one thing that stands between you and future credit—your credit report. If it weren't for this report, you could probably go out right now and purchase most anything you desired on credit. The credit report, then, is what we need to focus on during your quest for prosperity after bankruptcy.

If you truly want to take charge of your life and prosper after bankruptcy, you need to find out what your rights are under federal and state laws, and learn the tricks of lawyers and credit professionals. In this chapter, we're going to look at the federal and state laws that regulate credit reports and the companies that produce them. In the next chapter, we'll take your new-found knowledge, and turn it to practical use. So, if you're ready, open up your mind, and let's go!

Federal Law

There are many federal laws that protect your credit rights. The Equal Credit Opportunity Act prohibits creditors from denying credit based on sex, race, marital status, religion, national origin, or age. The Truth in Lending Act requires creditors to provide written disclosures about the cost of credit and terms of repayment before you enter into a credit transaction. The Fair Credit Billing Act establishes procedures for resolving billing errors on your credit card accounts. The Fair Debt Collection Practices Act prohibits debt collectors from using unfair or deceptive practices to collect overdue bills.

However, there's only one federal law that addresses our particular needs—the Fair Credit Reporting Act. The Fair Credit Reporting Act is the only federal law that directly addresses and regulates the credit reporting industry. The other federal laws may be important to you once you have reacquired credit. But until then, we need to focus on the Fair Credit Reporting Act.

The Fair Credit Reporting Act

Congress enacted the Fair Credit Reporting Act in 1970, to regulate the growing credit reporting industry. At that time, there were many credit reporting companies spread throughout the country. Congress found the need to regulate this industry, recognizing that errors in reporting consumer credit could be devastating.

The result of this congressional concern was the Fair Credit Reporting Act. The Act, and its subsequent amendments, specified the conditions and rules for accessing the credit history of American consumers. Among other things, the Act specified procedures for obtaining credit reports, identified parties that could obtain these reports, established procedures for reviewing disputed information, and designated the types of information that could appear in the reports.

The Fair Credit Reporting Act, then, contains the secrets to prosperity after bankruptcy. The Act will provide us with all the ammunition we need to fight the errors contained within your credit report. Knowledge is power, and you're about to become more powerful.

You'll find the full text of the Fair Credit Reporting Act in the next several pages. I've included the text of the Act in the body of this chapter, rather than in an appendix, because it's VERY IMPORTANT.

Take as much time as you need to study every section of the Act. Don't worry if you don't understand everything you read. We're going to discuss most of the sections in great detail over the course of this book. For now, just try to get a feel for it.

A Word About Section Numbers

Before we look at the Act, though, I want to say a word about the statute numbers. As you'll see in a moment, Congress divided the Fair Credit Reporting Act into sections. These sections are numbered from 1681 to 1681t, and indicate where you can find these sections in the official statute book for federal laws—the United States Code ("U.S.C.").

The U.S.C. is divided into titles and sections. The Fair Credit Reporting Act is in Title 15, sections 1681 through 1681t. Therefore, if you ever wanted to look this up yourself, you'd look for Title 15 of the U.S.C., and then locate section 1681. Pretty simple.

Unfortunately, many people refer to the Fair Credit Reporting Act by citing to its sections within the Consumer Credit Protection Act. You see, the Fair Credit Reporting Act is also Title VI of the Consumer Credit Protection Act, sections 601 through 622. Therefore, you may see one section of the Fair Credit Reporting Act cited in two different ways.

However, in this book I'm going to refer to the Fair Credit Reporting Act according to its U.S.C. section numbers. This is how attorneys refer to the Act. Be warned, however, that I will sometimes refer to some of the Act as "section 1681_ of the Fair Credit Reporting Act." This isn't technically correct, as it's really section 1681_ of Title 15. However, I hope you'll forgive this inaccuracy, as I do it with the intention of aiding your understanding.

What to do if the Law Changes

One final word before we look at the text of the Act. Congress has been trying for several years to amend the Fair Credit Reporting Act. Unfortunately, at the time of this book's publication, Congress has yet to pass any amendments. (They came very close during the 1992 session.) I'm very hopeful that the next Congress will finally address the problems with the Act and pass substantial amendments. If they do this, however, certain portions of this book will become obsolete.

If you want to stay up-to-date on the newest law, send a self-addressed, stamped envelope to:

Practical Publications, Inc.
P.O. Box 1244
Tallahassee, FL 32302

Then, if Congress does change the law in this area, I'll make sure you know about it. Additionally, you can subscribe to my bi-monthly newsletter, "How to Survive and Prosper in the 90's."

Text of the Fair Credit Reporting Act

§ 1681. Congressional findings and statement of purpose

(a) The Congress makes the following findings:

(1) The banking system is dependent upon fair and accurate credit reporting. Inaccurate credit reports directly impair the efficiency of the banking system, and unfair credit reporting methods undermine the public confidence which is essential to the continued functioning of the banking system.

(2) An elaborate mechanism has been developed for investigating and evaluating the credit worthiness, credit standing, credit capacity, character, and general reputation of consumers.

(3) Consumer reporting agencies have assumed a vital role in assembling and evaluating consumer credit and other information on consumers.

(4) There is a need to insure that consumer reporting agencies exercise their grave responsibilities with fairness, impartiality, and a respect for the consumer's right to privacy.

(b) It is the purpose of this title [15 USCS §§ 1681 et seq.] to require that consumer reporting agencies adopt reasonable procedures for meeting the needs of commerce for consumer credit, personnel, insurance, and other information in a manner which is fair and equitable to the consumer, with regard to the confidentiality, accuracy, relevancy, and proper utilization of such information in accordance with the requirements of this title [15 USCS §§ 1681 et seq.].

HISTORY: (May 29, 1968, P.L. 90-321, Title VI, § 602, as added Oct. 26, 1970, P.L. 91-508, Title VI, § 601, 84 Stat. 1128.)

§ 1681a. Definitions; rules of construction

(a) Definitions and rules of construction set forth in this section are applicable for the purposes of this title [15 USCS §§ 1681 et seq.].

(b) The term "person" means any individual, partnership, corporation, trust, estate, cooperative, association, government or governmental subdivision or agency, or other entity.

(c) The term "consumer" means an individual.

(d) The term "consumer report" means any written, oral, or other communication of any information by a consumer reporting agency bearing on a consumer's credit worthiness, credit standing, credit capacity, character, general reputation, personal characteristics, or mode of living which is used or expected to be used or collected in whole or in part for the purpose of serving as a factor in establishing the consumer's eligibility for (1) credit or insurance to be used primarily for personal, family, or household purposes, or (2) employment purposes, or (3) other purposes authorized under section 604 [15 USCS § 1681b]. The term does not include (A) any report containing information solely as to transactions or experiences between the consumer and the person making the report; (B) any authorization or approval of a specific extension of credit directly or indirectly by the issuer of a credit card or similar device; or (C) any report in which a person who has been requested by a third party to make a specific extension of credit directly or indirectly to a consumer conveys his decision with respect to such request, if the third party advises the consumer of the name and address of the person to whom the request was made and such person makes the disclosures to the consumer required under section 615 [16 USCS § 1681m].

(e) The term "investigative consumer report" means a consumer report or portion thereof in which information on a consumer's character, general reputation, personal characteristics, or mode of living is obtained through personal interviews with neighbors, friends, or associates of the consumer reported on or with others with whom he is acquainted or who may have knowledge concerning any such items of information. However, such information shall not include specific factual information on a consumer's credit record obtained directly from a creditor of the consumer or from a consumer reporting agency when such information was obtained directly from a creditor of the consumer or from the consumer.

(f) The term "consumer reporting agency" means any person which, for monetary fees, dues, or on a cooperative nonprofit basis, regularly engages in whole or in part in the practice of assembling or evaluating consumer credit information or other information on consumers for the purpose of furnishing consumer reports to third parties, and which uses any means or facility of interstate commerce for the purpose of preparing or furnishing consumer reports.

(g) The term "file," when used in connection with information on any consumer, means all of the information on that consumer recorded and retained by a consumer reporting agency regardless of how the information is stored.

(h) The term "employment purposes" when used in connection with a consumer report means a report used for the purpose of evaluating a consumer for employment, promotion, reassignment or retention as an employee.

(i) The term "medical information" means information or records obtained, with the consent of the individual to whom it relates, from licensed physicians or medical practitioners, hospitals, clinics, or other medical or medically related facilities.

§ 1681b. Permissible purposes of consumer reports

A consumer reporting agency may furnish a consumer report under the following circumstances and no other:

(1) In response to the order of a court having jurisdiction to issue such an order, or a subpoena issued in connection with proceedings before a Federal grand jury.

(2) In accordance with the written instructions of the consumer to whom it relates.

(3) To a person which it has reason to believe-

(A) intends to use the information in connection with a credit transaction involving the consumer on whom the information is to be furnished and involving the extension of credit to, or review or collection of an account of, the consumer; or

(B) intends to use the information for employment purposes; or

(C) intends to use the information in connection with the underwriting of insurance involving the consumer; or

(D) intends to use the information in connection with a determination of the consumer's eligibility for a license or other benefit granted by a governmental instrumentality required by law to consider an applicant's financial responsibility or status; or

(E) otherwise has a legitimate business need for the information in connection with a business transaction involving the consumer.

§ 1681c. Reporting of obsolete information prohibited

(a) Except as authorized under subsection (b), no consumer reporting agency may make any consumer report containing any of the following items of information:

(1) cases under title 11 of the United States Code [11 USCS §§ 101 et seq.] or under the Bankruptcy Act that, from the date of entry of the order for relief or the date of adjudication, as the case may be, antedate the report by more than 10 years.

(2) Suits and judgments which, from date of entry, antedate the report by more than seven years or until the governing statute of limitations has expired, whichever is the longer period.

(3) Paid tax liens which, from date of payment, antedate the report by more than seven years.

(4) Accounts placed for collection or charged to profit and loss which antedate the report by more than seven years.

(5) Records of arrest, indictment, or conviction of crime which, from date of disposition, release, or parole, antedate the report by more than seven years.

(6) Any other adverse item of information which antedates the report by more than seven years.

(b) The provisions of subsection (a) are not applicable in the case of any consumer credit report to be used in connection with-

(1) a credit transaction involving, or which may reasonably be expected to involve, a principal amount of $ 50,000 or more;

(2) the underwriting of life insurance involving, or which may reasonably be expected to involve, a face amount of $ 50,000 or more; or

(3) the employment of any individual at an annual salary which equals, or which may reasonably be expected to equal $ 20,000, or more.

§ 1681d. Disclosure of investigative consumer reports

(a) Disclosure of fact of preparation. A person may not procure or cause to be prepared an investigative consumer report on any consumer unless-

(1) it is clearly and accurately disclosed to the consumer that an investigative consumer report including information as to his character, general reputation, personal characteristics and mode of living, whichever are applicable, may be made, and such disclosure (A) is made in a writing mailed, or otherwise delivered, to the consumer, not later than three days after the date on which the report was first requested, and (B) includes a statement informing the consumer of his right to request the additional disclosures provided for under subsection (b) of this section; or

(2) the report is to be used for employment purposes for which the consumer has not specifically applied.

(b) Disclosure on request of nature and scope of investigation. Any person who procures or causes to be prepared an investigative consumer report on any consumer shall, upon written request made by the consumer within a reasonable period of time after the receipt by him of the disclosure required by subsection (a) (1), [shall]make a complete and accurate disclosure of the nature and scope of the investigation requested. This disclosure shall be made in a writing mailed, or otherwise delivered, to the consumer not later than five days after the date on which the request for such disclosure was received from the consumer or such report was first requested, whichever is the later.

(c) Limitation on liability upon showing of reasonable procedures for compliance with provisions. No person may be held liable for any violation of subsection (a) or (b) of this section if he shows by a preponderance of the evidence that at the time of the violation he maintained reasonable procedures to assure compliance with subsection (a) or (b).

§ 1681e. Compliance procedures

(a) Every consumer reporting agency shall maintain reasonable procedures designed to avoid violations of section 605 [15 USCS § 1681c] and to limit the furnishing of consumer reports to the purposes listed under section 604 [15 USCS § 1681b]. These procedures shall require that prospective users of the
information identify themselves, certify the purposes for which the information is sought, and certify that the information will be used for no other purpose. Every consumer reporting agency shall make a reasonable effort to verify the identity of a new prospective user and the uses certified by such prospective user prior to furnishing such user a consumer report. No consumer reporting agency may furnish a consumer report to any person if it has reasonable grounds for believing that the consumer report will not be used for a purpose listed in section 604 [15 USCS § 1681b].
(b) Whenever a consumer reporting agency prepares a consumer report it shall follow reasonable procedures to assure maximum possible accuracy of the information concerning the individual about whom the report relates.

§ 1681f. Disclosures to governmental agencies

Notwithstanding the provisions of section 604 [15 USCS § 1681b], a consumer reporting agency may furnish identifying information respecting any consumer, limited to his name, address, former addresses, places of employment, or former places of employment, to a governmental agency.

§ 1681g. Disclosures to consumers

(a) Every consumer reporting agency shall, upon request and proper identification of any consumer, clearly and accurately disclose to the consumer:

(1) The nature and substance of all information (except medical information) in its files on the consumer at the time of the request.

(2) The sources of the information; except that the sources of information acquired solely for use in preparing an investigative consumer report and actually used for no other purpose need not be disclosed: Provided, That in the event an action is brought under this title [15 USCS §§ 1681 et seq.], such sources shall be available to the plaintiff under appropriate discovery procedures in the court in which the action is brought.

(3) The recipients of any consumer report on the consumer which it has furnished-

(A) for employment purposes within the two-year period preceding the request, and

(B) for any other purpose within the six-month period preceding the request.

(b) The requirements of subsection (a) respecting the disclosure of sources of information and the recipients of consumer reports do not apply to information received or consumer reports furnished prior to the effective date of this title [180 days following Oct. 26, 1970; see effective date note to 15 USCS § 1681]except to the extent that the matter involved is contained in the files of the consumer reporting agency on that date.

§ 1681h. Conditions of disclosure to consumers

(a) Times and notice. A consumer reporting agency shall make the disclosures required under section 609 [15 USCS § 1681g] during normal business hours and on reasonable notice.

(b) Identification of consumer. The disclosures required under section 609 [15 USCS § 1681g] shall be made to the consumer-

(1) in person if he appears in person and furnishes proper identification; or

(2) by telephone if he has made a written request, with proper identification, for telephone disclosure and the toll charge, if any, for the telephone call is prepaid by or charged directly to the consumer.

(c) Trained personnel. Any consumer reporting agency shall provide trained personnel to explain to the consumer any information furnished to him pursuant to section 609 [15 USCS § 1681g].

(d) Persons accompanying consumer. The consumer shall be permitted to be accompanied by one other person of his choosing, who shall furnish reasonable identification. A consumer reporting agency may require the consumer to furnish a written statement granting permission to the consumer reporting agency to discuss the consumer's file in such person's presence.
(e) Limitation of liability. Except as provided in sections 616 and 617 [15 USCS §§ 1681n and 1681o], no consumer may bring any action or proceeding in the nature of defamation, invasion of privacy, or negligence with respect to the reporting of information against any consumer reporting agency, any user of information, or any person who furnishes information to a consumer reporting agency, based on information disclosed pursuant to section 609, 610, or 615 [15 USCS §§ 1681g, 1681h, or 1681m], except as to false information furnished with malice or willful intent to injure such consumer.

§ 1681i. Procedure in case of disputed accuracy

(a) Dispute; reinvestigation. If the completeness or accuracy of any item of information contained in his file is disputed by a consumer, and such dispute is directly conveyed to the consumer reporting agency by the consumer, the consumer reporting agency shall within a reasonable period of time reinvestigate and record the current status of that information unless it has reasonable grounds to believe that the dispute by the consumer is frivolous or irrelevant. If after such reinvestigation such information is found to be inaccurate or can no longer be verified, the consumer reporting agency shall promptly delete such information. The presence of contradictory information in the consumer's file does not in and of itself constitute reasonable grounds for believing the dispute is frivolous or irrelevant.
(b) Statement of dispute. If the reinvestigation does not resolve the dispute, the consumer may file a brief statement setting forth the nature of the dispute. The consumer reporting agency may limit such statements to not more than one hundred words if it provides the consumer with assistance in writing a clear summary of the dispute.
(c) Notification of consumer dispute in subsequent consumer reports. Whenever a statement of a dispute is filed, unless there is reasonable grounds to believe that it is frivolous or irrelevant, the consumer reporting agency shall, in any subsequent consumer report containing the information in question, clearly note that it is disputed by the consumer and provide either the consumer's statement or a clear and accurate codification or summary thereof.

(d) Notification of deletion of disputed information. Following any deletion of information which is found to be inaccurate or whose accuracy can no longer be verified or any notation as to disputed information, the consumer reporting agency shall, at the request of the consumer, furnish notification that the item has been deleted or the statement, codification or summary pursuant to subsection (b) or (c) to any person specifically designated by the consumer who has within two years prior thereto received a consumer report for employment purposes, or within six months prior thereto received a consumer report for any other purpose, which contained the deleted or disputed information. The consumer reporting agency shall clearly and conspicuously disclose to the consumer his rights to make such a request. Such disclosure shall be made at or prior to the time the information is deleted or the consumer's statement regarding the disputed information is received.

§ 1681j. Charges for disclosures

A consumer reporting agency shall make all disclosures pursuant to section 609 [15 USCS § 1681g] and furnish all consumer reports pursuant to section 611(d) [15 USCS § 1681i(d)] without charge to the consumer if, within thirty days after receipt by such consumer of a notification pursuant to section 615 [15 USCS § 1681m] or notification from a debt collection agency affiliated with such consumer reporting agency stating that the consumer's credit rating may be or has been adversely affected, the consumer makes a request under section 609 or 611(d) [15 USCS § 1681g or 1681i(d)]. Otherwise, the consumer reporting agency may impose a reasonable charge on the consumer for making disclosure to such consumer pursuant to section 609 [15 USCS § 1681g], the charge for which shall be indicated to the consumer prior to making disclosure; and for furnishing notifications, statements, summaries, or codifications to person designated by the consumer pursuant to section 611(d) [15 USCS § 1681i(d)], the charge for which shall be indicated to the consumer prior to furnishing such information and shall not exceed the charge that the consumer reporting agency would impose on each designated recipient for a consumer report except that no charge may be made for notifying such persons of the deletion of information which is found to be inaccurate or which can no longer be verified.

§ 1681k. Public record information for employment purposes

A consumer reporting agency which furnishes a consumer report for employment purposes and which for that purpose compiles and reports items of information on consumers which are matters of public record and are likely to have an adverse effect upon a consumer's ability to obtain employment shall-

(1) at the time such public record information is reported to the user of such consumer report, notify the consumer of the fact that public record information is being reported by the consumer reporting agency, together with the name and address of the person to whom such information is being reported; or

(2) maintain strict procedures designed to insure that whenever public record information which is likely to have an adverse effect on a consumer's ability to obtain employment is reported it is complete and up to date. For purposes of this paragraph, items of public record relating to arrests, indictments, convictions, suits, tax liens, and outstanding judgments shall be considered up to date if the current public record status of the item at the time of the report is reported.

§ 1681l. Restrictions on investigative consumer reports

Whenever a consumer reporting agency prepares an investigative consumer report, no adverse information in the consumer report (other than information which is a matter of public record) may be included in a subsequent consumer report unless such adverse information has been verified in the process of making such subsequent consumer report, or the adverse information was received within the three-month period preceding the date the subsequent report is furnished.

§ 1681m. Requirements on users of consumer reports

(a) Adverse action based on reports of consumer reporting agencies. Whenever credit or insurance for personal, family, or household purposes, or employment involving a consumer is denied or the charge for such credit or insurance is increased either wholly or partly because of information contained in a consumer report from a consumer reporting agency, the user of the consumer report shall so advise the consumer against whom such adverse action has been taken and supply the name and address of the consumer reporting agency making the report.

(b) Adverse action based on reports of persons other than consumer reporting agencies. Whenever credit for personal, family, or household purposes involving a consumer is denied or the charge for such credit is increased either wholly or partly because of information obtained from a person other than a consumer reporting agency bearing upon the consumer's credit worthiness, credit standing, credit capacity, character, general reputation, personal characteristics, or mode of living, the user of such information shall, within a reasonable period of time, upon the consumer's written request for the reasons for such adverse action received within sixty days after learning of such adverse action, disclose the nature of the information to the consumer. The user of such information shall clearly and accurately disclose to the consumer his right to make such written request at the time such adverse action is communicated to the consumer.

(c) Reasonable procedures to assure compliance. No person shall be held liable for any violation of this section if he shows by a preponderance of the evidence that at the time of the alleged violation he maintained reasonable procedures to assure compliance with the provisions of subsections (a) and (b).

§ 1681n. Civil liability for willful noncompliance

Any consumer reporting agency or user of information which willfully fails to comply with any requirement imposed under this title [15 USCS §§ 1681 et seq.] with respect to any consumer is liable to that consumer in an amount equal to the sum of-

(1) any actual damages sustained by the consumer as a result of the failure;

(2) such amount of punitive damages as the court may allow; and

(3) in the case of any successful action to enforce any liability under this section, the costs of the action together with reasonable attorney's fees as determined by the court.

§ 1681o. Civil liability for negligent noncompliance

Any consumer reporting agency or user of information which is negligent in failing to comply with any requirement imposed under this title [15 USCS §§ 1681 et seq.] with respect to any consumer is liable to that consumer in an amount equal to the sum of-

(1) any actual damages sustained by the consumer as a result of the failure;
(2) in the case of any successful action to enforce any liability under this section, the costs of the action together with reasonable attorney's fees as determined by the court.

§ 1681p. Jurisdiction of courts; limitation of actions

An action to enforce any liability created under this title [15 USCS §§ 1681 et seq.] may be brought in any appropriate United States district court without regard to the amount in controversy, or in any other court of competent jurisdiction, within two years from the date on which the liability arises, except that where a defendant has materially and willfully misrepresented any information required under this title to be disclosed to an individual and the information so misrepresented is material to the establishment of the defendant's liability to that individual under this title [15 USCS §§ 1681 et seq.], the action may be brought at any time within two years after discovery by the individual of the misrepresentation.

§ 1681q. Obtaining information under false pretenses

Any person who knowingly and willfully obtains information on a consumer from a consumer reporting agency under false pretenses shall be fined not more than $ 5,000 or imprisoned not more than one year, or both.

§ 1681r. Unauthorized disclosures by officers or employees

Any officer or employee of a consumer reporting agency who knowingly and willfully provides information concerning an individual from the agency's files to a person not authorized to receive that information shall be fined not more than $5,000 or imprisoned not more than one year, or both.

§ 1681s. Administrative enforcement

(a) Federal Trade Commission; powers. Compliance with the requirements imposed under this title [15 USCS §§ 1681 et seq.] shall be enforced under the Federal Trade Commission Act [15 USCS §§ 41 et seq.] by the Federal Trade Commission with respect to consumer reporting agencies and all other persons subject thereto, except to the extent that enforcement of the requirements imposed under this title [15 USCS §§ 1681 et seq.] is specifically committed to some other government agency under subsection (b) hereof. For the purpose of the exercise by the Federal Trade Commission of its functions and powers under the Federal Trade Commission Act [15 USCS §§ 41 et seq.], a violation of any requirement or prohibition imposed under this title [15 USCS §§ 1681 et seq.] shall constitute an unfair or deceptive act or practice in commerce in violation of section 5(a) of the Federal Trade Commission Act [15 USCS § 45(a)] and shall be subject to enforcement by the Federal Trade Commission under section 5(b) thereof [15 USCS § 45(b)] with respect to any consumer reporting agency or person subject to enforcement by the Federal Trade Commission pursuant to this subsection, irrespective of whether that person is engaged in commerce or meets any other jurisdictional tests in the Federal Trade Commission Act [15 USCS §§ 41 et seq.]. The Federal Trade Commission shall have such procedural, investigative, and enforcement powers, including the power to issue procedural rules in enforcing compliance with the requirements imposed under this title [15 USCS §§ 1681 et seq.] and to require the filing of reports, the production of documents,
and the appearance of witnesses as though the applicable terms and conditions of the Federal Trade Commission Act [15 USCS §§ 41 et seq.] were part of this title [15 USCS §§ 1681 et seq.]. Any person violating any of the provisions of this title [15 USCS §§ 1681 et seq.] shall be subject to the penalties and entitled to the privileges and immunities provided in the Federal Trade Commission Act [15 USCS §§ 41 et seq.] as though the applicable terms and provisions thereof were part of this title [15 USCS §§ 1681 et seq.].
(b) Other administrative bodies. Compliance with the requirements imposed under this title [15 USCS §§ 1681 et seq.] with respect to consumer reporting agencies and persons who use consumer reports from such agencies shall be enforced under-

(1) section 8 of the Federal Deposit Insurance Act [12 USCS § 1818], in the case of:

(A) national banks, by the Comptroller of the Currency;

(B) member banks of the Federal Reserve System (other than national banks), by the Federal Reserve Board; and

(C) banks insured by the Federal Deposit Insurance Corporation (other than members of the Federal Reserve System), by the Board of Directors of the Federal Deposit Insurance Corporation.

(2) section 8 of the Federal Deposit Insurance Act [12 USCS § 1818], by the Director of the Office of Thrift Supervision, in the case of a savings association the deposits of which are insured by the Federal Deposit Insurance Corporation;

(3) the Federal Credit Union Act [12 USCS §§ 1751 et seq.], by the Administrator of the National Credit Union Administration with respect to any Federal credit union;

(4) the Acts to regulate commerce, by the Interstate Commerce Commission with respect to any common carrier subject to those Acts;

(5) the Federal Aviation Act of 1958 [49 USCS Appx §§ 1301 et seq.], by the Secretary of Transportation with respect to any air carrier or foreign air carrier subject to that Act [49 USCS Appx §§ 1301 et seq.]; and

(6) the Packers and Stockyards Act, 1921 [7 USCS §§ 181 et seq.] (except as provided in section 406 of that Act [7 USCS §§ 226, 227]), by the Secretary of Agriculture with respect to any activities subject to that Act.

(c) Enforcement under other authority. For the purpose of the exercise by any agency referred to in subsection (b) of its powers under any Act referred to in that subsection, a violation of any requirement imposed under this title [15 USCS §§ 1681 et seq.]shall be deemed to be a violation of a requirement imposed under that Act. In addition to its powers under any provision of law specifically referred to in subsection (b), each of the agencies referred to in that subsection may exercise, for the purpose of enforcing compliance with any requirement imposed under this title [15 USCS §§ 1681 et seq.]any other authority conferred on it by law.

§ 1681t. Relation to State laws

This title [15 USCS §§ 1681 et seq.]does not annul, alter, affect, or exempt any person subject to the provisions of this title [15 USCS §§ 1681 et seq.] from complying with the laws of any State with respect to the collection, distribution, or use of any information on consumers, except to the extent that those laws are inconsistent with any provision of this title [15 USCS §§ 1681 et seq.], and then only to the extent of the inconsistency.

State Laws

Several states have passed consumer credit protection laws similar to the federal Fair Credit Reporting Act. However, because of the many problems with the statute, many of these states have passed fair credit reporting laws that go beyond the Fair Credit Reporting Act in regulating the credit reporting industry. And the credit reporting industry doesn't like that.

At the time of this book's publication, Arizona, California, Connecticut, Kansas, Maine, Maryland, Massachusetts, Montana, New Hampshire, New Mexico and New York have all passed comprehensive credit reporting laws. The legislatures of Florida, Illinois, Pennsylvania, and Washington are also considering comprehensive statutes as well. In addition, several other states have passed laws that also affect consumer credit reports.

Generally, the state laws mimic the federal law in most areas. However, there are several differences. For example, under section 1681c, a credit bureau can report adverse credit information indefinitely if the transaction involves (1) a credit transaction involving $50,000 or more, (2) a life insurance policy involving $50,000 or more, or (3) employment with an annual salary of $20,000 or more. Under California's Fair Credit Reporting Act, however, a credit bureau can also report adverse information beyond the obsolete period if the transaction involves renting a dwelling unit for over $1,000 per month. In addition, California's law changes the employment amount to $30,000.

Finally, California has just passed an amendment to its Fair Credit Reporting laws that imposes liability on any CREDITOR that supplies incorrect information to the credit bureaus. This is a big change in the law. Under most fair credit reporting laws, including the federal law, creditors are NOT liable for reporting incorrect information. Therefore, they have very little incentive to accurately report credit information, or to correct information on your credit reports. This law should change that very quickly.

You see, therefore, that you must become familiar with your own state's credit reporting law as well, if you live in one of the states that has enacted its own version of the Fair Credit Reporting Act. Diagram 3-1 lists the states that have passed comprehensive Credit Reporting Acts at the time of this book's publication. The Diagram also lists the applicable statute numbers and variations from the federal Fair Credit Reporting Act.

Diagram 3-1
State Credit Reporting Laws

State	Code Section	Comments
Arizona	44-1691 - 1696	Essentially similar to FCRA, except code requires credit bureau to admit or deny disputed information within 30 days.
California	1785.10 - .32	Essentially similar to FCRA, except that $ amounts for reporting obsolete information are different and includes dwelling unit rental above $1,000. Various other differences as well.
Connecticut	36-421 - 435	Not very comprehensive.
Kansas	50-706 - 719	Essentially similar to FCRA, although not as comprehensive.
Maine	10 ß 1311 - 1328	Essentially similar to FCRA, except code allows 200 word consumer statement, adds disability insurance greater than $1,000 per month to list of exceptions for obsolete information, and requires reinvestigation of disputed information within 21 days.
Maryland	14-1201 - 1218	Essentially similar to FCRA, except code requires reinvestigation of disputed information within 30 days.
Massachusetts	93-53 - 68E	Essentially similar to FCRA, although not as comprehensive.
Montana	31-3-101 - 153	Essentially similar to FCRA, except code eliminates exceptions for obsolete information.
New Hampshire	359-B:1 - 21	Essentially similar to FCRA.
New Mexico	56-3-1 - 8	Essentially similar to FCRA, except code eliminates exceptions for obsolete information, and not as comprehensive as FCRA.
New York	GBL ß 380-a - r	Essentially similar to FCRA, although not as comprehensive.

Chapter 4

Reviewing Your Credit File

If you don't know where you're going, you will probably end up somewhere else.

Laurence Johnston Peter

Whatever happened to the good old days? I'm talking about a time when you could walk into your local bank and everyone knew you by name. It was a time when the bank manager knew your family and your financial needs. If you needed a loan, you'd talk to the boss, and he'd listen.

Unfortunately, those days are gone. Today, you're lucky if the bank teller calls you by name. And forget the idea of talking to the boss about your financial needs—the boss is probably in another state and doesn't care about you anyway.

Yes, things are very different today. Large banks and retail stores have replaced the "mom and pop" banks and stores of yesterday. And with these large banks and stores have come layers and layers of people between you and the boss. Today, the people that make the loan decisions don't know you—you're just a name and some information on a financial report.

So you want a loan in today's modern world? O.K. The lending officer will first have you fill out a credit application. Then, the lending officer may fax your application to some centralized credit facility, probably located in another state. At this centralized credit facility, people that you've never met will decide whether you should receive the loan.

And how do these strangers decide your fate? They take the information from your credit application and "plug it in" to a variety of financial formulas and ratios. Additionally, they examine reports that explain your credit experience with other creditors. And throughout this entire process, you have no role whatsoever. The decision comes back as a "yes" or "no," and you're never able to talk with the people in charge. Yes, things have changed.

But, you don't have to suffer because of this. You just need to learn the system. As I said before, knowledge is power, and you're about to become more powerful. I'm going to teach you everything you need to know about the standardized forms and formulas that creditors use in making loan decisions. For our purposes here, this means I'm going to teach you all about the credit report—the report that explains your credit experience with other creditors. Therefore, we'll spend this entire chapter examining the credit report. We'll find out what the report is, who maintains it, who can access it, and how you can examine it. So read on!

The Credit Report

O.K. Let's start with the basics. What is a credit report? As I've already mentioned, a credit report is a written record that explains your experience with creditors. The credit report lists information from all of your creditors about how you've handled your loans or lines of credit. For example, the credit report will show which creditors you owe, and how much you owe them. It will also show whether you made your payments on time, were sometimes late, or completely failed to repay your loans. Yes, the credit report reveals a lot about you. Therefore, we're going to take a very close look at the various types of credit reports in Chapters 5, 6, and 7. But first, I want to introduce you to some credit report basics.

Probably the best place to begin is with the companies that produce your credit report—the credit bureaus. For a fee, these companies collect, maintain, and supply creditors and other interested parties with your credit information.

Credit Bureaus

You are the source of great interest—and profit—among several large companies. These companies, which the Fair Credit Reporting Act calls "consumer reporting agencies," gather financial and credit information about you and millions of other consumers from around the country. And what do they do with this information? That's right—they sell it. They collect as much information about you as they can, store this information in huge computer databases, and then sell the information as credit reports.

And who are their customers? Right again. Their customers are creditors that want to lend you money. These creditors use your credit report to decide whether they should grant your loan request, or toss your application in the reject pile. If your credit report contains "good" information, then you'll probably receive the loan. If, however, your credit report contains "bad" information, then your creditor will probably deny your request. We're going to examine the type of information contained in your credit report in just a moment. For now, though, let's take a closer look at the major credit reporting agencies.

Who are they?

There are currently three major players in the credit reporting business —Equifax, Inc., based in Atlanta, TRW Information Services, based in Cleveland, and, Trans Union Credit Information Co., based in Chicago. By acquiring other companies, these three credit reporting companies have taken control of the credit reporting business. These companies now each maintain credit files on more than 200 million consumers. And worst of all, these companies keep track of you from one end of the nation to the other. Therefore, if you move from California to Florida, your credit file follows you. It seems that the Big 3, like "Big Brother," are always watching.

At the top of the credit reporting business, then, are the "Big 3"— Equifax, Trans Union, and TRW. But, that's not the end of the story. There are also thousands of smaller credit reporting companies, called "credit bureaus." These smaller companies, or credit bureaus, work with the Big 3 to distribute your credit report to local creditors. Let's see how this works.

When you apply for a loan, your creditor will typically contact a local credit bureau. (The creditor has probably already signed an agreement with this credit bureau to supply the credit reports of local consumers.) To retrieve a copy of your credit report, the creditor probably enters some basic information about you into a computer terminal. From there, the credit bureau locates your credit information from its computer database, and sends a copy of your credit report to the creditor. This whole process usually takes just a few minutes. Yes, that's right. Your creditor knows everything about you in moments.

But where did the local credit bureau get the information about you? If you said the Big 3, you're right. Most of the local credit bureaus maintain close ties with at least one of the Big 3 credit reporting agencies. With this affiliation, the smaller credit bureaus don't have to gather information about you. Instead, they access the computer databases of the Big 3. Therefore, you don't have to worry about the information stored in the thousands of credit bureau databases around the country.

However, you do have to worry about the information stored in the computer databases of the Big 3. Therefore, we'll concentrate on these three companies throughout the rest of this book. To simplify our discussion, I'm going to call these three companies "credit bureaus," even though they're technically "credit reporting agencies." I hope you'll forgive me for this. Just remember that we're talking about the national credit reporting agencies, not the local affiliates.

Where the Information Comes From

Now that we've looked at the companies that produce your credit report, let's see where the information comes from. The information doesn't just appear in your credit report. It has to come from somewhere. And in our increasingly computerized world, it comes from many sources. However, the information generally comes from three sources— you, your creditors, and public records. Let's take a look at each of these sources and the information they reveal.

You

Yes, you! You unknowingly supply a great deal of information to credit bureaus. But how? Think about it. When you last applied for a loan or line of credit, what did you do? Yes, that's right. You filled out a credit application. Creditors will generally require you to complete a credit application whenever you want them to extend credit to you.

What kind of information do you reveal in a credit application? Well, let's start with the basics. You supply your full name, Social Security number, current and previous jobs, current and previous salary, and current and previous address. But that's not all the information you supply. You probably also supply information about your spouse, including Social Security number, current and previous employment, and current and previous salary.

After you've completed the credit application, your potential creditor transmits all of the information to the credit bureaus. This information then becomes a permanent part of your credit file. Therefore, it's important to accurately complete this information on credit applications. (Unfortunately, your creditors may incorrectly transmit your information to the credit bureau, and force mistakes into your credit file. We'll talk about this in later chapters.)

Your Creditors

Your current and former creditors also supply information for your credit report. As we've already discussed, these creditors tell the credit bureaus how you've paid your bills. However, not all of your creditors supply the same amount of information. Some of your creditors report your credit information to the credit bureaus every month. The credit bureaus call these creditors "automatic subscribers." However, other creditors only report certain types of information. The credit bureaus call these creditors "limited subscribers." Let's take a moment to examine these two types of creditors.

Automatic Subscribers

As I just mentioned, "automatic subscribers" are creditors that regularly supply information to the credit bureaus about your account with them. This information generally shows when the creditor first extended credit to you, the total amount of credit, and the repayment terms. Automatic subscribers will also report whether you make your payments on time, and if they've taken any collection action against you.

There are many types of automatic subscribers. Although I won't attempt to list them all, I've identified the major automatic subscribers in the following list.

Collection Agencies	- Generally report on collection efforts taken on behalf of any creditor
Finance Companies	- Generally report payment histories on loans
Large Banks	- Generally report on consumer and other loans
Large Credit Unions	- Generally report payment histories on loans
Large Department Stores	- Generally report payment histories on store accounts

Large Savings and Loans	- Generally report payment histories on loans
Major Credit Cards (American Express, Discover, MasterCard, Visa, etc.)	- Generally report payment histories

Limited Subscribers

Not all of your creditors automatically report credit information to the credit bureaus. Some creditors limit their association with the credit bureaus to making inquiries about your credit history. The credit bureaus call these creditors "limited subscribers," because they don't automatically report their experience in collecting timely payments from you. However, even these limited subscribers WILL notify the credit bureaus if you fail to repay your loan, or if they take any collection action against you.

There are many different types of limited subscribers. Again, I can't list them all, but the following list identifies the major ones.

Apartment Management Companies	Generally do not report terms or payment histories for apartment leases
Savings and Loans	Generally do not report terms or payment histories for home mortgages Generally do not report savings account information
Banks	Generally do not report savings or checking account information
Small Banks	Generally do not report small consumer loans
Credit Unions	Generally do not report savings or checking account information
Small Credit Unions	Generally do not report small consumer loans

Insurance Companies	Generally do not report terms and payments of insurance policies
Utility Companies	Generally do not report payment histories
Hospitals	Generally do not report medical payment histories

Why do you care whether your creditors are automatic or limited subscribers? Well, there are two reasons. First, your limited subscribers may or may not appear on your credit reports. It will help you to understand this before we look at your credit reports.

Second, if you run into financial problems again (you won't), it's generally better to pay your automatic subscribers before you pay your limited subscribers. Why? It's better because your automatic subscribers will report any late payments to the credit bureau. The limited subscribers, however, will only report serious delinquencies. Therefore, you can get away with a few late payments to limited subscribers, and not affect your credit report. (There's another consideration here, though. Although you won't affect your credit report, your limited subscribers might stop providing services to you if you don't pay them. This could be painful if it's a utility company. You'll need to take this into consideration.)

Public Records

The last source of information for your credit report comes from public records. Public records are government records that anyone can access. All local, state, and federal courts maintain court documents as public records. (For example, your bankruptcy case file is a public record.) Additionally, most state and federal agencies maintain information about you that is public record.

Whenever you're involved in matters of public record, ANYONE may review the complete history of the action. Generally, matters of public record that may appear in your credit report include bankruptcies, foreclosures, judgments, tax liens, and wage garnishments. Credit bureaus usually receive this information from private agencies that search the public records for adverse information.

When you filed your bankruptcy petition, someone discovered this information in the bankruptcy court files and reported it to the credit bureaus. (The person that discovered this information was probably an employee for a private research company. These companies hire workers to search public records for bad credit information.) Then, when the bankruptcy court discharged your debts, someone (maybe the same employee) discovered this information and reported that to the credit bureaus. Unfortunately, however, employees of these research agencies often make mistakes when recording and reporting public record information to the credit bureaus. A recent mistake by one of these companies caused the population of an entire town to temporarily lose their good credit rating. You'll learn to check the accuracy of your own public record information in Chapter 8.

What Your Credit Report Covers

Identification and Employment Information

Every credit file must begin with basic information about you. Remember, you probably supplied this information to one or more of your creditors. This information probably includes your full name, date of birth, current and previous addresses, Social Security number, current and previous employers, and your current income. Your credit file may also contain other information, such as your spouse's name, Social Security number, and employer.

Credit History

The credit history section is of particular interest to creditors. Most of your creditors probably subscribe to at least one of the Big 3 credit bureaus. All of the automatic subscribers, and perhaps even some of the limited subscribers, report information to the credit bureaus about their experience in collecting timely payments from you. The credit history section lists each creditor that has reported something about your credit history to that particular credit bureau.

The credit history section contains information reported by each of your creditors. For example, it shows when the creditor first extended credit to you, and the total or high amount of this credit. This section will probably also show the repayment terms, and the creditor's experience in collecting payments from you.

Typically, the creditor reports its payment collection experience by stating how often you've made late payments, and by how many days. For example, the creditor may notify the credit bureau that you've made four late payments. On two of these occasions, you made the required payment from 1-30 days after the due date. On one of these occasions, you made the payment 31-60 days after the due date. And on the fourth occasion, you made the payment, but were 61-90 days late. The credit history section will show each of these late payments.

Besides late payments, the credit history section will show serious problems with your loans. For example, if you fail to repay a loan (default), the creditor will report this to the credit bureau, and it will appear in the credit history section. Also, your creditor will report any actions it took against you because of your default. This could include giving your account to a collection company, or counting your account as a loss on its books. This too, will appear in the credit history section of your credit report.

But, there's more. The credit history section also shows who is responsible for repaying the debt. Although there are many subgroups, the credit history section shows three basic types of loan responsibility. You have "individual liability" if you are the only person responsible for repaying the debt. If you share responsibility for repaying the debt with someone else, then you have "joint liability." Finally, if you can use another person's credit line, but aren't responsible for repaying the debt at all, then you're an "authorized user." We'll come back to this section again when we examine the credit report in Chapters 5, 6, and 7.

Credit Inquiries

The credit inquiries section shows everyone that has reviewed your credit file. Whenever a creditor reviews your credit file, the credit bureaus record and report this information on your credit report. The Fair Credit Reporting Act requires that credit bureaus maintain a record of all creditors who have requested your credit history within the past six months. However, most credit bureaus report this information for at least two years after the inquiry. Potential creditors are interested in these credit inquiries because they may suggest your increased need for credit, or your inability to obtain credit from other creditors. Potential creditors will carefully review your credit request if your credit report shows many recent credit inquiries.

What Your Report Does Not Cover

Contrary to popular belief, your credit report does NOT contain information about your race, religion, sex, or personal life style. Additionally, your credit record does not contain information about your character, general reputation, or personal characteristics. Many people believe that credit bureaus derive this information based on personal interviews with family, friends, and associates. People probably believe this because credit applications typically ask for the names, addresses, and telephone numbers of family members and close friends. However, creditors don't ask for this information to gather private information about you. They do it to verify your employment history and to locate you should you fail to meet your scheduled payments.

(But here's something to worry about. Although your CREDIT RECORD doesn't contain this type of personal information about you, there MIGHT be another record that does contain this type of information. The Fair Credit Reporting Act calls this record an "Investigative Consumer Report." Specialized companies gather and maintain personal information about you and issue investigative consumer reports to interested parties. Fortunately, federal law requires that these companies notify you if they prepare an investigative consumer report on you. Although this is something to worry about, we're going to stay focused on credit reports. Just remember, credit reports and investigative consumer reports are different.)

Your credit file doesn't contain other information as well. (This one may surprise you.) Your credit file probably doesn't contain all of your credit history. As I mentioned earlier, many creditors are limited subscribers, and don't report your credit history with them to the credit bureaus. Also, many creditors don't belong to all of the Big 3 credit bureaus. Therefore, the credit reports from each of the Big 3 will probably show different parts of your credit history. To work with this, you'll have to get copies of your credit report from each of the Big 3. I'll show you how to do that in a moment. But first, let's see who can get a copy of your credit report.

Who Can Access Your Credit File and Why

Under section 1681b of the Fair Credit Reporting Act (remember—that's 1681b of Title 15), only certain people may access your credit file, and only for certain reasons. Generally, this means creditors to whom you have applied for credit. However, there are several other reasons that someone may see your credit file. For example, a potential employer may access your credit file when you apply for a job. Now take a look at the following list. It shows who can see your credit file, and for what reasons.

You. [Section 1681b(2).]

A court or federal grand jury. [Section 1681b(1).]

Retail Establishments—department stores, oil companies, airlines, etc. [Section 1681b(3)(A) and (E).]

Credit Card Issuers—American Express, Diner's Club, Discover, Mastercard, VISA, etc. [Section 1681b(3)(A) and (E).]

Lenders—Banks, Credit Unions, Finance Companies, Savings and Loans, Insurance Companies, etc. [Section 1681b(3)(A) and (E).]

Other Individuals or Companies that Extend Credit—Doctors, Home Improvement Companies, Hospitals, etc. [Section 1681b(3)(A) and (E).]

Other Individuals or Companies that intend to use the information in connection with employment, the underwriting of insurance, or certain government benefits. [Section 1681b(3)(B), (C), and (D).]

Other Individuals or Companies that have a legitimate business need for the information in connection with a business transaction involving you. [Section 1681b(3)(E).]

Only the individuals and companies that I've listed above may access your credit file. And, they may do so only for the specified reasons. If someone else accesses your credit file, they have violated federal law.

Obtaining Copies of Your Credit Report

Because credit reports are all about you, it only seems fair that you have the opportunity to examine the report for accuracy and truthfulness. Fortunately, Congress agrees with this idea. The Fair Credit Reporting Act guarantees you access to the information contained within your credit report. Credit bureaus aren't required to show you the actual report they send to creditors—this seems unfair—but they'll generally allow you access to most of it.

Direct Request

Under section 1681h of the Fair Credit Reporting Act, there are two ways that you may access your credit report. The first way is fairly straightforward. You request the information, and the credit bureau sends the report to you for a fee. Yes, that's right, the Fair Credit Reporting Act allows the credit bureaus to charge a reasonable fee for this service.

The second way that you can obtain your credit report depends upon your inability to receive credit. Section 1681j of the Fair Credit Reporting Act guarantees you a free credit report whenever a creditor denies you credit. However, this only applies if the creditor reviewed your credit report in making its decision, and if you act within 30 days.

In the next several sections, I'll tell you how to get a copy of your credit report from each of the Big 3. First, I'll tell you how to get your credit report if a creditor has NOT denied your credit request within the last 30 days. Then, I'll tell you how to get your credit report if a creditor HAS denied your credit request within the last 30 days. (Most credit bureaus will extend this period to 60 days.)

Section 1681g of the Fair Credit Reporting Act requires that credit bureaus allow you access to your credit file upon your request. The credit bureau must disclose the following information to you:

1. The nature and substance of all information (except medical information) in its files on you at the time of your request. [1681g(a)(1)].

2. The sources of the information. [1681g(a)(2)].

3. The identity of anyone that has received your credit report for employment purposes during the preceding two years. [1681g(a)(3)(A)].

4. The identity of anyone that has received your credit report for any other purpose during the preceding six months. [1681g(a)(3)(B)].

Cost

Section 1681j governs the cost of obtaining your credit report. If a creditor has not denied your credit request within the last 30 days, the credit bureau may charge you a "reasonable charge." This "reasonable charge" varies among the various credit reporting agencies. Additionally, some states regulate the "reasonable charge" that credit bureaus can impose on its consumers. Fortunately for all consumers, most credit bureaus have lowered the charge for receiving your credit report. (But, do you think they did this for your benefit? No, you're right. They did this because Congress and several states have threatened to impose stronger regulations on the credit reporting industry.)

At this time, TRW offers the best deal. Upon request, TRW will send your credit report at no cost to you once each year. If you want more than one credit report during the year, the cost is $8.00. Equifax and Trans Union have also lowered their charge for credit reports from $15 to $8. Unfortunately, Equifax and Trans Union do not plan to match the annual free report offered by TRW. (Remember, these charges are current as of the publication date for this book. The credit bureaus may have changed the price for obtaining your credit report. Therefore, you should contact the credit bureau before sending your request and payment.)

I've included the following list to give you an idea of the charges you can expect when you request your credit report from the Big 3. If you obtain your credit information from a local credit bureau, the charge may be different.

Equifax

$8 for each credit report for most states.
Maine residents - $3 for each report.
Maryland residents - First report free, then $5.
Vermont residents - First report free, then $7.50.

Trans Union

$8 for each individual credit report.
$16 for each joint (husband and wife) credit report.

TRW

One credit report each year at no cost. Additional reports during the year are $8 for most states.
Maine residents - $2 for additional reports.
Maryland residents - $5 for additional reports.

After Credit Denied

Now that you know how to pay for your credit report, let's look at how you can get your credit report for free. Under Section 1681j of the FCRA, the credit bureaus must give you a free copy of your credit report whenever a creditor rejects your credit request. However, Section 1681j only gives you 30 days to make this request, so you've got to act quickly. Also, you can only receive this free report if the creditor relied on information maintained by that particular credit bureau. Therefore, if the creditor only relied on a credit report prepared by Trans Union, then you're only entitled to a free credit report from Trans Union—you can't get a free report from Equifax or TRW. However, if the creditor relied on information from all three of the Big 3 credit reporting agencies, then you can get a free credit report from all three.

Remember, Section 1681j only allows you 30 days from the time of the credit denial to make your request. Therefore, you want to move fast. However, most credit bureaus will extend the statutory period to 60 days. This means that you can still get a free credit report even if you miss the 30-day time limit.

Procedure

Now that you know how much your credit report will cost, let me tell you how to get it. Section 1681h of the Fair Credit Reporting Act tells credit bureaus how to comply with your credit report request. Under 1681h, you can receive your credit report information in one of three ways. First, you may receive the information in person. To do this, you must visit the credit bureau during normal operating hours, and present proper identification. You can also receive your credit report information over the phone. To use this method, you must first send the credit bureau a written request. Also, if there's a charge for the call, you have to pay it. Finally, you may receive this information through the mail. To do this, you must send the credit bureau a written request. This is probably the most common method for obtaining credit reports.

Additionally, Equifax has just started a new service that allows you to request your credit report over the phone, if you have a major credit card. Equifax will then send your report to you within 12 hours. This service is only available if a creditor has NOT denied your credit request within the last 60 days. If a creditor HAS denied your credit request within the last 60 days, and you want a free report, then you'll have to send Equifax a written request. Also, if you don't have a major credit card (you will if you follow the procedures in this book!), you'll need to send Equifax a written request.

With any of the above methods, the credit bureaus will require some identification information. They need this information to prevent impostors from receiving your credit report, and to locate your credit file in their databases. These are reasonable goals. However, the credit bureaus are always after more information. Therefore, be careful about the type of information that you give them.

For example, if you visit a credit bureau in person, they may ask you to fill out an identification form. This form generally asks for identification information, such as your full name, date of birth, and Social Security number. However, the form may also request information about your current employment and marital status. It's difficult to see how information about your spouse or current employment will serve to identify you or to aid in locating your credit file information. If you feel uncomfortable about revealing this information—don't. There really isn't any need. Under Section 1681h, the credit bureau can only ask you for "proper identification." Your driver's license or other identification should be good enough.

Information to Include

Whichever method you choose, you should include the following information whenever you request your credit file information:

1. Your full name
2. Social Security Number
3. Current Address
4. Former Address
5. Spouse's Name (if applicable and if you want to reveal this)

You should include the above information whether you are seeking a direct credit request or if a creditor has denied your credit request within the last 30-60 days. However, if a creditor has rejected your credit request within the last 30-60 days, you'll need to include some more information. Most credit bureaus request that you also include a photocopy of the rejection notice. If you don't have the rejection notice, you should include the name and address of the creditor, and the date the creditor denied your credit request. (REMEMBER—If a creditor denied your credit request within the last 30-60 days, the credit bureau must give you a FREE copy of your credit report.)

One final thought on what you should include in your credit report request. If you want your yearly free credit report from TRW, you need to include one more thing. Besides the information we've already discussed, TRW requires that you include a photocopy of some identification that links you with your mailing address. This identification could include your driver's license, electric bill, telephone bill, etc. This is a reasonable request by TRW, and insures that someone else won't receive your credit report. Just be sure that the identification you send reveals information you don't mind sharing with TRW.

How to Contact the Credit Bureaus

Whenever a creditor denies your credit request, the creditor must send you a letter explaining the reason for the denial, and the source of credit information. This may be a local credit bureau, and not one of the Big 3. But remember, most of the local credit bureaus receive their information from the Big 3. The letter will contain the name and address of the credit bureau that furnished your credit information. Therefore, send your credit report request to that credit bureau at that address.

However, if a creditor has not refused your credit request within the last 30-60 days, then you may contact either a local credit bureau or one of the Big 3. You can locate a local bureau by looking in the Yellow Page directory of your telephone book. Additionally, you may request the names and addresses of credit bureaus in your area by contacting Bankcard Holders of America. Bankcard Holders of America will send you a list of credit bureaus in your region for a small fee. You may contact them at:

Bankcard Holders of America
650 Herndon Parkway, Suite 120
Herndon, VA 22070
703-481-1110

If you don't want to work with the local credit bureaus, you can go right to the source—the Big 3. You may contact them as follows:

Equifax

Equifax Information Service Center
P.O. Box 740241
Atlanta, GA 30375
(800) 685-1111

Trans Union

Trans Union Consumer Relations Center
25249 Country Club Boulevard
P.O. Box 7000
North Olmstead, OH 44070
(312) 408-1050 (Chicago telephone number)
(313) 689-3888 (Interactive Telephone Line)

TRW (To request your free credit report)

TRW
P.O. Box 2350
Chatsworth, CA 91313-2350

TRW (If you've already received your free credit report for the year, or if a creditor has denied your credit request within the last 60 days.)

TRW National Consumer Assistance Center
P.O. Box 749029
Dallas, TX 75374
(800) 392-1122
(214) 235-1200
(305) 962-5997

Sample Letters

To make this whole process less painful for you, I've included several sample letters. If you're like me, you probably hate to create your own letters. Therefore, you can steal mine. I've included three sample letters and three completed letters. The three completed letters should give you a better idea of how each letter should ultimately look. You may use these sample letters as they are, or tailor them to suit your particular writing style.

Use the first letter, Diagram 4-1(a), if a creditor has NOT denied your credit request within the last 30-60 days. Diagram 4-1(b) shows you how this letter would look if our fictional character, John Consumer, had completed it. Use the second letter, Diagram 4-2(a), if a creditor HAS denied your credit request within the last 30-60 days. Diagram 4-2(b) shows you how this letter would look if John Consumer had completed it. Use the third letter, Diagram 4-3(a), to request your free credit report from TRW. Diagram 4-3(b) shows you how this letter would look if John Consumer had completed it.

Diagram 4-1(a)
[Sample Letter Requesting Credit Report When Credit Has Not Been Denied]

Your Address
City, State Zip

Date

Credit Bureau Name
Credit Bureau Address
City, State Zip

Dear Sirs:

Please send me a copy of my credit report or any other information in your files that pertains to me. I have enclosed a check in the amount of $__ to cover the cost of this report. Additionally, I have included the following information to assist you in processing my request:

Name ______________________________

Social Security Number __-__-____

Date of Birth __________

Current Address ______________________________
____

Previous Address ______________________________
____

Thank you for your assistance in this matter.

Sincerely,

Your Name

Diagram 4-1(b)

5825 Red Wood Drive
Colonia, FL 32331

February 1, 1993

Trans Union Corporation
P.O. Box 7000
North Olmstead, OH 44070

Dear Sirs:

Please send me a copy of my credit report or any other information in your files that pertains to me. I have enclosed a check in the amount of $8 to cover the cost of this report. Additionally, I have included the following information to assist you in processing my request:

Name	John Joe Consumer
Social Security Number	123-45-6789
Date of Birth	1/18/57
Current Address	5825 Red Wood Drive Colonia, FL 32331
Previous Address	7825 Fort Knox Drive Texee, TX 18181

Thank you for your assistance in this matter.

Sincerely,

John J. Consumer

Diagram 4-2(a)
[Sample Letter Requesting Credit Report When Credit Has Been Denied in the Last 30-60 Days]

Your Address
City, State Zip

Date

Credit Bureau Name
Credit Bureau Address
City, State Zip

Dear Sirs:

I was recently denied credit by ___ Name of Creditor ___, based in part upon credit information supplied by your company. I understand that I am entitled to receive, at no cost, a copy of my credit report or other information maintained by your company about me. Therefore, I request that you send me a copy of my credit report or any other information in your files that pertains to me. I have enclosed a copy of the credit denial letter. [Or alternatively, give the name and address of the creditor in the blank section above labeled "Name of Creditor."] I have included the following information to assist you in processing my request:

Name ______________________________

Social Security Number ___-__-____

Date of Birth _________

Current Address ______________________________
____

Previous Address ______________________________
____

Thank you for your assistance in this matter.

Sincerely,

Your Name

Diagram 4-2(b)

5825 Red Wood Drive
Colonia, FL 32331

February 1, 1993

Equifax Information Service Center
P.O. Box 740241
Atlanta, GA 30375

Dear Sirs:

I was recently denied credit by First Bank, based in part upon credit information supplied by your company. I understand that I am entitled to receive, at no cost, a copy of my credit report or other information maintained by your company about me. Therefore, I request that you send me a copy of my credit report or any other information in your files that pertains to me. I have enclosed a copy of the credit denial letter. I have included the following information to assist you in processing my request:

Name	John Joe Consumer
Social Security Number	123-45-6789
Date of Birth	1/18/57
Current Address	5825 Red Wood Drive Colonia, FL 32331
Previous Address	7825 Fort Knox Drive Texee, TX 18181

Thank you for your assistance in this matter.

Sincerely,

John J. Consumer

Diagram 4-3(a)
[Sample Letter Requesting Free TRW Credit Report]

Your Address
City, State, Zip

Date

TRW
P.O. Box 2350
Chatsworth, CA 91313-2350

Dear Sirs:

I would like to take advantage of your free credit report offer. Please send me a copy of my credit report or any other information in your files that pertain to me. I have enclosed a photocopy of my [electric bill, driver's license, telephone bill, etc.] to verify my current address. I have also included the following information to assist you in processing my request:

Name ______________________

Social Security Number ___-__-____

Date of Birth __________

Current Address ______________________
____

Previous Address ______________________
____

Thank you for your assistance in this matter.

Sincerely,

Your Name

Diagram 4-3(b)

5825 Red Wood Drive
Colonia, FL 32331

February 1, 1993

TRW
P.O. Box 2350
Chatsworth, CA 91313-2350

Dear Sirs:

I would like to take advantage of your free credit report offer. Please send me a copy of my credit report or any other information in your files that pertains to me. I have enclosed a photocopy of my electric bill to verify my current address. I have also included the following information to assist you in processing my request:

Name	John Joe Consumer
Social Security Number	123-45-6789
Date of Birth	1/18/57
Current Address	5825 Red Wood Drive Colonia, FL 32331
Previous Address	7825 Fort Knox Drive Texee, TX 18181

Thank you for your assistance in this matter.

Sincerely,

John J. Consumer

Chapter 5

Your Equifax Credit Report

Know your opponent, know yourself. Do this and you shall never fail.

Sun Tzu

You should now have a copy of your credit report from each of the Big 3 credit reporting agencies, or their local representatives. If so, it's time to take a close look at these monsters. You've probably noticed several things about the different credit reports. First, you've probably noticed that the reports are very confusing. They all contain some type of code system and cryptic lettering. Second, you've probably noticed that all of the credit reports look different.

In this chapter, we'll look at the Equifax credit report format. Then, in Chapters 6 and 7, we'll look at the Trans Union and TRW credit report formats, respectively. Each of these sample credit reports should look something like the reports that you have in front of you. However, you may notice slight differences between the samples in this book and your credit reports. This may be because you received your report from a local credit bureau, or because the format has changed since the publication of this book. In any event, this chapter and Chapters 6 and 7 should give you a feel for the various credit report formats.

Remember, each credit bureau uses a different format for its credit report and different codes and symbols to represent information contained in the credit report. Therefore, we'll have to examine each report individually. In the next three chapters, we'll examine all of the codes that the Big 3 credit bureaus use on their reports. This should help you to understand what's in your credit report, and allow you to spot any errors. Then, we'll take this new knowledge and learn how to correct those errors in Chapter 9.

One final word before we start. In the next three chapters, I'll tell you everything you'll ever NEED to know about credit reports. Unfortunately, this may be more than you WANT to know. Because of this, my editors suggested that I remove these chapters from the book. But, as you can tell, I've refused this advice.

Why? Because I want you to have EVERYTHING you need to survive and prosper after bankruptcy. And part of that EVERYTHING is knowledge of your credit reports. As I've said so often before—knowledge is power. And if you let me, I'm going to make you more powerful. But, it's up to you.

Therefore, I recommend that you study the next three chapters and learn the various codes, abbreviations, and formats. Then, you'll be ready to face the credit bureaus. If, however, you're already familiar with the credit report formats, just skip ahead to chapter 8. Then, if you run into unfamiliar territory, you can always return to these chapters.

With all that said, it's time to start. So, get your Equifax credit report in front of you and let's go!

The Equifax Credit Report

Equifax uses a very condensed format for its credit report. This means that there is a great deal of information contained in a very small area. To get a feel for this, find Diagram 5-1, and take a look at it.

Diagram 5-1 is a sample Equifax credit report that lists credit information for our fictional character, John Consumer. Notice that all of John's credit information is contained on one page. You may have more credit information than this, so that your credit report is much longer.

Identifying Information

Let's look at the credit report. First, let's examine the identifying information on the credit report. (The credit bureau will probably get this information from your credit report request.) You'll find the credit bureau's address at the top left of the report. If you look at the top left corner of Diagram 5-1, you'll see that John Consumer obtained this report from "CB Colonia." This is a fictional credit bureau that obtained its information from Equifax. When you've found this information in Diagram 5-1, look at your Equifax credit report and compare it with the sample.

Now find your current address. You'll find it just below the credit bureau's address. In the sample, you'll see that John's current address information corresponds with the information that John supplied to the credit bureau in his credit report request.

O.K. You're getting the hang of this now. So, let's move faster. Now find the date the credit bureau prepared your credit report, your social security number, and your date of birth. You'll find the date that the credit bureau prepared your report to the right of your current address, and your social security number and date of birth just below this date. Diagram 5-1 shows that CB Colonia prepared John's report on February 14, 1993. It also shows that his social security number is "123-45-6789," and that he was born on January 18, 1957.

Make sure that all of your identifying information is correct on your Equifax credit report. If the report contains errors, you may be collecting another person's credit history. We'll talk about this in Chapter 8.

Credit History Section

Now let's look at the real meat of the credit report—the credit history section. Equifax appropriately labels this section "CREDIT HISTORY," and lists it just below the identifying information. The credit history section lists information that Equifax has gathered from all of your creditors that are Equifax subscribers. (Remember, the credit history section may not list all of your creditors. This could be because some of your creditors are limited subscribers, and only notify Equifax when you don't repay your loan. Or, it could be that some of your creditors don't subscribe to Equifax, and therefore don't report ANY credit information to them.)

Now look at the credit history section in Diagram 5-1. When you find it, you'll probably notice that Equifax divides the credit history section into several subcategories. These subcategories include: Company Name, Account Number, Whose Account, Date Opened, Months Reviewed, Date of Last Activity, High Credit, Terms, Balance, Past Due, Status, and Date Reported. These subcategories each tell a different story about your credit accounts.

Without getting too caught up in detail, let's try to examine each subcategory in the credit history section and discover what it reveals. Some subcategories are easy to understand, but others aren't. Therefore, we'll spend less time on some, and more time on others.

One final note before we start. Equifax lists one account on each line of the report. Therefore, all of the subcategories on one line apply to one account.

Company Name

The first subcategory lists the name of the creditor that extended credit to you on this particular account. This section could include banks, retail stores, gasoline dealers, or companies that issue major credit cards. In our sample Equifax credit report, "Checron" is the first "Company Name" in John Consumer's credit report.

Account Number

The "Account Number" subcategory lists the identifying number that the creditor has assigned to your account. This helps the creditor and the credit bureau identify your account. Diagram 5-1 shows that Checron has assigned account number "123571919245" to John's account.

Whose Account

The "Whose Account" subcategory shows your association with the account and your liability for repaying the account balance. Equifax uses the following designations:

J — Joint contractual liability. You share the account with another person, and you're each responsible for repaying the entire account balance. If one person fails to pay, the creditor may go after the other person for the entire debt.

I — Individual Liability. You are the only user of the account, and you are the only one responsible for repaying the account balance.

U — Undesignated. The creditor has not identified this account as a joint, individual, or other type of account.

A — Authorized User. You may use the account, but someone else is responsible for repayment.

T Terminated. You are no longer responsible for repayment, but you don't have access to the account.

M Maker. You signed a negotiable instrument (generally a promissory note) and are responsible for its payment.

C Co-Maker. You signed a negotiable instrument with one or more other people, and are responsible for its payment along with the others.

S Shared. You share this account and responsibility for its repayment with someone other than your spouse.

P Participant in shared account. The credit bureau can't determine whether you have joint contractual liability on this account or whether you're an authorized user of the account.

To give you an idea of how these designators work, look at Diagram 5-1. You'll find an "S" in the Whose Account subcategory for John's Checron account. If you look at the list above, you'll see that "S" means a"shared" account. Therefore, John and another person share responsibility for repaying the Checron account balance.

Date Opened

The "Date Opened" subcategory shows when the creditor first extended credit to you on this account. Diagram 5-1 shows that Checron opened John's account in February 1989.

Months Reviewed

The "Months Reviewed" subcategory shows how many months the credit bureau has reported information about this account. It may or may not correspond with the number of months that the account has been open. Diagram 5-1 shows that Equifax has reported information about John's Checron account for 32 months.

Date of Last Activity

The "Date of Last Activity" subcategory shows when the creditor last did something in your account. This could include crediting a payment, or charging off the debt because of a bankruptcy filing. Diagram 5-1 shows that the Date of Last Activity for the Checron account is December 1992.

The Date of Last Activity is very important because it helps to identify obsolete information that the credit bureau must remove from your credit report. To decide if your credit information is obsolete, the credit bureau must count how many years have passed since the Date of Last Activity on your account. If this period is more than the Fair Credit Reporting Act allows, the credit bureau must remove the account information from your credit report. We'll talk more about this in Chapter 9.

High Credit

The "High Credit" subcategory shows the highest amount you've ever owed on the account. For fixed payment accounts, the high credit amount is the amount of the original loan. For open or revolving accounts, the high credit amount equals your greatest balance on that account. Diagram 5-1 shows that the high credit for John's Checron account is $125.

Terms

The "Terms" subcategory shows how much your payments are, and how often you must make them. If you look at Diagram 5-1, you'll see that the Terms subcategory doesn't list any payment terms for John's Checron account. This may be because Checron requires John Consumer to pay the balance in full every month. Also, this could be because Checron doesn't report the terms of John's account for some reason.

To see an example of an account that lists the terms, look just below the line containing the Checron account. This is the "EPSC" account. Look under the Terms section for the EPSC account, and you'll see that John Consumer must pay $250 each month on this account.

Balance

The "Balance" subcategory shows how much you owed the creditor on this account when the creditor last reported your credit information to Equifax. Diagram 5-1 shows that the balance of John's Checron account is $55.

Past Due

The "Past Due" subcategory shows any past due amounts on the account when the creditor last reported this information to Equifax. You'll notice that Diagram 5-1 doesn't list a past due amount in the Checron account. However, look at the Wands account. The credit report shows that John was $160 past due on the Wands account when Wands last reported John's account information to Equifax.

Status

The "Status" subcategory shows whether you are up-to-date on your payments for this account. Equifax uses one letter and one number to show this status. The letter identifies the type of account, and the number shows whether the account is current or past due. Let's look at each of these indicators. First we'll look at the letter indicator, which identifies the type of account.

Type of Account

A creditor can extend credit to you in many ways. The creditor may want you to repay your loan in full each month, or give you many months or years to repay it. To show what type of credit arrangement you have, Equifax uses a letter indicator. To give you an idea of how this works, look at the following table. In it, I've listed the various letter indicators that Equifax uses and explained each indicator.

O Open Account. You promise to repay the full balance owed each month. Travel and entertainment cards, such as American Express, and charge accounts with local businesses, generally require this type of repayment.

R Revolving or Option. You may pay your balance in full each month or make a minimum payment based on some percentage of your total outstanding balance. Bank cards, such as Visa and Mastercard, department stores, and gas and oil companies, generally issue credit cards based on a revolving credit plan.

I Installment. You repay a fixed amount of your loan during a specified period. Automobile, furniture, and major appliance dealers usually finance your purchase with an installment loan. Banks, credit unions, and finance companies also use installment loans.

With this information in mind, look at Diagram 5-1. Notice that under the status column for the Checron account is the notation "O1." From the table above, we know that the "O" identifies the Checron account as an "open account." Therefore, John Consumer must pay the balance in full each month. This corresponds with our prediction under the "Terms" section. Because John must pay the balance in full each month, there are no monthly payments, and therefore nothing to list under the "Terms" category.

Manner of Payment Indicator

Now that we know about the first part of the Status indicator, let's look at the last part of it—the "Manner of Payment Indicator." The Manner of Payment Indicator shows whether you make your payments on time, or are sometimes late. It will also show if a bankruptcy court discharged the account. The following table lists the standard abbreviations and explanations that Equifax uses for the manner of payment indicator.

00 Your creditor has not rated this account because it is too new, or because you haven't used it yet.

01 You always make your payments within 30 days of the due date. Your report will also list this indicator if your payments aren't due each month, and you're less than one payment late.

02 Your payment is more than 30 days late, but not yet 60 days late. Your report will also list this indicator if your payments aren't due each month, and you're more than one, but less than two, payments late.

03 Your payment is more than 60 days late, but not yet 90 days late. Your report will also list this indicator if your payments aren't due each month, and you're more than two, but less than three, payments late.

04 Your payment is more than 90 days late, but not yet 120 days late. Your report will also list this indicator if your payments aren't due each month, and you're more than three, but less than four, payments late.

05 Your payment is more than 120 days late. You report will also list this indicator if your payments aren't due each month, and you're more than four payments late.

07 You are making regular payments under a Chapter 13 wage earner plan or similar arrangement.

08 The creditor has repossessed your vehicle.

8A You voluntarily abandoned your vehicle to the creditor.

09 The creditor has given up on your account. This is a bad debt, and the creditor has probably charged it off on its books as a loss.

Now, let's take this new information and learn to read the credit report. Look at Diagram 5-1. In the Status subcategory, you'll find the notation "O1." To decipher this notation, compare it with the table we've just reviewed. When you do this, you'll find that the "1" following the "O" means that John's Checron account was current when Checron last reported his information to Equifax. Therefore, John made his Checron payment on time, or at least wasn't more than 30 days late.

Before we go on to other areas of the credit report, let's look at a few more things under the Credit History section. We'll examine the following topics: Prior Paying History, Closed Accounts, Accounts included in Bankruptcy, and Involuntary Repossession.

Prior Paying History

Look again at Diagram 5-1, and find the "NE BANK" notation under the Company Name column. First, let's look at the account itself. The account number is 80905742. The Whose Account subcategory lists this account as a "U." This means that the credit bureau isn't sure about whose account it is. Now look to the right under the Balance column. Notice that this column is empty. That's because John Consumer doesn't currently owe NE Bank any money. But now let's look a little closer at this account.

Look again at the "NE BANK" reference and find the "PRIOR PAYING HISTORY" notation just below it. The credit report lists John's NE BANK account as "R1." Therefore, this account is currently in good standing. However, the Prior Paying History shows that John had problems with this account in the past. Notice the series of numbers located to the right of the "PRIOR PAYING HISTORY" notation. The notations are "30(01) 60(01) 90+(00) 11/85 - R3, 10/85 - R2." These notations show that John made one payment more than 30 days late—the "30(01)"—and made another payment more than 60 days late—the "60(01)."

The Prior Paying History subcategory also shows the Status indicators for these late payments. Look at the "11/85 - R3, 10/85 - R2" notations. These letters and numbers correspond to the letters and numbers that we examined in the "Status" section. The "R" is the "type of account" indicator, and identifies this account as a revolving account. The numbers are the "manner of payment" indicators, and show whether John made timely payments on the account. We see now that he did not.

Now let's look very closely at the Prior Paying History subcategory and see what it tells us about John's account. In October of 1985, John Consumer was more than 30 days late with one payment. This was probably the payment that he should have made in September of 1985. Because John failed to make this payment, the credit bureau downgraded his status for this account from "1" to "2." Not terrible, but not great either. Then, in November of 1985, John again failed to pay NE Bank. Now the September payment was more than 60 days late, and the October payment was more than 30 days late. Because of the missed September payment, the credit bureau then downgraded John's NE Bank account from a "2" to a "3." Now John was getting into bad credit territory.

Closed Account

Fortunately, John managed to repay NE Bank. However, for some reason, the account is now closed. This may have been at John's request, but may also have been NE Bank's idea. In either case, Equifax shows the "closed" status of John's account by listing "CLOSED ACCOUNT" just below the "PRIOR PAYING HISTORY" notation.

Account Included in Bankruptcy

Now look at the Househeld and Siti Prvs accounts. Follow them over to the right and look under the "Terms" column. You should see the notation "INCLUDED IN BANKRUPTCY" for these two accounts. This notation shows that John included these accounts in his bankruptcy filing. Therefore, the credit report doesn't list any terms, balance, past due amounts, or status for these accounts.

Your credit report should show similar notations for any account that you included in your bankruptcy case. However, you may find that many of your accounts don't reflect their true status. This is true in the sample credit report as well. Notice that the GMAK and AMAX accounts report the status as "8" and "9," respectively. But, if you look back at the sample schedules that John Consumer filed, you'll see that John included the GMAK and AMAX accounts in his bankruptcy case. Therefore, the credit report should show "INCLUDED IN BANKRUPTCY" for these accounts, just like the Househeld and Siti Prvs accounts. But, it doesn't.

We'll look at this problem in great detail in Chapter 9, and examine what you can do with your credit report mistakes. For now, though, let's keep familiarizing ourselves with the credit report format.

Involuntary Repossession

Look at the GMAK account. Notice that Equifax lists the notation "INVOLUNTARY REPOSSESSION" just beneath and to the right of the GMAK name. This notation shows that the creditor took John's car without his permission. State laws allow this under certain circumstances. If this notation is on your credit report, you'll find it very difficult to locate a bank or automobile dealer that will sell you a car on credit. You'll also notice that the Status subcategory shows this repossession with the type of account indicator "I," followed by the manner of payment indicator "8."

Collection Accounts

Now let's get away from the Credit History Section—finally! The next section in the Equifax credit report is the "Collection Accounts" section. This section will list any accounts that your creditors turned over to collection companies. Notice that Diagram 5-1 does not contain a "COLLECTION ACCOUNTS" section. That's because John included all of his bad credit accounts in his bankruptcy case. This SHOULD be the case with you as well. If you DO have accounts listed in this section, it's probably because your previous creditors are reporting them as collection accounts, and not bankruptcy accounts. If so, we'll take care of that in Chapter 9.

Public Record Information

The next section in the Equifax credit report is the "Courthouse Records" section. This is where you'll find any public record information that Equifax has collected about you. Look at Diagram 5-1. Under the Courthouse Records section, you'll find information about John Consumer's bankruptcy case. There's quite a bit of information here. The credit report correctly lists the date of filing as May 1986, and the date of discharge as September 1986. This section also lists John's case number, 86-00258, and shows that he filed an individual bankruptcy.

You should also find information about your bankruptcy case in the Courthouse Records section of the Equifax credit report. Examine the information closely. In the next chapter, we'll talk about fixing any errors that you find.

Additional Information

The next section below the Courthouse Records section lists your former addresses and your current and former employment. Equifax labels this section "Additional Information." Examine the information presented in this section in Diagram 5-1, and then look at your credit report. Make sure that the information is correct. If not, we'll take care of it in Chapter 9.

Inquiries

The final section in the Equifax credit report is the inquiry section. Equifax calls this section "Companies That Requested Your Credit History." In this section, you'll find information about individuals and companies that have requested your credit report within the last two years. Section 1681g(a)(3)(B) of the Fair Credit Reporting Act requires that credit bureaus report this information for six months. However, most credit bureaus report this information for two years.

Now look at Diagram 5-1. You'll see "2/14/93 CONS COPY" on the far left side of this section. This notation shows that John Consumer requested a copy of his credit report on that date. You'll also see four other entries under this section. Each entry includes the date of the credit report request, and the name of the company that requested the report.

Now look at your credit report. Find the inquiries section and examine the entries. We'll come back to this section in Chapter 8 to look for mistakes. For now, though, let's go on to the next credit report. (Congratulations! You made it through the first credit report.)

Diagram 5-1
[Sample Equifax Credit Report]

CB COLONIA
150 BORDEAUX RD
P.O. BOX 51
COLONIA, FL 32333

JOHN CONSUMER
5825 RED WOOD DR
COLONIA, FL 32331

DATE 02/14/93
SOCIAL SECURITY NUMBER 123-45-6789
DATE OF BIRTH 01/18/57

CREDIT HISTORY

Company Name	Account Number	Whose Acct.	Date Opened	Months Reviewed	Date of Last Activity	High Credit	Terms	All Items as of Date Reported			DATE REPORTED
								Balance	Past Due	Status	
CHECRON	123571919245	S	02/89	32	12/92	125		55		O1	12/92
EPSC	24304758392	I	07/90	20	11/92	23K	250	21K		I1	12/92
SITIBK-MC	175832419685	I	10/88	14	10/92	2000	50	1500		R1	12/92
JC PICKEY	2424382942	A	10/87	30	11/92	800	40	500		R1	12/92
WANDS	3838029535	J	10/87	19	9/92	1500	80	1400	160	R2	12/92
NE BANK	80905742	U	10/85		11/86	250		0		R1	2/90
>>> PRIOR PAYING HISTORY - 30(01) 60(01) 90+ (00) 11/85 - R3, 10/85 - R2 <<<											
CLOSED ACCOUNT											
HOUSEHELD	25-2872-34572	I	5/83	05	5/86	INCLUDED IN BANKRUPTCY					8/86
SITI PRVS	427138254914	I	1/84	12	5/86	INCLUDED IN BANKRUPTCY					7/86
GMAK	20043748	I	4/85		5/86	15K	48	15K		I8	9/86
INVOLUNTARY REPOSSESSION											
AMAX	56568966674	I	3/84	20	8/86	500		500	500	R9	10/87
AMAX	56568966674	I	3/84	20	8/86	758		758	758	R9	10/87

************** COURTHOUSE RECORDS **************

>>> BANKRUPTCY FILED 05/86, BANKRUPTCY, CASE NUMBER - 86-00258/ DISCH 09/86, PERSONAL INDIVIDUAL, DISCHARGED

************** ADDITIONAL INFORMATION **************

>>> FORMER ADDRESS 7825 FORT KNOX DR, TEXEE, TX, 18181
>>> FORMER ADDRESS 1325 NORWALK LANE, ATLEE, GA 10528
>>> CURRENT EMPLOYMENT - MANAGER, HOT DOG HEAVEN
>>> FORMER EMPLOYMENT - SCIENTIST, NASA

************** COMPANIES THAT REQUESTED YOUR CREDIT HISTORY ************

1/15/93	CONS COPY	06/25/91	BARKETT	6/10/91	NIXXAN
5/10/90	FT CASSAL	1/9/90	SE BANK		

Chapter 6

Your Trans Union Credit Report

He who knows others is wise; He who knows himself is enlightened.

Lao-tzu

O.K. One credit report finished, two more to go. It's time to tackle the Trans Union credit report. Find Diagrams 6-1(a) and 6-1(b). These diagrams represent two pages of a typical Trans Union credit report. Notice the differences between this report and the Equifax credit report represented by Diagram 5-1. They look a lot different, don't they?

Fortunately for us, though, the main difference between the two reports is structure. They really convey most of the same information; they just report it differently. Therefore, in this chapter, we'll examine the Trans Union credit report piece by piece, and compare it to the Equifax credit report. By the end of the chapter, you should have a strong understanding of both reports.

However, as we talked about before, this may bore you to tears. But don't let me or this chapter do that to you. Take it easy. Try to take in as much information as you can. Then, come back later for some more. You WILL learn what you need to know. (I promise!)

O. K. With all that said, let's get down to business and take a close look at the Trans Union credit report. Now, get your report, and Diagrams 6-1(a) and 6-1(b) in front of you. When you're ready, let's begin.

Identifying Information

For

Let's start with the identifying information at the top of the report. In the top left corner of the report is a box labeled "FOR." This box identifies who requested your credit report. In John Consumer's sample report, you'll find the code "(I) ZTA 5250" in the "FOR" box. Trans Union uses this code to show that you requested a copy of your own report. Therefore, John requested this report from Trans Union.

The "I" shows that this credit report is an individual credit report. If John were married, and his report contained information about his wife, the code would list "J" for joint. You probably have similar codes in this box on your report.

Market Sub

To the right of the "FOR" box is another box labeled "MARKET SUB." The MARKET SUB box identifies the location of the report according to the Trans Union coding system. In the sample, this box contains the notation "17 NF."

In File Since

To the right of the "MARKET SUB" box is another box labeled "IN FILE SINCE." This box shows when Trans Union first started to collect your credit information. In the sample, this box contains the notation "10/80." Therefore, Trans Union has collected John's credit information since October 1980.

Date and Time of Issue

To the right of the "IN FILE SINCE" box is the final box in the row, labeled "DATE" and "TIME OF ISSUE." These labels are self-explanatory. Trans Union prepared this sample credit report for John Consumer on February 14, 1993 at 4:45 local time. You'll notice that Trans Union uses the 24-hour clock to report the Time of Issue.

Name and Social Security Number

Below the first line is a long box that lists your name and Social Security number. This information is self-explanatory.

Birth Date

To the right of the Name and Social Security Number box is a smaller box that lists your year of birth. The sample report lists John's year of birth as "57-E." The "57" shows that John was born in 1957.

Watch Criteria

To the right of the "BIRTH DATE" box is the final box in this row, labeled "WATCH CRITERIA." The Watch Criteria box warns potential creditors that you may be a special risk.

Unfortunately, I see two major problems with the Watch Criteria box. First, Trans Union may not show you this information. Therefore, you may not know whether the information is true or not. This seems to go against the spirit and purpose of the Fair Credit Reporting Act.

Second, the Watch Criteria box looks like a rating system. Credit bureaus have always claimed that they don't "rate" your credit. But, if this claim were true, Trans Union wouldn't need shorthand warning signals like the Watch Criteria.

Fortunately, at least one major credit bureau will soon report the Watch Criteria on your copy of the credit report. Equifax has recently reached a settlement agreement with several states, to avoid legal action that the states had brought against it. One condition of this settlement requires that Equifax tell you about any watch criteria or rating system that it uses. In addition, it looks like Trans Union and TRW will also agree to this. This is great news for all of us.

Current and Previous Addresses

In the third row, you'll find a large box that shows your current and previous addresses. This box also shows when someone last reported these addresses to Trans Union. This information is self-explanatory.

Telephone Number and Spouse's Social Security Number

To the right of the address box are two boxes. One box lists your telephone number. The other box lists your spouse's name and Social Security number. Again, this information is self-explanatory.

Current and Former Employment

The last row contains information about your current and former employment. This information can be quite extensive, or very incomplete. You'll notice that the sample report lists NASA as John's current employer. However, we know that John has left his former job to work at Hot Dog Heaven. You'll probably find that your employment information is incomplete or inaccurate as well.

Now that we've looked through John's identification information, take a moment to review yours. Locate the identification section on your Trans Union credit report, and look through each box. You'll probably find inaccurate or missing information here. If so, remember the problems, and we'll correct them in Chapter 9.

Credit History

Now let's turn our attention to the credit history section of the credit report. The Trans Union credit history section doesn't look like the Equifax credit history section. However, it's very easy to find.

Locate the box in the middle left-hand side of the report labeled "SUBSCRIBER NAME." This entire section from left to right, which contains three major columns, is the credit history section. And although there are differences between this section and the credit history section of the Equifax credit report, you'll recognize many of the same concepts and symbols.

However, one main difference between each report format is that Trans Union reports three lines of information for each account. Equifax, however, uses only one line of information for most accounts. Therefore, we'll examine the Trans Union report a little differently.

Throughout the rest of this chapter, we'll examine each account by major column. For example, we'll look first at the sections contained within the first major column. These sections are subscriber name, subscriber code, date opened, account number, terms, ECOA, and collateral. Then, we'll move on to the next major column, and end with the third. This should make it easier to follow the information.

The First Major Column

Subscriber Name

O.K. Let's start our review with the first major column. Find the box labeled "SUBSCRIBER NAME." The Subscriber Name section identifies which company owns each account. Does this sound familiar? Yes, that's right. The Subscriber Name section shows the same information as the "Company Name" section in the Equifax credit report. Trans Union just calls it something else.

(Are you wondering why Trans Union calls your creditors "subscribers" instead of companies? If so, think back to our discussion of automatic and limited "subscribers." Subscribers are just "members" of the credit bureau. If they don't belong to a credit bureau—because they haven't paid the required fees—then they aren't subscribers of that credit bureau. Consequently, Trans Union won't list credit information from any of your creditors that don't subscribe to Trans Union's services.)

To get a feel for this, find "Checron" in the Subscriber Name section. (Hint—You'll find it on the second page of the credit report, Diagram 6-1(b).)

Subscriber Code

Now, let's move on. Find the box to right of the "Subscriber Name" section, labeled "SUBSCRIBER CODE." This section identifies the identification number that the credit bureau has assigned to this subscriber. (It is NOT the same number as the account number section that we examined in the Equifax credit report. We'll see in a minute that Trans Union also lists your account numbers.) The subscriber code for Checron in the sample report is 104T002.

Date Opened

Now find the box labeled "DATE OPENED." It's to the right of the Subscriber Code section. The Date Opened section shows when your creditor first gave you credit on each account. (Yes, that's right. It's just like the Date Opened section in the Equifax credit report.) The sample report shows that Checron opened John's account in February 1989.

Account Number

Now find the box labeled "ACCOUNT NUMBER." It's just below the Subscriber Name and Subscriber Code sections. As in the Equifax credit report, the Account Number section in the Trans Union report lists the number that your creditor uses to identify your account. In the sample, the account number for the Checron account is 123571919245.

Terms

Now find the box labeled "TERMS." It's to the right of the Account Number section. The Terms section shows how often you must pay your creditor, and the amount of each payment. Therefore, it's just like the Terms section in the Equifax credit report.

As in the sample Equifax report, the Trans Union credit report doesn't list anything under the Terms section. As we discovered earlier, this is because Checron requires that John pay his entire balance each month. Therefore, to learn how the Terms section works, we'll need to find another account that does list this information.

One account that does list its terms is the "SITIBANK" account. You'll find it just below the Checron account, with the notation "MIN50." The "MIN" stands for "minimum," and the "50" shows the required payment amount. Therefore, John must pay Sitibank at least $50 each month, although his real payment could be higher.

ECOA

Now find the box labeled "ECOA." It's just below the Account Number section. The "ECOA" stands for the Equal Credit Opportunity Act. This Act makes it illegal for creditors to deny your credit request based on your sex, race, marital status, religion, national origin, age, or because you receive public assistance.

The ECOA "designators" identify whether you are responsible for repaying any balance amounts on each account. The designators also show how you're associated with each account. (The ECOA section in the Trans Union credit report is just like the Whose Account section in the Equifax credit report. Therefore, if you've forgotten what the designators stand for, review the Whose Account section in the Equifax credit report. There, you'll find a complete list of the ECOA designators and explanations for each.)

In the sample credit report, the ECOA designator for John's Checron account is "P." This designator stands for "participant in a shared account which cannot be distinguished as joint contractual liability or authorized user." Therefore, in the sample report, Trans Union can't decide whether John shares repayment responsibility with another person, or is merely an authorized user of the account.

Collateral

Now let's look at some information that Equifax doesn't report. Find the box labeled "COLLATERAL." It's to the right of the ECOA section. The Collateral section identifies any assets that you've used to "secure" your debt. (Review Chapter 2 if you've forgotten the meaning of collateral, and secured and unsecured debt.)

The Second Major Column

High Credit

O.K. We've completed the first major column. Now it's time to move on to the second major column. Find the box labeled "HIGH CREDIT." It's the next box to the right of the Date Opened section. The High Credit section shows the greatest amount you've ever owed to this creditor for this account. Therefore, it's just like the High Credit section in the Equifax credit report. In the sample report, John Consumer's high credit for the Checron account is $125.

Date Verified

Now find the box labeled "DATE VERIFIED." It's the next box to the right of the High Credit section. The Date Verified section shows when your creditor last reported your account information to Trans Union. (The Date Verified section is just like the Date Reported section in the Equifax credit report.)

Besides the date, Trans Union includes a "date indicator" in the Date Verified section. The date indicator is a letter, generally an "A," that shows how Trans Union received this information from your creditor. For example, the "A" shows that your creditor uses some automated process to report account information to Trans Union.

Now look at John's Checron account in Diagram 6-1(b). In the Date Verified section, you'll find the notation "12/92A." The "12/92" shows that Checron reported John's account information to Trans Union in December 1992. The "A" shows that Checron used an automated process to report the information.

Another date indicator that you may find in the Date Verified section is "V." This date indicator shows that your creditor has verified your account information. The "V" symbol will appear if you ask Trans Union to verify information in your report. (You'd do this if you thought the information was inaccurate. We'll talk about this in Chapter 9.) We'll talk more about date indicators when we look at the "date closed" section.

Balance Owing

Now find the box labeled "BALANCE OWING." It's to the right of the Date Verified section. The Balance Owing section shows how much you owed on the account when your creditor last reported your account information to Trans Union. (The Balance Owing section is just like the Balance section in the Equifax credit report.) In our example, the Balance Owing section shows that John owed Checron $55 as of December 1992.

Amount Past Due

Now find the box labeled "AMOUNT PAST DUE." It's to the right of the Balance Owing section. The Amount Past Due section shows the total of your late payments when your creditor last reported to Trans Union. (The Amount Past Due section is just like the Past Due section in the Equifax credit report.) If you look at the sample report, you'll see that John wasn't late with any Checron payments when Checron last reported to Trans Union.

Credit Limit

Now find the box labeled "CREDIT LIMIT." It's just below the High Credit section. The Credit Limit section shows the maximum amount of credit on your account when your creditor last reported to Trans Union. (The Equifax credit report doesn't contain a section that shows this information.)

The Credit Limit amount may be the same amount as in the High Credit section, or it may be a different amount. Why would the two sections be different? Several things may cause them to be different. For example, your creditor might lower your credit line if you make late payments. Or, your creditor might let you exceed the stated credit limit. This would raise the amount listed in the High Credit section.

To see how this works, look at the HOUSEHELD FN account on the first page of the credit report, Diagram 6-1(a). You'll notice that the high credit amount is $1,500, but the credit limit amount is $0. Why is there a difference in the amounts? It looks like Househeld closed John's credit line when he failed to pay his payments on time.

Now look at the Checron account. You'll notice that the Credit Limit section doesn't list a Credit Limit amount for this account. As we discussed before, this is because Checron requires that John pay his entire balance each month. (Similarly, the Credit Limit section will be blank for any of your accounts that require payment in full each month, such as American Express.)

Because the Checron Credit Limit section is blank, let's look at another account. Find the SITIBANK account just beneath the Checron account. You'll see that John's credit limit for the SITIBANK account is $2,000, and that his High Credit amount is also $2,000.

Date Closed

Now find the box labeled "DATE CLOSED." It's to the right of the Credit Limit section. The Date Closed section shows when your creditor closed your account. As in the date verified section, you'll probably find a date, followed by a letter. (The Equifax credit report doesn't show when a creditor closes an account.)

Now look at the sample credit report. You won't find any information in the Date Closed section for John's Checron account. This is because the account is not closed. It's a current account.

However, look again at the HOUSEHELD FN account. You'll see the notation "5/86F" under the Date Closed section. The "5/86" notation shows that Househeld closed John's account in May 1986. The "F" notation is a date indicator that shows that Househeld "wrote off" John's account from its books, or turned it over to a collection company. A creditor will write off an account if it gives up hope that you'll repay the loan.

In John's case, the "F" notation is an inaccurate indicator for his account. Why? It's inaccurate because John included the Househeld account in his bankruptcy case. Therefore, the account should list a different date indicator. We'll talk more about that in Chapter 8. For now, let's look at the various date indicators that might appear on your credit report.

A Automated. Your creditor used an automated process to report this information to the Trans Union. (We saw this one under the Date Opened section.)

C Closed. Your account is closed.

D Declined. Trans Union rarely uses this indicator.

F Repossessed/Written Off/Collection. Your creditor has probably given up hope of ever collecting the money you owe them on this account. Therefore, it has written your account off its books or turned it over to a collection company.

H Hired. Trans Union rarely uses this indicator.

I Indirect. Trans Union rarely uses this indicator.

M Manually Frozen. Trans Union has stopped its computer tape from updating certain information about your account. This prevents unwanted information from recurring on your credit report. For example, Trans Union might manually freeze the accounts you included in your bankruptcy. They would do this to prevent the balance amounts from reappearing each month.

N No Record. Trans Union rarely uses this indicator.

P Paid Out. You have completely repaid this account.

R Reported but not Verified. Your creditor reported this account information, but has not yet responded to Trans Union's request to verify the information.

S Slow Answering. Trans Union rarely uses this indicator.

T Terminated or Temporarily Frozen. Trans Union rarely uses this indicator.

U Never/Not Used Account. You have access to this account, but you haven't used it. This indicator generally appears when the account is new.

V Verified. Your creditor has checked the accuracy of your credit information and told Trans Union that the information is correct.

X No Reply. Your creditor has not responded to a request from Trans Union to verify your account information.

Maximum Delinquency

Now find the box labeled "MAXIMUM DELINQUENCY," and the three smaller boxes labeled "DATE," "AMOUNT," and "MOP." These boxes are to the right of the Date Closed section. The Maximum Delinquency section lists late payment information about your account.

Now look at the three smaller boxes. These boxes are subcategories of the Maximum Delinquency section. The Date subcategory shows when your payments first became late. The Amount subcategory shows the greatest amount past due when your creditor last reported your account information.

The third subcategory is the MOP section. The "MOP" stands for your "manner of payment." The MOP subcategory shows how late your delinquent payments were. The MOP subcategory is just like the Status section of the Equifax credit report, except that it shows information about the delinquent amount. The Status section, however, shows your CURRENT standing.

Let's see how this works. Your credit report could show that you made a payment more than 30 days late. However, your creditor would show your account as current if you later made your payment and brought your account up to date. But, the MOP subcategory might still show your delinquent credit history. We'll talk more about the current Manner of Payment section when we get to the third major column.

Remarks and Type of Loan

Now find the box labeled "REMARKS TYPE LOAN." It's the bottom box in the second major row. Trans Union uses this section to add miscellaneous remarks about your account, and to identify the specific type of loan.

To get a feel for this, find the Househeld FN account in Diagram 6-1(a). Now look in the Remarks Type Loan section. You should see the notation "PROFIT-AND-LOSS WRITEOFF" for the Househeld FN account. This notation shows that Househeld has given up any hope that John will repay his account balance. Therefore, Househeld has removed John's account from its receivables account. Househeld may also have transferred the account to a collection company.

Unfortunately, the "PROFIT-AND-LOSS WRITEOFF" notation doesn't reflect the true status of John's account. John included the Househeld FN account in his bankruptcy case. Therefore, his account should show "BANKRUPTCY." Instead, the "PROFIT-AND-LOSS WRITEOFF" notation signals other creditors that John is ignoring his current accounts—not just those he included in his bankruptcy.

To see the correct notation, look at the "SITIBANK" account. In the Remarks section, you'll find the "BANKRUPTCY" notation. This is the true status of John's Sitibank account. And, as we've already discussed, it's also the true status of John's Househeld FN account. Therefore, the Househeld account should list "BANKRUPTCY" as well. We'll talk more about correcting errors like this one in Chapter 9.

The Third Major Column

Payment Pattern

Now we're in the third major column. The first section in this column is the Payment Pattern section. You'll find it to the right of the Present Status section, in a box labeled "PAYMENT PATTERN." The Payment Pattern section shows how you've paid your account over the last 24 months. To do this, Trans Union uses "1's" and "X's" for each month. The "1's" show that you made your payment on time, and the "X's" show that you were late.

Let's see how this works. Look just below the Payment Pattern section, and you'll see two boxes. The top box shows the notation "1-12 MONTHS" and the bottom box shows the notation "13-24 MONTHS." These boxes represent the last 24 months of your account.

The first row will show "1's" and "X's" for each of the first 12 months. The second row will show "1's" and "X's" for each of the next 12 months. Therefore, if your account is less than one year old, there will only be one row of "1's" and "X's." If your account is more than one year old, then there will be two rows of "1's" and "X's."

If your account IS more than two years old, Trans Union will only show the last 24 months of your account information. The most recent payment information will be in the second row, labeled "13-24 MONTHS." The year before the current year will be in the first row, labeled "1-12 MONTHS." If you have any account information before that, this section will not list it. Therefore, the Payment Pattern section will only show, at most, the last two years of payment information, even if the account has been open for more than two years.

I know this sounds confusing. So, let's look at an example. Find the Checron account on the sample credit report. Under the payment pattern section, you'll see 11 "1's" and one "X" on the first row. The 11 "1's" on the first row show that John Consumer paid the Checron payment on time for 11 months last year. The "X" shows, however, that he was late on one payment out of that 12-month period.

On the second row, you'll see nine "1's" and three "X's." The nine "1's" show that John paid the Checron payment on time for nine months in the current year. However, the three "X's" show that John missed a few more due dates this year than last.

The payment pattern section in the Trans Union credit report is more accurate than the Status section in the Equifax report. The "1's" and "X's" allow potential creditors to see whether you are slow with your payments, and may show a trend of increasing credit problems. Notice that although John missed three due dates in the current year for the Checron account, the status in the Equifax credit report still shows a top rating of "01." The Historical Status and MOP sections of the Trans Union credit report also reflect this status. Yes, I know. We haven't talked about those sections yet. Well, this seems like a good time to talk about them.

Historical Status

Find the long box labeled "HISTORICAL STATUS." It's just below the Payment Pattern section. The Historical Status section shows how many months the credit bureau has received information on your account. This section also shows how often you've missed your payment deadline and by how many days. To do this, it will show the number of times you missed the due date by 30-59 days, 60-89 days, and more than 90 days. You'll find this information under the boxes labeled "No. Month," "30-59," "60-89," and "90+."

Let's see an example of this. Look again at the Checron account in the sample report. You'll see the notation "29" under the No. Month section. This shows that Trans Union has received information on this account for 29 months.

Now look under the boxes labeled "30-59," "60-89," and "90+." You'll find a "0" under each box. This shows that over the last 24 months, John has never missed a payment deadline by more than 30 days. Therefore, even though John has missed the due date four times over the last two years, he's always paid the required payment within 30 days of the due date.

Type of Account and MOP

Now find the box labeled "TYPE ACCOUNT & MOP." It's to the right of the Payment Pattern section. As you remember from our discussion in the Equifax credit report, the Type of Account section shows how you must repay the loan. There are many ways to repay your creditor. Trans Union uses the following indicators to show what each of your creditors requires:

O Open Account. You must repay your entire balance over 30, 60, or 90 days.

R Revolving or Option. You must repay some percentage of your entire balance with regular payments. Most credit cards are revolving accounts.

I Installment. You must repay a fixed amount of your entire balance over a fixed period. Most car loans are installment accounts.

M Mortgage. You must repay your entire balance over a fixed period. Home loans are generally mortgage accounts.

C Check credit (line of credit). You can draw on a line of credit by writing checks. You must then repay your balance according to the terms of your agreement with the creditor.

Now let's see an example of this. Look again at the Checron account. You'll notice the notation "R01" under the Type Account & MOP section. The "R" shows that the Checron account is a revolving account. (But, is this right? Look again at the Equifax report. The Equifax report shows that the Checron account is an open account. This is the correct information.) The "01" shows that John is not currently more than 30 days late on any payment. (If you've forgotten the MOP—or Manner of Payment—symbols, look back to the explanation of the Status section in the sample Equifax credit report.)

Inquiries

O.K. We've finally completed the Credit History section. Now it's time to move on. The next section in the Trans Union credit report is the Inquiries section. As in the Equifax report, the Inquiries section lists anyone that's requested your credit report within the last two years. You may remember from our earlier discussion that the Fair Credit Reporting Act only requires that the credit bureau maintain this information for six months. However, as we discovered, most credit bureaus will maintain this information for two years.

Locate the Inquiries section in the sample Trans Union credit report. You'll find it on the second page of the report, Diagram 6-1(b). Look just below the "WANDS" account information. You'll see the following notation: "INQR 4." This shows that Trans Union has received four requests for John's credit report within the last two years.

Now find the notations "DATE," "ECOA," "SUBCODE," "SUBNAME," "TYPE," and "AMT." You'll find them just below the "INQR 4" notation. These notations show the name of the individual or company that requested your credit report, and the date that they made the request.

In the sample, the Inquiries section only lists John's request for his own report. You'll notice that this information corresponds to the information at the top of the credit report. For example, the Date section identifies February 14, 1993 as the date for this request. We know that this is the day that John Consumer made this request. Under the Subname category in the sample report, you'll see "CONSUM DISCL." This stands for "consumer disclosure," and correctly reports the purpose of this report.

O.K., seems fairly simple. But, I said there were four inquiries. Where are the other three? Believe it or not, just below the first one. Look at the single line of numbers and letters directly beneath the consumer disclosure line. The line begins with "0S00385006." You'll notice that there are two commas in this line. The two commas separate the remaining three inquiries.

Yes, that's right. The notation "0S00385006 (SCT) - 6/25/92I" is a credit inquiry. It relays the same type of information about the credit inquiry as the consumer disclosure line we just examined. In our example, the "0S00385006" is the subcode that the credit bureau uses to identify inquirers. The "(SCT)" is the subname that the credit bureau has assigned to this inquirer. The "6/25/92" is the date of the inquiry. And finally, the "I" shows that this is John's individual credit report.

So why can't the credit bureau just put inquiry information in an understandable form? That's a good question. Trans Union used to present the inquiry information in an understandable format, but has since gone to this cryptic language. If you want to find out who has been searching through your credit information, you'll need to contact Trans Union and have them decipher the codes for you. This seems ridiculous, doesn't it?

Collection Accounts

Now find the section labeled "COLLECTION." This section will list any accounts that your creditors turned over to collection companies. (It's just like the Collection Accounts section in the Equifax credit report.) Notice that Diagrams 6-1(a) and 6-1(b) do not contain a "COLLECTION" section. That's because John included all of his past due accounts in his bankruptcy case. This SHOULD be the case with you as well. If you do have accounts listed in this section, it's probably because your previous creditors are reporting them as collection accounts, and not bankruptcy accounts. If so, we'll take care of that in Chapter 9.

Public Record Information

Now let's look at the section of the Trans Union credit report that contains public record information. You'll find this section under the notation "PUBLIC RECORD." (The Public Record section in the Trans Union credit report is similar to the Courthouse Records section in the Equifax credit report.) You'll remember from our earlier discussion that public record information is information contained in government records that anyone can access. The type of information that normally appears in credit reports as public record information includes judgments, liens, and most important to our discussion, bankruptcies.

Locate the Public Record section of the sample Trans Union credit report. You'll find it on the second page of the report, Diagram 6-1(b), labeled "PUBLIC RECORD." Let's take a quick look at the various subsections that you're likely to find here.

Source

Find the notation "SOURCE." It's directly below the "PUBLIC RECORD" notation. The Source section shows how Trans Union found out about this information. Generally, credit bureaus receive this information from companies that search public records to find adverse information about you. In the sample report, the source code is "Z 6054062." Unfortunately, that really doesn't do much for us. Even if we could decipher the code, it probably wouldn't help us to know the name of the company that located the information.

Court

Now find the section labeled "COURT." It's to the right of the Source section. The Court section shows which court maintains the public record information about you. In the sample report, you'll see the notation "FE" under the Court section. This shows that a federal district court maintains public record information about John's bankruptcy case.

If the Public Record section lists your bankruptcy, you'll also have the notation "FE." However, the Public Record section will also list other court abbreviations if you've been involved in other matters of public record, such as a lien or judgment. The following table lists other court abbreviations you may encounter in this section:

AS	Associate Court	GS	General Session
CA	County Auditor	IC	Inferior Court
CC	County Clerk's Office	JU	Justice of the Peace
CH	Chancery Court	MA	Magistrate Court
CI	Circuit Court	MU	Municipal Court
CL	County Court at Law	M1	1st Magisterial Court
CN	Conciliation Court	M2	2nd Magisterial Court
CO	Common Claims	M3	3rd Magisterial Court
CP	Common Pleas	M4	Quarterly Court
CT	County Court	PC	Parish Court
CY	City Court	PR	Probate Court
DC	District Court	RD	Recorder of Deeds
DO	Domestic Court	SC	Small Claims
DS	District Judge System	ST	State Court
FE	Federal District Court	SU	Superior Court

Date

Now find the section labeled "Date." The Date section lists the date of the public record information. For bankruptcies, the Date section will list the date of filing, the date of discharge, or both. In the sample credit report, the Date section lists May 1986, as the date that John filed his bankruptcy.

Liabilities

If the Public Record section does list your bankruptcy, you'll probably see a section labeled "LIAB." The Liabilities section shows the total dollar amount of your liabilities when you filed your bankruptcy petition. In the sample credit report, John had $40,000 in debts when he filed his bankruptcy petition.

Type

The section labeled "TYPE" shows what form of bankruptcy you filed. To get a feel for this, look at the sample credit report. Under the Type section, you'll see the notation "DC." This notation shows that John's bankruptcy is discharged. You'll also see the notation "I." This notation shows that John filed an individual bankruptcy.

Assets

Now find the section labeled "ASSETS." This section shows the total value of your assets when you filed your bankruptcy petition. In the sample report, John Consumer had $5,000 in assets when he filed his bankruptcy petition.

Paid

Now find the section labeled "PAID." The Paid section shows whether you repaid the debt. This information generally applies to liens and judgments.

Docket Number

Now find the section labeled "DOCKET NUMBER." You'll remember from our earlier discussion that the docket number is the identification number that the bankruptcy court assigns to your case. We found your docket number, or case number, in Chapter 2. The Docket Number section lists your bankruptcy docket number. The docket number for John's bankruptcy case is 86258.

Plaintiff/Attorney

Now find the section labeled "PLAINTIFF/ATT." The Plaintiff/Attorney section lists your bankruptcy attorney. Don't worry if this section doesn't show any information about your case. In the sample report, the Plaintiff/Attorney section doesn't list the name of John Consumer's attorney. This could be because John handled the bankruptcy case himself, or because Trans Union hasn't received this information.

TransAlert Message

After the Public Record section, you may find one or more additional messages. The first message that you may find is a "TransAlert message." This message will appear on your credit report if one of several events occurs.

First, the TransAlert message will appear if Trans Union discovers conflicting information in your file. Let me give you an example of how this could happen. Suppose that you apply for credit at a local store. You complete a credit application, and the store transmits this information to Trans Union. Trans Union then takes this information, locates your credit file, and sends a copy to the creditor. This is generally a smooth process.

But what happens if the person that transmits your information to Trans Union makes a typing error, or incorrectly reads your credit application? A discrepancy occurs in the information that Trans Union has just received and the information contained within your files. If this happens, you'll probably get a TransAlert message on your credit report that shows the discrepancy.

How does this affect you? It makes you look like you're trying to defraud your creditors by using alternate information. This won't help your credit rebuilding efforts.

The second reason that a TransAlert message may appear on your credit report is if your Social Security number doesn't match Trans Union's table of valid Social Security numbers. Like the problem above, a typing error could cause this problem.

Finally, a TransAlert message may appear on your credit report if there were four or more inquiries about your report in the last 60 days. The idea behind this is to warn potential creditors that you seem to have a sudden need for credit. This could show that you have a deteriorating financial situation and would make a bad credit risk.

HAWK ALERT

The next type of message that may appear on your credit report, and the last one that we'll talk about here, is a "Hawk Alert." The Hawk Alert message will appear if Trans Union believes that your residential address is really a commercial address. The idea behind this is to prevent you from giving inaccurate addresses or to warn creditors of potential fraud. Trans Union will also issue a Hawk Alert on your credit report to highlight any other information that it believes will interest your creditors.

Final Words

Congratulations! You've completed the second credit report format, and there's only one more to go. So, if you're ready, turn the page, and let's do it.

Diagram 6-1(a)
[Sample Trans Union Credit Report]

OPER NO.	BATCH NO.	DPT	RPT TYPE
	57	28	104

FOR	MARKET SUB	IN FILE SINCE	DATE	TIME OF ISSUE
(I) ZTA 5250	17 NF	10/80	2/14/93	16:45

REPORT ON	SSN	BIRTH DATE	WATCH CRITERIA
CONSUMER, JOHN J	123-45-6789	57 - E	

TELEPHONE: 725-1234

CURRENT ADDRESS	DATE REPORTED
5825 RED WOOD DR., COLONIA FL 32331	7/91 R
FORMER ADDRESS	
7825 FORT KNOX DR., TEXEE TX 18181	7/90R
1325 NORWALK LANE, ATLEE GA 10528	

SPOUSE'S NAME / SSN:

CURRENT EMPLOYER AND ADDRESS	POSITION / INCOME	EMPL. DATE	DATE REPORTED
NASA			4/83R
FORMER EMPLOYER AND ADDRESS			
SPOUSE'S EMPLOYER AND ADDRESS			

SUBSCRIBER NAME / ACCOUNT NUMBER / ECOA	SUBSCRIBER CODE / TERMS / COLLATERAL	DATE OPENED	HIGH CREDIT / CREDIT LIMIT	DATE VERIFIED / DATE CLOSED	BALANCE OWING	AMOUNT PAST DUE	PAYMENT PATTERN 1-12 MONTHS / 13-24 MONTHS / HISTORICAL STATUS (No month, 30-59, 60-89, 90+)	TYPE ACCOUNT & MOP
HOUSEHELD FN 25-2872-34572 I	F 2371707 35M50	5/83	$1500 $0	8/86A 5/86F	$1500	$0		I09
			*PROFIT-AND-LOSS WRITEOFF					
SITIBANK 427138254914 I	B 65ED003	1/84		7/86A 5/86F	$0	$0		R09
			*BANKRUPTCY					
AMERICAN AXP 56568966674 I	N 657N002	3/84		10/87A 8/86F	$0	$0		R09
			*BANKRUPTCY					
AMERICAN AXP 56568966674 I	N 657N002	3/84		10/87A 8/86F	$0	$0		O09
			*BANKRUPTCY					
GMAK 20043748 I	F 5200032	4/85	$15K	5/86A	$0			R08
			*BANKRUPTCY					
J C PICKEY 2424382942 A	D 5300019	10/87	$800	11/92	$500	$0	11111XX11X11 11XX1 17 0 0 0	R01

PAGE 1 CONT

Diagram 6-1(b)
[Sample Trans Union Credit Report]

ORDER NO.	BATCH NO.	DPT	RPT TYPE
	57	28	104

FOR	MARKET SUB	IN FILE SINCE	DATE	TIME OF ISSUE
(I) ZTA 5250		10/80	2/14/93	16:45

REPORT ON: CONSUMER, JOHN J
SSN:
BIRTH DATE: 57 - E
WATCH CRITERIA:
TELEPHONE: 785-4231

CURRENT ADDRESS: 5825 RED WOOD DR., COLONIA FL 32331 — DATE REPORTED: 7/91 R
SPOUSE'S NAME / SSN:

FORMER ADDRESS:
7825 FORT KNOX DR., TEXEE, TX 18181 — 7/90 R
1325 NORWALK LANE, ATLEE, GA 10528

CURRENT EMPLOYER AND ADDRESS	POSITION / INCOME	EMPL. DATE	DATE REPORTED
NASA			5/83 R
FORMER EMPLOYER AND ADDRESS			
SPOUSE'S EMPLOYER AND ADDRESS			

SUBSCRIBER NAME / ACCOUNT NUMBER / ECOA	SUBSCRIBER CODE / TERMS / COLLATERAL	DATE OPENED	HIGH CREDIT / CREDIT LIMIT	DATE VERIFIED / DATE CLOSED	PRESENT STATUS: BALANCE OWING / MAXIMUM DELINQUENCY: DATE / REMARKS	AMOUNT PAST DUE / AMOUNT / MOP / TYPE LOAN	PAYMENT PATTERN: 1-12 MONTHS / 13-24 MONTHS / HISTORICAL STATUS: No month, 30-59, 60-89, 90 +	TYPE ACCOUNT & MOP
CHECRON 123571919245 P	O 104T002	2/89	$125	12/92A	$55	$0	11111111X111 111111XX111X 29 0 0 0	R01
SITIBANK 175832419685 I	B 65ED003 MIN50	10/88	$2000 $2000	12/92A	$1500	$0 / CREDIT CARD	111111111111 1111111X1111 32 0 0 0	R01
WANDS 3838029535 C	D 44CC001	10/87	$1500	12/92A	$1400	$0	1111X1X11111 1 16 0 0 0	R01

INQR 4

DATE	ECOA	SUBCODE	SUBNAME	TYPE AMT
2/14/93	I	ATZ5350	CONSUM DISCL	

0S00385006 (SCT)- 6/25/92I,CTA2114-6/21/92I,DTC3778-6/10/92I

PUBLIC RECORD

SOURCE	COURT	DATE	LIAB	TYPE	ASSETS	PAID	DOCKET NUM.	PLAINTIFF/ATT
Z 6054062	FE	5/86	$40.0K	DC I	$5000		86258	VOL BANKRUPTCY

DISCHARGED BANKRUPTCY

Chapter 7

Your TRW Credit Report

There is only one good, knowledge, and one evil, ignorance.

Socrates

Finally, we're down to the last credit report—TRW. Fortunately for us, the TRW credit report is straightforward and easy to understand. And by now, you're an expert! Therefore, this chapter should be smooth sailing. So, roll out your sails and let's begin.

Identifying Information

Let's start, as we have in the last two chapters, with the identifying information. To locate the identifying information, turn to the sample TRW credit report in Diagrams 7-1(a) and 7-1(b). You'll find the identifying information at the top of the first page, Diagram 7-1(a).

Identifying information is the information that TRW used to locate your credit file in its data base. Remember that TRW has credit information on more than 200 million consumers. The identifying information allows TRW to locate your file from among all the rest. Identifying information includes your Social Security number, date of birth, and present and former addresses. You'll see this information for John Consumer at the top of the sample credit report.

Now look at the next row of boxes below the first box. These boxes contain self-explanatory information about the request for this credit report, such as the page number, date of request, and time that TRW printed the report. However, there are a few more boxes here that may need explanation.

Important Notice: This chapter presents the credit report format that TRW has used for several years. Unfortunately, TRW completely revised this format just as we were going to press. But don't worry—the new format is straightforward and easy to understand. TRW has taken a bold step in the right direction, and I applaud their efforts. But, you're still not off the hook. TRW representatives have told me that they will continue to use the "old" format for reporting any changes. Therefore, you'll still need to know all the sections and symbols presented in this chapter.

Port and H/V

The boxes labeled "PORT" and "H/V" list information about TRW's computer system. You can ignore these boxes.

Last Name and City Identification

Now find the box to the right of the "H/V" section. This box lists your last name, and your city and state according to the information in TRW's database. To get a feel for this, look at the sample report in Diagram 7-1(a). You'll see that TRW lists John's last name, Consumer, in this box. You'll also see the notation "CFL2." This stands for Colonia, Florida, John's city and state.

Consumer Identification Number

Now look at the final box in this row. Just above this box, you'll find the notation "IDENTIFICATION NUMBER." The Identification section shows the number that TRW has assigned to your credit information. TRW asks that you include this number whenever you contact them about your credit information. In the sample report, TRW has assigned the number "57-425678-32" to John's credit information.

Name and Address

Now look at the long box just below the "PAGE," "DATE," and "TIME" sections. This box lists your name, address, and the date that TRW received this information. In the sample report, you'll see that TRW has correctly listed John's name and address. This section also shows that TRW received this information in February 1993. (Incidentally, TRW received this information from John. That's right. John gave this information to TRW when he requested his credit report. This is one way that credit bureaus get you to update their files.)

Employment Information

Now find the information about your current employment. It's in the same long box, but to the right of the name and address information. This employment information may or may not be current, depending upon how long it's been since someone last reported it to TRW. In the sample report, TRW incorrectly lists "NASA" as John's current employment. You may remember that Equifax correctly reported John's current employment with Hot Dog Heaven, and the NASA position as previous employment. This is a common error in credit reports.

Social Security Number and Year of Birth

Now locate your Social Security number and year of birth. You'll find this information in the same long box, but to the right of the employment information. In the sample credit report, TRW correctly lists John's Social Security number as "123-45-6789," and his year of birth as "1957."

FACS+ Summary

Before we get to the meat of the report, let's look at a section that TRW calls the "FACS+ SUMMARY." You'll find this information at the top of the Credit History section.

TRW uses the FACS+ SUMMARY to warn creditors about potential problems with your credit report. First, the FACS+ SUMMARY shows whether your reported Social Security number is valid. Second, this section shows whether TRW believes your reported residential address is really a commercial address. Finally, this section shows how many subscribers have requested your report during the last 120 days. This might alert potential creditors that you have some financial problem and suddenly need credit. (As you can probably tell, the FACS+ SUMMARY is very similar to the TransAlert and HAWK ALERT messages in the Trans Union credit report.)

To see an example of this section, locate the "FACS+ SUMMARY" notation on the first page of the credit report. You'll notice that John's credit report doesn't list any information under the "FACS+ SUMMARY" notation. This means that TRW hasn't found any unusual problems with his Social Security number, or with his address. Additionally, the notation "FROM 10/15/91 NUMBER OF INQS WITH THIS SS# =0"shows that John hasn't applied for credit in the last 120 days.

Credit History Information

Credit Accounts

Now it's time to look at the Credit History section, the "meat" of the TRW credit report. At the beginning of this chapter, I said that the TRW credit report is straightforward and easy to understand. I said that because TRW uses a simplified credit "rating" system to report your credit information.

TRW uses a simple three-part "account profile," instead of the 01-09 Status system that Equifax and Trans Union use. Under this system, TRW lists your accounts as "positive," "non-evaluated," or "negative." Therefore, your creditors can quickly review your account information.

(Unfortunately, it looks to me like TRW's account profile system "rates" your credit. Credit bureaus have always claimed that they don't "rate" your credit, but only supply information to your creditors. Then, the story goes, your creditors decide what that information means to them. But what do the labels "positive" and "negative" mean to you? I think they mean good and bad. This sure seems like a rating system to me. Oh well, enough of that. Let's look at the credit history section.)

Account Profile

Well, we didn't get very far. We're back to this simplified account system that doesn't rate your credit. As we discussed just a moment ago, the account profile section breaks all of your accounts down into three categories—positive, non-evaluated, and negative. Look at the sample TRW credit report in Diagram 7-1(a). You'll see the Account Profile section just below the name and address section.

The Account Profile section contains three columns, one for each of its categories. To see how this works, look at the "HOUSEHELD" and "SITIBANK MASTERCHARGE" accounts. To the left of each of these accounts, you'll see an "A." For the HOUSEHELD account, the "A" is in the column labeled "Neg" for negative. For the "SITIBANK MASTERCHARGE" account, the "A" is in the column labeled "Pos" for positive. A creditor, then, could look at each of these accounts, and see how TRW "rates"—I mean, classifies—them. This is a simple system that doesn't rely on codes like the Equifax and Trans Union systems.

Incidentally, the "A" in the columns shows that your creditor used an automated system to report your credit information to TRW. The three columns could also contain an "M." This would show that your creditor manually reported your credit information to TRW.

To see an example of this, look at the second page of the sample TRW credit report, Diagram 7-1(b). To the left of the NIXXAN entry, you'll see an "M" in the non-evaluated column. Therefore, NIXXAN manually reported John's credit information to TRW.

The NIXXAN entry also shows how TRW uses the "non-evaluated" category. As you might imagine, a credit inquiry doesn't really show whether you're able or willing to repay a loan. Therefore, TRW doesn't try to "rate"—there's that word again—inquiries. However, there are other uses for this non-evaluated category.

Look back to the first page of the sample report, Diagram 7-1(a), and locate the "NE BANK" account. You'll find an "A" in the non-evaluated column. The "NE BANK" account is not an inquiry. It's a true credit account. However, TRW lists this account in the non-evaluated column. Why? They do this because NE BANK has closed John's account.

Although John's bankruptcy "closed" other accounts in the technical sense, NE BANK closed this account for another reason. Therefore, TRW doesn't "evaluate" the account. An account may appear in the non-evaluated column if you successfully repay the entire balance, but had earlier problems with the account.

Subscriber Name/Court Name

Now find the box labeled "Subscriber Name/Court Name." It's to the right of the Account Profile section. The Subscriber Name/Court Name section shows who supplied your credit or public record information to TRW. This should be one of your creditors, or a court or government agency. (The Subscriber Name/Court Name section is just like the Subscriber Name section of the Trans Union report, and the Company Name section of the Equifax report.)

Status Comment

Now find the box labeled "Status Comments." It's just below the Subscriber Name/Court Name section. TRW uses the Status Comment section to provide miscellaneous comments about your accounts. (The Status Comment section is just like the Remarks section of the Trans Union report.) TRW uses a variety of abbreviations in the Status Comment section. In the following table, I've listed the abbreviations you might find in the Status Comment section, and explained each of them.

BK ADJ PLN	You included this account in your Chapter 13 repayment plan.
BK LIQ RE	You included this account in your Chapter 7, 11, or 12 bankruptcy case.
CHARGE OFF	Your creditor has reported this account as a loss.
CLOS INAC	Your account is closed and inactive.
CLOS NP AA	Your creditor has closed your credit line for this account. Additionally, you've agreed to repay the loan, but are not doing so.
COLL ACCT	Your account is seriously past due. Therefore, your creditor has assigned your account to a collection agency, attorney, or in-house collection department.
CO NOW PAY	Your creditor initially reported this account as a charge-off. However, you subsequently started to repay the debt.
CR CD LOST	Your creditor has reported that your credit card was lost or stolen.
CR LN CLOS	Your creditor has closed your credit line for this account for some unknown reason, or at your request. You may still have a balance due on the account.

CR LN RNST	Your account was a closed account. However, you are now in good standing and can use the account.
CURR ACCT	Your account is either an open or closed account. If the account is open, you probably can use it, and there may be a balance. If the account is closed, then your creditor has reported no account balance or past due payments.
CURR WAS COL	Your account was previously a collection account, insurance claim, or government claim. However, you subsequently repaid all past due amounts, and the account is current.
CURR WAS DL	Your account was previously past due. However, you subsequently repaid all past due amounts, and the account is current.
CURR WAS FOR	Your creditor began foreclosure procedures on your account. However, you subsequently repaid all past due amounts, and the account is current.
CURR WAS 30	Your account was more than 30 days past due. However, you subsequently repaid all past due amounts, and the account is current.
CURR WAS 30-2	Your account was more than 30 days past due for the number of times shown. However, you subsequently repaid all past due amounts, and the account is current.
DECEASED	You are dead. (I hope you don't see this one on your credit report!)
DEED IN LIEU	You gave your creditor a deed to your property to prevent the creditor from foreclosing on your mortgage.
DELINQ 60 (etc.)	Your account is past due for the number of days shown.
DEL WAS 90	Your payments for this account were more than 90 days past due. However, you subsequently made payments on the account, but are still 30 or 60 days late.
DEL WAS 120	Your payments for this account were more than 120 days past due. However, you subsequently made payments on the account, but are still 30, 60, or 90 days late.
GOVCLAIM	The government has filed a claim against you because you failed to repay your student loan.
FORECLOSURE	Your creditor has seized and sold your property to repay your mortgage.

FORE PROC	Your creditor has started a foreclosure process on your property because you've failed to repay your mortgage.
INQUIRY	This creditor has requested a copy of your TRW credit report.
INS CLAIM	Your creditor has filed a claim against you based on the insured portion of your account balance that you've collateralized with real estate.
NOT PAY AA	You've agreed to repay the balance of your account, but aren't making payments according to that agreement.
PAID ACCT	Your account is closed and has no balance. Your creditor has not rated the account.
PAID SATIS	Your account is closed, and you repaid it according to the terms of your credit agreement.
PD BY DLER	The seller of the merchandise underlying your account paid the account in full.
PD CHG OFF	Your creditor reported your account as a charge-off. However, you subsequently repaid the account in full.
PD COLL AC	Your creditor originally reported your account as a collection account. However, you subsequently repaid the account in full.
PD FORECLO	Your creditor began a foreclosure process on your account. However, you subsequently repaid the account in full.
PD NOT AA	Your creditor initially reported that you failed to make some payments according to a repayment agreement. However, you subsequently repaid the account in full.
PD REPO	Your creditor repossessed your property because you failed to make scheduled payments. However, you subsequently repaid the account in full.
PD VOL SUR	You voluntarily returned property to your creditor to avoid repossession. However, you subsequently repaid the account in full.
PAID WAS 30	Your account was more than 30 days past due. However, you subsequently repaid the account in full.
PAID WAS 30-2	Your account was more than 30 days past due for the number of times shown. However, you subsequently repaid the account in full.
REDMD REPO	Your creditor repossessed your property because you failed to repay the loan. However, you subsequently regained possession of your assets.

REFINANCED	Your creditor has renewed or refinanced your account.
REPO	Your creditor seized your property because you failed to repay your loan.
SCNL	Your creditor can't find you.
SCNL NWLOC	Your creditor previously reported that it couldn't find you. However, your creditor has subsequently located you.
SETTLED	You have legally satisfied the obligations of your account by paying less than the full amount due.
TERM DFALT	Your creditor has terminated your account before the expiration of its original terms because you defaulted on the original agreement.
TRANSFERRED	Your creditor moved your account to another office.
VOL SURR	You voluntarily surrendered your property to prevent your creditor from repossessing.
30 DAY DEL	You are currently 30 or more days late on one or more payments for your account.
30 2 TIMES (etc.)	You are currently 30 or more days late on one or more payments for your account, for the number of times shown.
30 WAS 60	You were more than 60 days late with one or more payments for your account. However, you subsquently made payments on the account, but are still more than 30 days late.

That's a lot of abbreviations. Fortunately, you don't have to memorize them all. Just review this table whenever you find an abbreviation that you don't understand.

Now let's see how TRW uses these abbreviations. Look at the first page of the sample TRW report, Diagram 7-1(a). Just below the "HOUSEHELD" account, you'll find the "BK LIQ REO" notation. Now look at the Status Comment table above. You'll see that the "BK LIQ REO" notation shows that John included the HOUSEHELD in his Chapter 7 bankruptcy case.

O.K., let's do another one. Find the "CURR ACCT" notation just below the "SITIBANK MASTERCHARGE" account. Now look at the Status Comment table above. You'll see that the "CURR ACCT" notation shows that John's Sitibank account is current and in good standing.

All right, one more. Find the "CHARGE OFF" notation just below the "AMERICAN AXPRESS" account. This notation shows that AMERICAN AXPRESS reported a loss on John's account. However, as we discussed earlier with another account, this is wrong. John included this AMERICAN AXPRESS account in his Chapter 7 bankruptcy case. Therefore, the status comment should reflect this. We'll talk more about this type of problem, and how to correct it, in Chapter 9. For now, though, let's continue our exploration of the TRW credit report.

Status Date

Now find the box labeled "Status Date." It's to the right of the Status Comment section. The Status Date section shows when your creditor last reported the status of your account—you know, all the comments we just examined.

Date Opened

Now find the box labeled "Date Opened." It's to the right of the Status Date section. The Date Opened section shows when your creditor opened your account. (It's just like the Date Opened sections in the Equifax and Trans Union reports.)

Subscriber Number

Now find the box labeled "Subscriber #." It's to the right of the Subscriber Name/Court Name section. The Subscriber Number section lists the identification number that TRW has assigned to your creditor. (It's just like the Subscriber Code section in the Trans Union report. Equifax doesn't list the subscriber number.)

Type

Now find the box labeled "Type." It's just below the Subscriber # section. The Type section shows the purpose of your loan. To do this, TRW uses many abbreviations. In the following table, I've listed those abbreviations and explained each of them.

ADD	Address information for mailing	AUT	Auto
A/M	Account monitored by subscriber	BUS	Business
CCP	Combined Credit Plan	CHG	Charge Account
CLS	Credit Line Secured	COL	Collection attorney
COM	Co-maker, not borrower	CPS	Consumer service Creditentials
CRC	Credit card	CRD	Consumer relations display
C/C	Credit check or line of credit	DCP	Data correction profile
DCS	Debt counseling service	D/C	Debit card
EDU	Educational	EMP	Employment
FHA	FHA home improvement	F/C	FHA co-maker, not borrower
F/S	Family support	GEA	Government employee advance
GFS	Government fee for service	GMD	Government miscellaneous debt
GOP	Government overpayment	G/B	Government benefit
G/F	Government fine	G/G	Government grant
H/E	Home equity	HHG	Secured by household goods
H/I	Home improvement	H + O	Secured by household goods and other collateral
IDV	Address information for the government	INS	Insurance claims
ISC	Installment sales contract	I/L	Installment loan
LEA	Lease	MED	Medical debt
M/H	Mobile home	NCM	Note loan with co-maker
NTE	Note loan	PHC	Prescreen/extract report
PIA	Prescreen/invitation to apply	PMI	Prescreen/extract promotion inquiry
PPO	Prescreen/preapproved offer	PPI	Prescreen/post prescreen inquiry
PSC	Solicitation	P/S	Partially secured
QST	Account reviewed by subscriber	RCK	Returned check
REC	Recreational merchandise	REN	Rental agreement
RVW	Account reviewed by subscriber	R/C	Conventional real estate mortgage, terms are in years
R/E	Real estate/specific type unknown, terms are in years	R/F	FHA real estate, terms are in years

R/O	Real estate mortgage with or without other collateral- usually a 2nd mortgage, terms are in years	R/V	VA real estate mortgage, terms are in years
SCO	Secured by a co-signer	SDL	Government secured direct loan
SEC	Secured	SGL	Government secured guaranteed loan
SUM	Summary of accounts with the same status	UDL	Government unsecured direct loan
UGL	Government unsecured guaranteed loan	UNK	Unknown
UNS	Unsecured		

Again, we have quite a list of abbreviations to learn. Remember, though, you don't have to memorize them. If you find a Type abbreviation you don't understand, just refer to the Type of Account table. To give you a better feel for this, let's look at some examples from the sample report.

First, find the "HOUSEHELD" account. Now find the "ISC" notation in the Type section. Now look at the "Type" abbreviation table. You'll see that "ISC" stand for an "installment sales contract." Therefore, John agreed to make regular payments to Househeld over a certain period to repay his account.

O.K. Let's look at another one. Find the "SITIBANK MASTER-CHARGE" account. It's just below the Househeld account. Now find the "CRC" notation in the Type section. When you've done that, look again at the Type abbreviation table. You'll find that "CRC" stands for "credit card account." Therefore, John can access his Sitibank Mastercard account by using a credit card.

One more? All right. Find the "GMAK" account. It's near the bottom of the page. Under the Type section for this account, you'll find the "LEA" notation. The "LEA" notation stands for "lease." Therefore, John leased some type of property from GMAK.

Code

Now find the box labeled "Code." It's to the right of the Subscriber # box. The Code section shows who has financial responsibility for the account. Therefore, it's just like the ECOA section in the Trans Union report, and the Whose Account section in the Equifax report. However, TRW uses a different code system. TRW uses letters and numbers to identify the responsible party, while Equifax and Trans Union only use letters. In the following table, I've listed the codes that TRW uses for this section, and explained each of them.

0 UNDESIGNATED. Accounts reported before 1977.

1 INDIVIDUAL. You are the only person associated with this account. (Termination code H appears if the account is a mortgage loan that others assumed.)

2 JOINT/CONTRACTUAL. You've signed an agreement that requires you to repay all debts on this account. However, other people associated with this account may also have contractual responsibility. (Termination code B appears if someone ends this association.)

3 JOINT/AUTHORIZED USER. You can use this joint account. However, another person is contractually responsible for repayment of the account. (Termination code C appears if someone ends this association.)

4 JOINT/UNDESIGNATED. You can use this account. However, TRW cannot determine whether you have contractual responsibility for repayment of this account, or if you're an authorized user. (Termination code D appears if someone ends this association.)

5 CO-MAKER. You guaranteed this account and will assume financial responsibility if the maker defaults.

6 ON BEHALF OF. You signed an application to help another person obtain credit. (Termination code F appears if someone ends this association.)

7 MAKER. You are responsible for this account, and a co-maker has guaranteed repayment.

X DECEASED. You are dead. However, there may be other people associated with this account.

Terms

Now find the box labeled "Terms." It's just below the Code section. The Terms section shows how long you have to repay your account balance. It's similar to the Terms sections in the Equifax and Trans Union reports. However, the TRW Terms section only identifies the number of periods for repayment—probably months.

To see how this works, look at the sample report, Diagram 7-1(a). Find the "HOUSEHELD" account at the top of the page. You should see the notation "36" under the Terms column for this account. The "36" shows that John must repay his Househeld account over 36 months.

Let's look at another example. Find the "GMAK" account. Under the Terms column you should see the notation "48." As you might expect, this shows that John must repay his GMAK account over 48 months.

One more example? O.K. Find the "CHECRON" account. Under the Terms section you should see the notation "REV." What's this? It's something new. This is another way that the TRW Terms section differs from the Equifax and Trans Union Terms sections. The "REV" notation shows that John's Checron account is a revolving account. With a revolving account, your creditor won't set a fixed period for repayment. Generally, you must pay some percentage of your balance each month as a minimum payment. Most credit card accounts are revolving accounts. These accounts will have the "REV" notation under the Terms section.

But we're not finished yet. I said that TRW only shows how long you have to repay your account balance. Therefore, you're probably thinking that TRW doesn't list your payment amount. But that's not true. Let me show you what I mean.

Find the "SITIBANK MASTERCHARGE" account. Now find the "SCH MONTH PAY $50" notation in the third row of information for this account. This notation shows that John's scheduled payments for this account are $50.

If TRW doesn't know the exact amount of your payment, they might try to estimate the amount. Let me show you an example. Find the "WANDS" account. Now look at the last row of information for the Wands account. You should see the notation "EST MONTH PAY $80." This shows that TRW has estimated that John's monthly Wand's payment is $80.

Amount

Now find the box labeled "Amount." It's to the right of the Code and Terms sections. The Amount section shows your total credit line for the account. Therefore, it's just like the CREDIT LIMIT section in the Trans Union report, and the HIGH CREDIT section in the Equifax report.

To show your credit line, TRW uses abbreviations called "Amount Qualifiers." These abbreviations show many things about your account. In the following table, I've listed TRW's Amount Qualifiers and explained each of them.

ORIGL	This is the original amount of the loan.
LIMIT	This is your credit limit amount.
HIBAL	This is the highest balance that your creditor has ever reported for your account.
UNKWN	Your creditor has not reported a credit limit for your account.
C/OAM	Your creditor charged off this amount.

O.K. Let's see how this works. Find the HOUSEHELD account again. Now look under the Amount section. You should see the notation "ORIGL" and the notation "$1,500" just below it. These notations show that John's original credit limit for the Househeld account was $1,500.

All right. Let's do one more. Find the "CHECRON" account. Now look under the Amount section. You should see the notation "HIBAL" and the notation "$125" just below it. These notations show that the highest balance CHECRON ever reported to TRW for John's account was $125.

Balance

Now find the box labeled "Balance." It's to the right of the Amount section. The Balance section shows how much you owed your creditor on this account when your creditor last reported to TRW. It's just like the Balance section in the Equifax report, and the Balance Owing section in the Trans Union report.

Account/Docket Number

Now find the box labeled "Account/Docket Number." It's to the right of the Balance section. The Account/Docket Number section lists two types of identification numbers. First, this section will show the identification number that your creditor has assigned to your account. Second, this section will show the identification number that a court has assigned your court case. (The Account Number is similar to the Account Number sections in the Equifax and Trans Union reports. However, TRW is the only credit bureau that lists the docket number with the regular credit account numbers.)

Let's look at an example. Find the "HOUSEHELD" account. Now look under the Account/Docket Number section. You should see the notation "25-2872-34572." This is the correct account number for John's Househeld account.

We'll talk about the docket number in a moment. For now, though, let's look at the "Balance Date" and "Amount Past Due" sections.

Balance Date

Now find the box labeled "Balance Date." It's just below the Account/ Docket Number section. The Balance Date section shows when your creditor last reported your account information to TRW. Therefore, it's just like the DATE REPORTED section in the Equifax report, and the Date Verified section in the Trans Union report.

Amount Past Due

Now find the box labeled "Amount Past Due." It's to the right of the Balance Date section. The Amount Past Due section shows whether you're late with any payments, and by how much. It's just like the Past Due section in the Equifax report, and the Amount Past Due section in the Trans Union report.

To see an example of this section, find the "WANDS" account. Now look in the Amount Past Due section. You should see the notation "$80." This notation shows that John is late on $80 in payments to Wands. This is incorrect, by the way, but we'll talk about that in the next chapter.

Last Payment

You won't find a box for the Last Payment section. However, you'll find this information just below the Balance Date and Amount Past Due sections. The Last Payment section shows when you last paid your creditor. To show this, TRW uses the notation "LASTPAY."

Let's look at an example. Find the "SITIBANK MASTERCHARGE" account. Now look under the Balance Date and Amount Past Due sections. You should see the notation "LASTPAY 12-15-92." This notation shows that John last paid Sitibank on December 15, 1992.

Payment Profile

Now find the box labeled "Payment Profile." It's to the right of the Account/Docket Number section. The Payment Profile section shows how you've paid your account during the last 24 months. Creditors can look at this section and see whether you made your payments on time or not. To show this, TRW lists a letter or number for each month of your payment history. Therefore, it's similar to the Historical Status section in the Trans Union report. However, TRW uses the letter "C" to show a current status for the month. Trans Union uses a "1" to show a current status for the month. In the following table, I've listed the symbols that TRW uses for the Payment Profile section, and explained each of them.

C	Current	5	150 days past due date
1	30 days past due date	-	No history reported for that month
2	60 days past due date		
3	90 days past due date	Blank	No history maintained
4	120 days past due date	N	Current/Zero balance reported

Let's look at an example. Find the "CHECRON" account on the first page of the sample report. Now look in the Payment Profile section. You should see several "C's" and "N's" on two rows. Each "C" and "N" represent one month, and each row represents 12 months. Therefore, the two rows together represent the last 24 months for this account. The most recent 12-month period is on the second row.

The Checron account lists eight "C's" and four "N's" on the first row, and five "C's" and seven "N's" on the second row. The "C's" show that John made his required payments on time for those months. The "N's" show that John didn't owe Checron any money for those months.

Now look at the "WANDS" account at the bottom of the first page. In the Payment Profile section for this account, you should see 11 "C's" and one "-" in the first row. In the second row, you should see 11 "C's" and one "1." The "1" shows that John is more than 30 days late with his required payment. (The Status Comment section also showed this late payment by listing the "DELINQ" notation.)

The Payment Profile section gives your potential creditors a very precise view of each of your credit accounts. It provides the details about your accounts that the simplified three-part Account Profile section fails to do.

Inquiries

O.K. We're finally finished with the Credit History section. Now let's move on to the Inquiries section. TRW lists inquiries just after your Credit History information. The Inquiries section lists information about subscribers that request your credit information. For example, it will list the subscriber's account number and the date of the inquiry.

The Inquiries section also shows whether the subscriber used an automatic or manual system to receive your credit report. However, as we discussed earlier, TRW lists the "A" or "M" notations in the non-evaluated column of the Account Profile section. TRW does this because it doesn't "rate" the significance of an inquiry.

Let's look at an example. Find the "NIXXAN" notation on the second page of the sample report, Diagram 7-1(b). Now look below this notation. You should see the notation "INQUIRY." This shows that Nixxan requested a copy of John's credit report. This section also lists Nixxan's subscriber number as "1895000" and shows that Nixxan requested John's credit report on June 10, 1992.

Public Record Information

Now we're down to the Public Record section. TRW lists your public record information just after the last inquiry. As we discussed earlier, the Public Record section lists any information about you that TRW has pulled from public records. This information includes liens, judgments, and bankruptcies.

As you might expect, TRW uses many abbreviations to show the different forms of public record information. In the following table, I've listed the abbreviations that TRW uses, and explained each of them.

BK 7,11,12,13 FILE. You filed a voluntary bankruptcy case under Chapter 7, 11, 12, or 13 of the Bankruptcy Code. This could also mean that a creditor has filed an involuntary bankruptcy case against you.

BK 7,11,12 DISC. The bankruptcy court has discharged your Chapter 7,11, or 12 bankruptcy case.

BK 7,11,12,13 DISM. The bankruptcy court has dismissed your Chapter 7,11, or 12 bankruptcy case. Therefore, you're still responsible for all debts.

BK 13-COMP. You successfully completed a Chapter 13 repayment plan.

JUDGMENT. A Court entered judgment against you.

JUDGMT SAT. A court entered judgment against you. However, you subsequently paid the judgment.

JUDG SAT VAC. A court vacated a judgment, either before or after you satisfied it.

NT RESPON. You have disclaimed responsibility for the debt. For example, a husband or wife may claim that they are not responsible for debts incurred by the other spouse.

TX LN. Some entity has filed a tax lien against you. This may be a city, county, state, federal, or mechanic's lien.

TX REL. Some entity had filed a tax lien against you. However, they have subsequently released you from that lien.

SUIT. Someone has started legal action against you.

SUIT DISMD. Someone had started legal action against you. However, they have subsequently stopped the action, or a court has dismissed it.

WAGE ASIGN. Someone has convinced a court to seize some of your wages to repay a debt.

W/A RELEASE. Someone had convinced a court to seize some of your wages to repay a debt. However, they have subsequently released you from this action.

O.K. Let's look at an example to see how these public record indicators work. Find the Inquiries section in the sample report. It's just below the "CHASTE" inquiry. You should see the notations "BK 7 - File" and "5-14-86." These notations show information about John's bankruptcy case.

To figure out what they mean, look at the Public Record Indicators table. The "BK 7 - File" notation shows that John filed a Chapter 7 bankruptcy case. The "5-14-86" notation shows that John filed his case on May 14, 1986. We know that this information is correct.

TRW also shows other information about John's bankruptcy case. For example, the "US BKPT CT" notation shows that a federal bankruptcy court maintains the information about John's bankruptcy. The "FL - COLONIA" notation shows the location of that court—Colonia, Florida. And the notation "00860258" shows the docket number for John's bankruptcy case. Finally, TRW shows—rates—John's bankruptcy as a negative account in the Account Profile section.

Checkpoint and File Variation

The final section of the TRW report that we'll look at is the "Checkpoint" and "File Variation" sections. TRW places warning messages labeled "CHECKPOINT" and "FILE VARIATION" to report suspicious information on your credit report. This suspicious information is information that your creditors report about you that doesn't match up with TRW's information.

For example, let's suppose that you're completing a credit application. However, you've forgotten your Social Security number and try to fill it in from memory. Unfortunately, you transpose two of the numbers. Your potential creditor will send this information to TRW, along with your incorrect Social Security number. When TRW locates your credit file, it will notice the discrepancy in Social Security numbers, and report this problem on your credit report. To do this, it will list either the "CHECKPOINT" or "FILE VARIATION" message. These warning messages alert your potential creditors that you might be trying to create an alternate credit file using a different Social Security number. This could prevent you from receiving ANY credit.

Unfortunately, you're probably not even responsible for any errors on your report. It's just as likely that one of your creditors made an error when it sent your credit information to TRW. Therefore, your credit report would list the "CHECKPOINT" or "FILE VARIATION" messages, even though you didn't do anything wrong. We'll talk more about the "CHECKPOINT" and "FILE VARIATION" messages in Chapter 9. For now, though, let's look at an example.

Find the "CHECKPOINT" notation on the second page of the sample credit report. It's just below the Public Record section. You should see the notation "SS# IS 123-44-6789, STREET INIT IS R, ZIP IS 32331." This CHECKPOINT message warns John's potential creditors that he may be using a Social Security number other than his own to apply for credit. But as you can see, it's very likely that one of John's creditors incorrectly reported this information to TRW. Now John has one more problem on his credit report. We'll talk about correcting this problem in the next chapter. And guess what? We're finally there!

Diagram 7-1(a)
[Sample TRW Credit Report]

Updated CREDIT PROFILE Report

TCR3 JDJD2 3599954 CONSUMER JOHN J 32331,P-7825 F 18181, S-123456789, Y-1957, M-5825 RED WOOD DR, COLONIA FL 32331

IDENTIFICATION NUMBER

PAGE	DATE	TIME	PORT	H/V			
1	2/14/93	10:50:02	DO3	107	CONSUMER	CFL2	57-425678-32

2-93	JOHN J. CONSUMER	1-85 NASA	SS# 123456789
U	5825 RED WOOD DR	KENNEDY SC	
	COLONIA FL 32331	PORT CANAVERAL FL	YOB - 1957

ACCOUNT PROFILE			Subscriber Name / Court Name			Subscriber #	Code	Amount		Account/Docket Number		Payment Profile
			Status Comment	Status Date	Date Opened	Type	Terms		Balance	Balance Date	Amount Past Due	
Pos	Non	Neg										
>>>	>>>		FACS+ SUMMARY									
>>>												
>>>	>>>		FROM 10/15/91 NUMBER OF INQS WITH THIS SS# = 0									
		A	HOUSEHELD			1200710	1	ORIGL		25-2872-34572		
			BK LIQ REO	5-86	5-83	ISC	36	$1500				
A			SITIBANK MASTERCHARGE			1217575	1	LIMIT		175832419685		
			CURR ACCT	12-92	10-88	CRC	REV	$2000	$1500	12-31-91		CCCCCCCCCCCC
						SCH MONTH PAY			$50	LAST PAY 12-15-92		CCCCCCCCCCCC
		A	FREEDMAN CARD CENTER			1310052	1			4357701104136		
			BK LIQ REO	7-87	5-83	CRC	REV	$1800				
			** CREDIT LINE CLOSED - REPORTED BY SUBSCRIBER									
A			CHECRON			1357825	2	HIBAL		123571919245		
			CURR ACCT	12-92	2-89	CRC	REV	$125	$55	12-31-91		CCCNCCNNNCCC
												CCNNNNCCNNCN
		A	AMERICAN AXPRESS CO			1455113	1			56568966674		
			CHARGE OFF	8-86	3-84	CRC	REV	$758	$758	8-30-86	$758	
		A	AMERICAN AXPRESS CO			1455113	1			56568966674		
			CHARGE OFF	8-86	3-84	CRC	1	$500	$500	8-30-86	$500	
A			J C PICKEY			1500234	3			2424382942		
			CURR ACCT	11-92	10-87	CHG	REV	$800	$500	11-31-91		CCCCC-CCCCCC
						SCH MONTH PAY			$40	LAST PAY 11-15-92		CCCCCCCCCCCC
		A	GMAK			1555321	1			20043748		
			REPO	5-86	4-85	LEA	48	$15000				
		A	SITIBANK PREFERRED VISA			1603122	1			427138254914		
			BK LIQ REO	5-86	1-84	CRC	REV	$5000				
	A		N E BANK			1719453	1	LIMIT		80905742		
			CUR WAS 60	11-85	10-84	HHG	12	$250				
A			WANDS			1759876	2	HIBAL		3838029535		
			DELINQ	12-92	10-87	CHG	REV	$1500	$1400	12-15-91	-	CCCCCCC-CCCC
						EST MONTH PAY			$80		$80	CCCCCCCCCCC1

Diagram 7-1(b)
[Sample TRW Credit Report]

Updated CREDIT PROFILE Report

JDJD2 3599954 CONSUMER JOHN J. ,5825 R 32331

IDENTIFICATION NUMBER

PAGE	DATE	TIME	PORT	H/V		
2	2/14/93	10:50:02	DO3	107	CONSUMER CFL2	57-425678-32

ACCOUNT PROFILE Pos	Non	Neg	Subscriber Name / Court Name / Status Comment	Status Date	Date Opened	Subscriber # / Type	Code / Terms	Amount	Balance	Account/Docket Number / Balance Date	Amount Past Due	Payment Profile
	M		NIXXAN			1895000						
			INQUIRY	6-10-92								
	A		BARKETT			1952287						
			INQUIRY	6-25-92								
	A		DISKOVER CARD			2270059						
			INQUIRY	1-07-91								
	M		CHASTE			2359287						
			INQUIRY	5-14-91								
		M	US BKPT CT - FL - COLONIA			1006007				00860258		
			BK 7 - FILE	5-14-86				UNKN				

\>>>>>>> CHECKPOINT >>>>>>> SS# IS 123-44-6789, STREET INIT IS R, ZIP IS 32331

12-92 JOHN J. CONSUMER
5825 RED WOOD DR
COLONIA FL 32331

-------------- END -- TRW

Chapter 8

Finding the Mistakes

For every man the world is as fresh as it was at the first day, and as full of untold novelties for him who has the eyes to see them.

Thomas Henry Huxley

Congratulations! You made it through all three credit report formats. Therefore, you know what information the credit bureaus include in your credit report. But, that's only the first step. Now you need to find out if that information is correct.

In this chapter, we'll do that. We'll review each of your credit reports and find the mistakes. To help you in this task, I'll have you organize your financial records, and compare them with your credit reports. Then, to help you find the mistakes, I'll have you transfer this information to a worksheet. So if you're ready—let's go!

Get Your Records Together

To find the mistakes in your credit reports, you'll have to know which information is correct, and which information is incorrect. Therefore, you'll need to get all of your financial records together. Then you can compare the information in your records against the information in your credit reports.

Current Records

First, find any information you have about your current accounts. These accounts may include retail store credit cards, store accounts without credit cards, bank cards, etc. (You know, those accounts that eat up your paychecks every month!) However, you don't need to find your electric bills, phone bills, or rental payment records. These types of accounts probably won't appear on your credit reports.

Non-Current or Closed Accounts

Now find any information about your old accounts. These are probably the accounts that you included in your bankruptcy. Therefore, you'll want to find your bankruptcy schedules. (This is why we spent so much time reviewing your bankruptcy file in Chapter 2.)

As you remember, your bankruptcy schedules list all of your creditors at the time of your bankruptcy petition— secured creditors, unsecured creditors, creditors with priority, and creditors without priority. Your bankruptcy schedules also list information about your accounts with those creditors. For example, you should find account numbers and balance amounts for every account you included in your bankruptcy. We'll use this information to check the accuracy of your credit reports. Unfortunately, your credit reports will probably contain many errors regarding your inactive accounts. Fortunately, however, your bankruptcy schedules will allow you to quickly identify these errors.

To do this, find any schedule that lists your debts when you filed your bankruptcy petition. If you filed your bankruptcy petition after August 1, 1991, you should find the following three schedules: Schedule D - Creditors Holding Secured Claims, Schedule E - Creditors Holding Unsecured Priority Claims, and Schedule F - Creditors Holding Unsecured Non-priority Claims.

If you filed your bankruptcy petition before August 1, 1991, you should find the following three schedules: Schedule A-2 - Creditors Holding Security, Schedule A-1 - Creditors Having Unsecured Claims With Priority, and Schedule A-3 - Creditors Having Unsecured Claims Without Priority.

Other Records

Besides the records we've already discussed, you can probably think of other records—old and new—that will help you in this chapter. If so, go ahead and dig them out of your closet or file cabinet. Then, you'll be ready to go when you sit down with your credit reports.

Recording the Information and Identifying the Mistakes

By this point, you should have all of your financial records together. If so, it's time to find and record the errors in your credit reports. To help you with these tasks, I've included a worksheet that I call the Credit Report Summary. (I should probably call it something more interesting, like "Find the Stupid Errors Worksheet." Unfortunately, I think my legal education has killed my creativity. Sorry about that.)

O.K. Our first job is to record all of the important information from your credit reports. We'll do this —actually, you'll do this—by transferring this important information from your credit reports to the Credit Report Summary, Diagram 8-1. The Credit Report Summary will summarize the important information contained within each of your credit reports.

After you've recorded your credit information onto the Credit Report Summary, you'll be able to find any mistakes. I've constructed it to make this easy. With one glance at your Summary, you should be able to see any discrepancies among the different credit bureaus. Then in Chapter 9, we'll take this information and start the process of repairing your credit. Sound good? All right, let's do it!

Review the Credit Report for Mistakes

All right. Let's start from the beginning. The first step in this process is to review your credit reports from the Big 3 credit bureaus. While doing this, you need to find and record any mistakes. Therefore, you MUST examine them very carefully. That's why I created the Credit Report Summary. It will force you to examine every section in each of your credit reports. I know that sounds like a lot of work, but it will be worth your time and energy. Believe me!

Before we go on though, let me make a small confession. I don't usually use worksheets and lists. I resist anything that makes me organize my affairs. But, I know that other people do like organization. That's why I created the Credit Report Summary.

But guess what happened after I created it? That's right. I used it myself to record my account information. Thanks to the Credit Report Summary, I found mistakes I'd never noticed before. And you will too! Therefore, give it a try, even if you hate organization as much as I do. With that said, let's look at the Credit Report Summary.

Overview of the Credit Report Summary

Find the Credit Report Summary. It's the three pages at the end of this chapter labeled Diagram 8-1(a), 8-1(b), and 8-1(c). Now look at the first page, Diagram 8-1(a). Near the top of this page, you should see the notation "Section I - Personal Identification Information." In this section, you'll record the identification information that each credit bureau lists in your credit report.

It's important that the credit bureaus maintain your correct personal identification information. If not, they may be reporting another person's credit history in your report. And that person's history may be worse than yours! Therefore, you'll need to find any errors.

To do this, I'll have you record the personal identification information from each of your credit reports. When you place this information on the Credit Report Summary, you'll be able to see any discrepancies among the different credit bureaus.

Now look at the second page, Diagram 8-1(b). Near the top of the page, you should see the notation "Section II - Credit History Information." Section II is probably the most important section of the Credit Report Summary, because this is where the credit bureaus usually make mistakes.

To find the errors in Section II, I'll have you record the credit history information for EACH of your accounts. The entire page represents ONE account. Therefore, you'll need to photocopy this page. Make one copy for EACH of your credit accounts—current and closed.

Now look at the last page, Diagram 8-1(c). Near the top of the page, you should see the notation "Sections III and IV - Inquiries and Public Record Information." In these sections, I'll have you record information about your credit inquiries and public records. As with the other pages of the Credit Report Summary, you'll be able to see any discrepancies among the three credit bureaus.

It's important that you review each section thoroughly. The Inquiries section is important because it helps you find any unauthorized inquiries. Remember, under the Fair Credit Reporting Act, there are only a few specific reasons that someone can access your credit report. If someone obtains a copy of your credit report for the wrong reason, then the inquirer and the credit bureau have violated the law.

Why should you care about your credit inquiries? If too many inquiries appear on your report, a creditor may be reluctant to extend you credit. Therefore, review this section carefully to make sure that you know the reason behind each inquiry.

The Public Records section, Section IV, is also important. This section should list information about your bankruptcy, and any other information that is freely available to the public. You'll want to make sure that this information is correct.

Complete the Credit Report Summary

All right. That's it. That's your grand tour of the Credit Report Summary. Now it's time to start.

Section I - Personal Identification Information

Now that you know what's in the Credit Report Summary, let's begin. Find the first page of the Credit Report Summary, Diagram 8-1(a), and put it next to one of your credit reports. Then, transfer the relevant information to each box in Section I.

To do this, read each item in section I, and use your credit report to complete the box. For example, print your full name in the appropriate box in row A-1. Row A-1 contains the notation "Full Name."

Remember, however, don't just print your full name here. We're trying to find mistakes in your credit reports. Therefore, record ALL personal identification information as it appears IN YOUR CREDIT REPORT. If the credit bureau spelled your name wrong, then record your name just as they spelled it. (This is how we'll spot any inconsistencies in your reports. For example, Equifax and Trans Union might report John Consumer's first name as "John." But, if TRW reports his name as "Joan," then John can quickly see the problem.)

Although some items in Section I require you to actually list the information from your credit reports, other items only require your response. For example, Row B-2 asks whether the credit bureaus have correctly listed your address. For this box, you don't need to list your address. Just write "Yes" or "No." Other items might not even apply to you. If they don't apply, just write "N/A" for not applicable. Finally, if one of your credit reports doesn't list some information, just write "Not Listed" in the appropriate box.

O.K. Now that you know what Section I is all about, go ahead and complete all the boxes. Start with one credit report and answer all the personal identification items. Then, move on to the next credit report. When you've completed the third credit report, you can start Section II of the Credit Report Summary.

Section II - Credit History Information

When you've completed Section I of the Credit Report Summary, it's time to start Section II. However, remember to make copies of Section II BEFORE you record any information.

As I said earlier, Section II is probably the most important section of the Credit Report Summary. In this section, you'll record credit history information about all of your accounts—current and closed. This is the type of information that the credit bureaus usually get wrong. Therefore, you need to pay special attention to it.

To complete Section II, start by recording information from your records into the column labeled "Your Records." I would probably start with your closed or inactive accounts.

You'll find most of the information about your closed or inactive accounts in your bankruptcy schedules. To record this information, get your bankruptcy schedules in front of you. Then transfer every account from your bankruptcy schedules to the boxes in Section II. (Remember, each page of Section II lists information about ONE of your accounts. Therefore, if you have 10 credit accounts, you should have 10 copies of Section II.) Include as much information as you can. At a minimum, you should list the name of each creditor, account numbers, account balances, and date of last payment. This should take care of your closed or inactive accounts.

Then, get your current account information together and transfer this information to Section II. Remember to complete each item in Section II, or at least as much as you can. As with the closed accounts, list the name of each creditor, account numbers, account balances, and date of last payment.

When you've completed the column labeled "Your Account," it's time to record the credit history information from your credit reports. As with Section I, record every item in Section II for one credit report, then record the information from another credit report. When you've finished the third credit report, I'll bet you'll find several errors. Then, in the next chapter, we'll take your discoveries and use them to repair your credit.

Because Section II contains some items that may confuse you, let's quickly review each of them.

1. Creditor Name and I.D. Number - O.K. This one probably won't confuse you. Record your creditor's name and the identification number that each credit bureau has assigned to your creditor. (This is NOT the same number as your account number. You'll record that one next.)

2. Account # - Record the identification number that your creditor assigned to your account.

3. Balance - Record how much you owe this creditor. However, you should NOT have a balance for any account that you included in your bankruptcy case. Therefore, your credit reports should list a "0" balance for any of your bankruptcy accounts. If so, just list "0" in this box. If your bankruptcy accounts list any other balance amount, go ahead and record that amount. Then we'll fix this problem in the next chapter.

4. Date Opened - Here's another easy one. Just record the date you opened this account.

5. Date Closed - O.K. This is the last easy one. Record the date that your creditor closed your account. Remember, if you have any current accounts, they won't list this date.

6. Date of Last Activity - This item is more difficult. The Date of Last Activity is the last date that "something" happened in your account. This may or may not be the same as the "Date Closed."

Unfortunately, there are two reasons why you might find it difficult to check this information. First, some credit bureaus don't report the date of last activity on your credit report. Second, you may not know when something last happened in your account. Therefore, even if the credit bureau reports it on your credit report, you won't be able to verify the date. Just do the best that you can with this information.

7. Current Status - Now record the current status of your account. Your current status should show whether your account is a current, closed, collection, or bankruptcy account. For your Equifax report, you'll find this information in the High Credit, Terms, and Balance sections. For your Trans Union report, you'll find it in the Remarks section. Finally, for your TRW report, you'll find the current status in the Status Comment section.

8. Credit Limits - Record how much credit you had, or have, for this account.

9. Whose Account - Record who has primary responsibility for repaying your account. The Whose Account section should show whether your account is an Individual, Joint, Authorized User, or other type of account. For your Equifax report, you'll find this information in the Whose Account section. For your Trans Union report, you'll find it in the ECOA section. Finally, for your TRW report, you'll find the Whose Account information in the Code section.

10. MOP Indicator - You might have to review one of the last three chapters for information about the Manner of Payment Indicator. Or, you might remember that the MOP indicator shows whether your account is current. If your account is not current, the MOP Indicator shows that your payment is late, and by how many days.

For your Equifax report, you'll find this information in the Status section. The MOP Indicator will be a number from "0 "to "9" that follows a letter indicator. For your Trans Union report, you'll find it in the Type Account & MOP section. As with the Equifax report, the MOP Indicator will be a number from "0" to "9" that follows a letter indicator.

For your TRW report, you'll find this information in the Account Profile section. Remember though, TRW uses a different reporting system than the other credit bureaus. For TRW, record which of the three columns, labeled "Pos," "Non," or "Neg," contains a letter indicator.

11. Delinquency Amounts - Record whether you're late with any payment for this account. This SHOULD only apply to your current accounts. If you included this account in your bankruptcy case, you probably don't owe your creditor any money. Therefore, this item should be "0." However, you'll probably find that some credit bureaus report delinquency amounts for these bankruptcy accounts.

Section III - Inquiries

When you've completed Section II, it's time to move on to Section III. You'll find this section on the third page of the Credit Report Summary, Diagram 8-1(c). To complete Section III, find the Inquiries section of each credit report, and transfer the relevant information to the Credit Report Summary. You'll probably find the Inquiries section just after the Credit History section in each credit report. As with the other sections, carefully review each item and complete the appropriate boxes. Complete one credit report, and then start with the next. Contact the credit bureau if you can't decipher the code it used to identify the inquiries.

Section IV - Public Record Information

Now it's time to complete the Credit Report Summary. Find Section IV. It's just after Section III, on the last page of the Credit Report Summary. To complete Section IV, find the Public Record section of each credit report, and transfer the relevant information to the Credit Report Summary. You'll probably find the Public Record section just after the Inquiries section in each credit report. As with the other sections, carefully review each item and complete the appropriate boxes. Complete one credit report, and then start with the next.

The public record information section should contain information about your bankruptcy petition and discharge. If so, make sure that all of the information relating to your bankruptcy is correct. For example, make sure that the dates of filing and discharge are correct. Also, review the amount discharged and the docket number.

You'll also want to look in this section for other types of public record information. This could include liens, judgments, suits filed against you, etc. If other public record information appears here, closely check this information against your records. You will probably find that the credit bureaus have incorrectly listed some of this information. If so, you can dispute this information with the credit bureau.

John Consumer's Credit Report Summary

To show you how your completed Credit Report Summary should look when you've completed it, I've included John Consumer's completed Credit Report Summary. You'll find this sample Worksheet in Diagrams 8-2(a) - 8-2(c).

You'll notice that I didn't include some of John's credit accounts in Diagram 8-2(b). That's because I didn't want to bore you with too much detail. However, I've included the accounts that show some common credit reporting errors. Now, let's quickly review John's Credit Report Summary.

Diagram 8-2(a) - Personal Identification Information

Look at Diagram 8-2(a). In this diagram, John has completed Section I of his Credit Report Summary - Personal Identification Information. You'll notice that all of the credit bureaus correctly identified John, even though they don't include his full name in any of the reports.

However, two of the reports incorrectly list John's current employment with NASA. This is a common error in credit reports. It's difficult for credit bureaus to keep up with employment changes. Therefore, you need to help them out as much as possible. You should update this information if you want the credit bureau to report your current employment.

Diagram 8-2(b) - Credit History Information

Now look at Diagrams 8-2(b)(1) - (7). These diagrams show several of John's accounts and point out various problems with them. In the next several sections, we'll go through each of these accounts and discuss them.

Diagram 8-2(b)(1) - The GMAK Account

Diagram 8-2(b)(1) represents a completed Section II of the Credit Report Summary for John's GMAK account. You'll notice that the Credit Report Summary allows John to easily compare his records for the GMAK account against the records of the three credit bureaus.

Look at the "Balance" section of the Summary. You'll see that John's records, Trans Union, and TRW all report that John has a "$0" balance on this account. However, the Equifax report shows that John still owes GMAK $15,000. We know this isn't true because John's bankruptcy discharge eliminated his GMAK debt. Therefore, John doesn't owe GMAK any money on this account.

John will need to contact Equifax and correct this error. We'll look at the letter he should use in the next chapter. For now, though, let's look at the next account.

Diagram 8-2(b)(2) - The Househeld Finance Account

Look at Diagram 8-2(b)(2). This diagram represents John's Househeld Finance account. Again, you'll see that the Summary allows us to easily spot the errors in the credit reports. In the "Balance" section of the Summary, you'll notice that Trans Union lists John's Househeld account balance as $1,500. However, Equifax, TRW, and John's records show that he doesn't owe Househeld anything.

This is the same problem as before. John doesn't owe Househeld any money on this account because his bankruptcy discharge eliminated John's Househeld debt. Again, John will need to contact the credit bureau and correct this mistake.

Unfortunately, the incorrect balance amount isn't the only problem with this account. Look at the "Current Status" section of the Summary. John's records, Equifax, and TRW report that John included the Househeld account in his bankruptcy case. However, Trans Union reports John's account as a "PROFIT-AND-LOSS WRITEOFF."

The "PROFIT-AND-LOSS WRITEOFF" indicator shows that Househeld took a loss on its books for John's unpaid debt. This may be technically correct for Househeld's books. However, this indicator makes it look like John failed to repay debts that he didn't include in his bankruptcy case. Potential creditors will see the indicator, and think that John is still neglecting his creditors. Therefore, John will need to correct this mistake by contacting the credit bureau.

Diagram 8-2(b)(3) - The Candlelight Hospital Account

Diagram 8-2(b)(3) represents John's Candlelight Hospital account. I've included this diagram to show you that many of your accounts won't appear on ANY of your credit reports. In this case, that's good for John. Of course, he shouldn't contact the credit bureaus about this "mistake."

Diagram 8-2(b)(4) - The Freedman Card Center

Diagram 8-2(b)(4) represents John's Freedman Card Center account. I've included this diagram to show you that some of your accounts will only appear on one or two of your credit reports. TRW has correctly reported this account, while Equifax and Trans Union don't report it at all. Therefore, John shouldn't notify Equifax or Trans Union about it.

I have one final comment about this diagram. You'll notice that TRW doesn't list the date that Freedman closed John's account and that John doesn't have this information either. John should search through his records and find this date, or contact the creditor for this information. Why? Credit bureaus can only report bad credit information for a certain period after the closing date of the account. After that, the credit bureau must remove any reference to the account. We'll talk more about that in the next chapter.

Diagram 8-2(b)(5) - The American Axpress Account

Diagram 8-2(b)(5) represents John's American Axpress account. The credit bureaus have really messed this account up. First, you'll notice that Equifax and TRW report a balance of $500 for one account, and $758 for the other account. As before, this information is incorrect because John's bankruptcy discharge eliminated these debts. Therefore, the balance should show the notation "$0."

Additionally, Equifax reports the current status of these accounts as "Delinquent," and TRW reports their current status as "CHARGE OFF" accounts. This information is incorrect for the same reason as above. These reports should show that John included these American Axpress accounts in his bankruptcy.

Finally, Equifax and TRW report that John is delinquent by $500 for one account and $758 for the other account. As with the balance amounts, this is incorrect because John doesn't owe American Axpress ANY money on these accounts. Therefore, John will need to contact the credit bureaus and correct this information, along with the errors on the balance amount and current status.

Diagram 8-2(b)(6) - The Wands Account

Diagram 8-2(b)(6) represents John's Wands account—a current account. John did not include the Wands account in his bankruptcy case. Unfortunately, there are mistakes with this account as well. Although John's records show that he is current with all payments to Wands, Equifax and TRW have reported a delinquency.

First, let's look at the "Current Status" section for the TRW report. You'll notice that TRW lists John's current status for this account as "Delinquent." However, John's records, Equifax, and Trans Union all correctly report that the account is current.

The next problem with this account is in the MOP section of the Summary. You'll notice that Equifax lists this account as "R2," meaning that John is currently more than 30 days past due on this account. Again, this information is not correct.

Finally, Equifax reports that John owes Wands $160 in past due payments and TRW reports that he owes $80 in past due payments. Each of these indications is wrong. Therefore, John will need to contact the credit bureaus and correct this information, and the incorrect Current Status and MOP indicators. As with all the information on John's credit report, he needs to make sure that the credit bureaus correctly report this information.

Diagram 8-2(b)(7) - The Sitibank Preferred Visa Account

Diagram 8-2(b)(7) represents John's Sitibank Preferred Visa account. I've included this diagram to show you that the credit bureaus CAN report your account information without ANY errors. After the next chapter, I hope that all of your accounts will be free from errors as well!

Final Thoughts

If you've done your job in this chapter, you've probably found several mistakes in your credit reports. If so, these mistakes will provide the ammunition for your upcoming complaints to the credit bureaus. In Chapter 9, I'll show you how to correct these mistakes and repair your credit. And guess what? We're here!

Diagram 8-1(a)
Credit Report Summary

Section I - Personal Identification Information				
	Your Records	Equifax	Trans Union	TRW
A. Name				
1. Full Name?				
2. Jr., Sr., Etc.?				
3. Designation listed?				
4. Designation listed incorrectly?				
B. Address				
1. Current Address correct?				
2. Previous Address correct?				
C. Employment				
1. Current Employment				
2. Job Description accurate?				
3. Salary correct?				
D. Spouse Information				
1. Marital Status correct?				
2. Name correct?				
3. Current and correct employer?				

Diagram 8-1(b)
Credit Report Summary

Section II - Credit History Information				
	Your Records	Equifax	Trans Union	TRW
1. Creditor Name and I.D. Number				
2. Account Number				
3. Balance				
4. Date Opened				
5. Date Closed				
6. Date of Last Activity				
7. Current Status				
8. Credit Limits				
9. Whose Account or ECOA				
10. MOP Indicator				
11. Delinquency Amounts				

Diagram 8-1(c)
Credit Report Summary

Sections III and IV - Inquiries and Public Record Information				
	Your Records	Equifax	Trans Union	TRW
III. Inquiries				
1. How many inquiries are listed?				
2. Can you account for every inquiry?				
3. List any unauthorized inquiries.				
IV. Public Record Information				
1. Is your bankruptcy listed?				
2. Date of filing?				
3. Date of discharge?				
4. Amount discharged?				
5. Docket/Case number?				
6. Other public record information?				
6. Listed correctly?				

Diagram 8-2(a)
Credit Report Summary

Section I - Personal Identification Information				
	Your Records	Equifax	Trans Union	TRW
A. Name				
1. Full Name?		John Consumer	John J. Consumer	John J. Consumer
2. Jr., Sr., Etc.?		No	No	No
3. Designation listed?		N/A	N/A	N/A
4. Designation listed incorrectly?		N/A	N/A	N/A
B. Address				
1. Current Address correct?		Yes	Yes	Yes
2. Previous Address correct?		Yes	Yes	Not Listed
C. Employment				
1. Current Employment		Yes	No	No
2. Job Description accurate?		Yes	No	No
3. Salary correct?		Not Listed	Not Listed	Not Listed
D. Spouse Information				
1. Marital Status correct?		N/A	N/A	N/A
2. Name correct?		N/A	N/A	N/A
3. Current and correct employer?		N/A	N/A	N/A

Diagram 8-2(b)(1)
[Incorrect Balance Amount]

Section II - Credit History Information				
	Your Records	Equifax	Trans Union	TRW
1. Creditor Name	**GMAK**	**GMAK**	**GMAK**	**GMAK**
2. Account Number	**20043748**	**20043748**	**20043748**	**20043748**
3. Balance	**- 0 -**	**$15,000**	**- 0 -**	**- 0 -**
4. Date Opened	**4/13/85**	**4/13/85**	**4/13/85**	**4/13/85**
5. Date Closed	**?**	**?**	**?**	**?**
6. Date of Last Activity	**?**	**5/86**	**?**	**?**
7. Current Status	**BANKRUPTCY ACCOUNT**	**INVOLUNTARY REPOSSESSION**	**BANKRUPTCY**	**REPO**
8. Credit Limits	**$15,000**	**$15,000**	**$15,000**	**$15,000**
9. Whose Account or ECOA	**Individual**	**I**	**I**	**1**
10. MOP Indicator		**I8**	**R08**	**NEG Column**
11. Delinquency Amounts	**- 0 -**	**- 0 -**	**- 0 -**	**- 0 -**

Diagram 8-2(b)(2)
[Improper Current Status and Incorrect Balance Amount]

Section II - Credit History Information				
	Your Records	Equifax	Trans Union	TRW
1. Creditor Name	**Househeld Finance**	**HOUSEHELD**	**HOUSEHELD FN**	**HOUSEHELD**
2. Account Number	**25-2872-34572**	**25-2872-34572**	**25-2872-34572**	**25-2872-34572**
3. Balance	**- 0 -**	**- 0 -**	**$1,500**	**- 0 -**
4. Date Opened	**5/15/83**	**5/83**	**5/83**	**5/83**
5. Date Closed	**?**	**Not Listed**	**?**	**Not Listed**
6. Date of Last Activity	**?**	**5/86**	**Not Listed**	**Not Listed**
7. Current Status	**Bankruptcy Account**	**INCLUDED IN BANKRUPTCY**	**PROFIT AND LOSS**	**BK LIQ REO**
8. Credit Limits	**$1,500**	**Not Listed**	**- 0 -**	**$1,500**
9. Whose Account or ECOA	**Individual**	**I**	**I**	**1**
10. MOP Indicator		**Not Listed**	**I09**	**NEG Column**
11. Delinquency Amounts	**- 0 -**	**- 0 -**	**- 0 -**	**- 0 -**

Diagram 8-2(b)(3)
[Account not listed in any credit report]

Section II - Credit History Information				
	Your Records	Equifax	Trans Union	TRW
1. Creditor Name	**Candlelight Hospital**	**Not Listed**	**Not Listed**	**Not Listed**
2. Account Number	**2178319**			
3. Balance	**- 0 -**			
4. Date Opened	**12/17/85**			
5. Date Closed	**?**			
6. Date of Last Activity	**?**			
7. Current Status	**Bankruptcy Account**			
8. Credit Limits	**?**			
9. Whose Account or ECOA	**Individual**			
10. MOP Indicator				
11. Delinquency Amounts	**- 0 -**			

Diagram 8-2(b)(4)
[Account listed in only one credit report]

Section II - Credit History Information

	Your Records	Equifax	Trans Union	TRW
1. Creditor Name	**Freedman Card Center**	**Not Listed**	**Not Listed**	**FREEDMAN CARD CENTER**
2. Account Number	**4357701104136**			**4357701104136**
3. Balance	**- 0 -**			**- 0 -**
4. Date Opened	**?**			**Not Listed**
5. Date Closed	**?**			**Not Listed**
6. Date of Last Activity	**?**			**Not Listed**
7. Current Status	**Bankruptcy Account**			**BK LIQ REO**
8. Credit Limits	**$1,800**			**$1,800**
9. Whose Account or ECOA	**Individual**			**1**
10. MOP Indicator				**NEG Column**
11. Delinquency Amounts	**- 0 -**			**- 0 -**

Diagram 8-2(b)(5)
[Improper Current Status and Incorrect Balance and Delinquency Amounts]

Section II - Credit History Information				
	Your Records	Equifax	Trans Union	TRW
1. Creditor Name	**American Axpress**	**AMAX**	**AMERICAN AXP**	**AMERICAN AXPRESS CO**
2. Account Number	**56568966674**	**56568966674 Shows 2 accounts**	**56568966674 Shows 2 accounts**	**56568966674 Shows 2 accounts**
3. Balance	**- 0 -**	**$500 for one, $758 for one**	**- 0 - for both accounts**	**$500 for one, $758 for one**
4. Date Opened	**?**	**3/84**	**3/84**	**3/84**
5. Date Closed	**?**	**Not Listed**	**8/86**	**Not Listed**
6. Date of Last Activity	**?**	**8/86**	**Not Listed**	**Not Listed**
7. Current Status	**Bankruptcy Account**	**DELINQUENT**	**BANKRUPTCY**	**CHARGE OFF for both accounts**
8. Credit Limits	**$1,258**	**$500 for one, $758 for one**	**Not Listed**	**$500 for one, $758 for one**
9. Whose Account or ECOA	**Individual**	**I for both accounts**	**I for both accounts**	**1 for both accounts**
10. MOP Indicator		**R9**	**R09 for one, O09 for one**	**NEG Column for both accounts**
11. Delinquency Amounts	**- 0 -**	**$500 for one, $758 for one**	**- 0 - for both accounts**	**$500 for one, $758 for one**

Diagram 8-2(b)(6)
[Improper Current Status and MOP Indicator, and Incorrect Delinquency Amounts]

Section II - Credit History Information				
	Your Records	Equifax	Trans Union	TRW
1. Creditor Name	**Wands**	**WANDS**	**WANDS**	**WANDS**
2. Account Number	**3838029535**	**3838029535**	**3838029535**	**3838029535**
3. Balance	**$1,450**	**$1,400**	**$1,400**	**$1,400**
4. Date Opened	**10/5/87**	**10/87**	**10/87**	**10/87**
5. Date Closed	**N/A**	**N/A**	**N/A**	**N/A**
6. Date of Last Activity	**?**	**9/91**	**Not Listed**	**Not Listed**
7. Current Status	**Current**	**CURRENT**	**CURRENT**	**DELINQUENT**
8. Credit Limits	**$1,500**	**$1,500**	**$1,500**	**$1,500**
9. Whose Account or ECOA	**Joint**	**J**	**J**	**2**
10. MOP Indicator		**R2**	**R01**	**POS Column**
11. Delinquency Amounts		**$160**	**- 0 -**	**$80**

Diagram 8-2(b)(7)
[Correct Account Information for all credit reports]

Section II - Credit History Information				
	Your Records	Equifax	Trans Union	TRW
1. Creditor Name	**Sitibank**	**SITI PRVS**	**SITIBANK**	**SITIBANK PREFERRED**
2. Account Number	**427138254914**	**427138254914**	**427138254914**	**427138254914**
3. Balance	**- 0 -**	**- 0 -**	**- 0 -**	**- 0 -**
4. Date Opened	**1/14/84**	**1/84**	**1/84**	**1/84**
5. Date Closed	**?**	**Not Listed**	**5/86**	**Not Listed**
6. Date of Last Activity	**?**	**5/86**	**Not Listed**	**Not Listed**
7. Current Status	**Bankruptcy Account**	**INCLUDED IN BANKRUPTCY**	**BANKRUPTCY**	**BK LIQ REO**
8. Credit Limits	**$4,985**	**Not Listed**	**Not Listed**	**$5,000**
9. Whose Account or ECOA	**Individual**	**I**	**I**	**1**
10. MOP Indicator		**Not Listed**	**R09**	**NEG Column**
11. Delinquency Amounts	**- 0 -**	**- 0 -**	**- 0 -**	**- 0 -**

Chapter 9

Repairing Your Credit

The wheel that squeaks the loudest is the one that gets the grease.

Josh Billings [Henry Wheeler Shaw]

We've finally reached the chapter that you've been waiting for—the one that tells you how to "repair" your credit. In this chapter, I'll tell you everything you need to know to make your credits reports more appealing to potential creditors.

To do this, I'll teach you a complete credit repair system. I call it the "CARE" system—Correct, Add, Remove, Explain. This system will help you correct mistakes, add good credit information, remove bad information, and explain anything that's left over. By the time you've completed the CARE system, your credit report should look a lot better than it does now.

I'll also show you a step-by-step process that you can use to put all four parts of the CARE system into action. I call it the WDTF process—Write, Document, Track, Follow-Up. You'll want to use this process whenever you communicate with the credit bureaus or your creditors.

The WDTF process will prevent the credit bureaus and your creditors from ignoring your requests, and help you to organize your credit repair efforts. I'll show you all four parts of this process in Section I. Then, in Sections II, III, IV, and V, I'll teach you the CARE system of credit repair.

I. The WDTF Process

All right. Let's talk about the WDTF process—Write, Document, Track, Follow-Up. The first part of the process—WRITE—reminds you to put EVERYTHING in writing. Let me tell you what I mean.

Put Everything in Writing

Write—Don't Talk

Whenever you communicate with the credit bureaus or your creditors, make sure that you have something in writing. The best way to do this is to avoid telephone conversations and in-person visits. ALWAYS send a letter to the credit bureaus or your creditors, don't just pick up the phone or visit them.

There are two reasons that I tell you to do this. First, a written letter will prevent the credit bureaus or your creditors from forgetting what you want. If you put your request in writing, they can't forget. Second, your written letter, combined with other documentation, proves that you DID make the request. Therefore, as a general rule, always write, don't talk.

However, I know that you MIGHT need to talk to a credit bureau employee or one of your creditors. Sometimes, this is the only way to get something done. But, if you do this, still put it in writing. Let me tell you how I do this.

If I talk to another lawyer on the telephone, and we verbally agree to do something, I make a written record of the conversation. To do this, I send the other lawyer a letter that restates our verbal conversation. The letter usually starts out like this: "As we discussed during our February 3, 1993, telephone conversation ... "

The main reason I do this is to prevent mistakes. People sometimes hear different things during a telephone conversation. I want to make sure that we each understood the same thing during our conversation. If not, my letter should clear up any misunderstandings.

But there's another reason I do this. As I said before, people often "forget" their side of an agreement. I've had many cases where another lawyer would agree to do something, and then "forget" that promise several months later. However, because I always send a letter that restates my verbal conversations, I have proof of these promises.

You should be as cautious with the credit bureaus and your creditors as I am with other lawyers. Therefore, record your verbal conversations IN WRITING. (You don't need to do this for every conversation. If no one says anything important, don't worry about sending a written version.)

All right. I think you probably get the idea—put everything in writing. But, if you're like me, you probably hate to create your own letters. Therefore, to make it easy for you, I've included many sample letters in this chapter. These sample letters should cover just about anything you're likely to encounter in your credit repair efforts. You may use the letters as they are or tailor them to your individual writing style. However, I'd like to give you a word of warning about copying the sample letters word for word—watch out for the "frivolous or irrelevant dispute" clause.

The "Frivolous or Irrelevant Dispute" Clause

Under section 1681i of the Fair Credit Reporting Act, credit bureaus must reinvestigate any information on your credit report that you disagree with. If the credit bureaus can't verify the information, or it's wrong, they must remove the information from your report. However, section 1681i also gives the credit bureaus a "loophole" to avoid this process. Under section 1681i, a credit bureau can refuse your request if it "has reasonable grounds for believing the dispute is frivolous or irrelevant."

Some credit bureaus have used this loophole to avoid their obligations under the Fair Credit Reporting Act. One way that they've done this is to deny requests from consumers who appear to have received assistance in drafting their letters. This means that the credit bureau may deny your request or complaint as "frivolous" if you send them a "polished" letter. Additionally, the credit bureaus might deny your request if everybody starts sending them copies of my sample letters. Therefore, to avoid this problem, it's probably better if you use the sample letters as guides and tailor them to fit your own writing style.

However, don't let this loophole frighten you too much. If you want to use my sample letters word for word, then go ahead. If the credit bureaus deny your request as frivolous, I'll tell you how to remedy this in the next chapter.

Document Everything

Now let's talk about the second part of the WDTF process—Document. Whenever you write the credit bureaus or your creditors, you need to keep proof of this communication. Lawyers call this "documenting."

In the legal world, lawyers document EVERYTHING they do. They do this to keep a record of every step in the process. You see, it's often important to know who received a letter, and when they received it. Let me give you an example.

I once handled a mortgage foreclosure on a large commercial shopping mall. The owners of the mall—seven different companies—had stopped paying their mortgage payments and the bank wanted my firm to seize the property. However, under state law, a mortgagee (the bank) must notify the mortgagors (the companies) that it intends to foreclose on the mortgage. If the mortgagors fail to respond within 10 days, then the bank can seize the property. (I've simplified this a bit.)

Therefore, I had to send a letter to each company. I also needed to make sure that the letters reached the companies and that I knew when they reached them. But most important, I had to have proof of the whole process. I did this by copying the letters, and sending the originals by Certified Mail - Return Receipt Requested.

Under Certified Mail - Return Receipt Requested, the Postal Service will have the recipient sign and date a receipt for your letter. Then, the Postal Service mails this receipt to you. This shows who got your letter, and when they got it.

And you know, it's a good thing that I did this. Two of the companies told the judge that they never received any notice, while a third company responded 15 days after they received my letter.

When the judge asked me about this, I sent him copies of my letter and the return receipts for all three companies. These receipts proved that the two companies DID receive notice. Therefore, they lost.

The certified receipts also showed when the third company had received my letter. Because this company took 15 days to respond, and the law only allowed them 10 days, they lost too. With the proof provided by the return receipts, I easily won the case.

You can win your cases too, if you document your letters. Therefore, make sure that you follow the two-step documenting process. First, make photocopies of EVERYTHING you send to the credit bureaus or your creditors. Or, save your files if you use a computer to write your letters.

Remember, letters have a way of disappearing. If the credit bureaus or your creditors lose your letter, you'll still have a copy. Additionally, it will be easier for you to keep track of the specific complaints you've made to each credit bureau and creditor if you keep copies of all your letters.

The next step is to make sure you send your letters by Certified Mail - Return Receipt Requested. Remember, when you send a letter by Certified Mail, the Postal Service makes the recipient sign and date a receipt for the letter. Then, the Postal Service will return the signed and dated receipt to you for your records.

To send a letter by Certified Mail, take your letter to the post office and tell the clerk that you want to send it by Certified Mail - Return Receipt Requested. The postal clerk will have you complete a form by identifying your name and address and the name and address of the credit bureau or creditor. This service will cost you a little bit more than a normal first class stamp, but the rewards are worth the money.

There are two reasons why you should send your letters by Certified Mail - Return Receipt Requested. First, the receipt of delivery will contain the signature of the employee that accepts your letter. This will prove that the credit bureau or creditor received it.

Second, the receipt of delivery will show when the credit bureau or creditor accepted your letter. This is important because the credit bureau must respond to your request within a "reasonable time" period. If they don't, they must remove the disputed information from your report.

This is just like the company that replied 15 days after they received my letter. They took too long to respond, so they lost. If the credit bureaus take too long to respond to your letters, they'll lose too. We'll talk about this idea in a moment. For now though, let's look at the next part of the WDTF process.

Track Your Complaints

The third part of the WDTF process—Track—reminds you to keep organized records of your credit repair efforts. To help you with this, I've included another work sheet. I've named this work sheet the "Complaint Sheet." You'll find it in Diagram 9-1.

The Complaint Sheet will help you to follow every request and complaint you send to the credit bureaus or your creditors. By using the Complaint Sheet, you'll know what credit information you've complained about, and whether someone has responded.

Additionally, the Complaint Sheet will help you follow how long the credit bureaus take to respond to your requests. Remember, they must respond within a "reasonable time." If they don't, they must remove the information you've complained about. Therefore, it's very important to know when the credit bureaus received your request. The Complaint Sheet will help you keep track of this.

Before we look at the final part of the WDTF process, take a moment to review the Complaint Sheet. To make it easy for you, I've also included detailed instructions on how to use it. You'll find these instructions just after the Complaint Sheet.

When you find the Complaint Sheet, you'll probably notice that it follows three separate complaints. (If you send out more than this—and you probably will—you'll need to make photocopies of the Complaint Sheet BEFORE you complete it.) The first six sections track your FIRST letter to the credit bureau or your creditor. The last three sections track your SECOND letter. Therefore, if the credit bureau responds to your first letter within 30 days, you WON'T need to complete the last three sections. You'll only need to complete these last sections if the credit bureau DOES NOT respond to your first letter within 30 days.

O.K. I think you get the idea. Now, let's look at the last part of the WDTF process.

Follow-Up on Your Complaints

The final part of the WDTF process—Follow-Up—reminds you to stay on top of your requests. Don't let the credit bureaus or your creditors ignore your requests. If the credit bureaus fail to respond to your initial requests within 30 days, send them another letter. If your creditors ignore you, send them another letter.

This is probably the most important part of the WDTF process. When you're repairing your credit, persistence pays off. If you let the credit bureaus and your creditors ignore your requests, they will. So, don't let them ignore you. In the next section, I'll tell you how to do this.

O.K. Now you know about the WDTF process. Use this process EVERY time that you communicate with the credit bureaus or your creditors. If you do, you'll avoid mistakes and problems during your credit repair efforts.

Now that you know how to talk to the credit bureaus and your creditors, it's time to repair your credit. As I told you at the beginning of this chapter, the best way to repair your credit is to use the CARE system—Correct, Add, Remove, Explain. In the next several sections, I'll show you each part of the system. So, if you're ready, let's start from the beginning.

II. Correct Any Mistakes in Your Reports

In the first part of the CARE system, you CORRECT any mistakes in your credit report. If you've completed the Credit Report Summary from Chapter 8, you've probably found several of them. If so, it's your right under section 1681i of the Fair Credit Reporting Act to force the credit bureaus to reinvestigate this information. If you're right, the credit bureau must correct the information, or remove it from your credit report. In the process, you've "repaired" your credit.

Unfortunately, correcting the mistakes in your credit report isn't always that easy. Sometimes, a credit bureau investigation proves that the information is correct—even when it's not. But how can this happen?

The main obstacle to correcting mistakes in your credit report is the investigation process. When you complain about a mistake in your credit report, the credit bureau reinvestigates the information. And do you know who they ask about the mistake? That's right. They ask your creditor. And guess who probably gave the credit bureau the wrong information in the first place? You're right again—your creditor.

If your creditor's records are wrong, your creditor will verify the incorrect information when the credit bureau contacts it about your account. The credit bureau then happily reports to you that the information is correct, and that your creditor has verified it. If this happens, you haven't repaired your credit.

If your creditor does verify information that you know is wrong, you'll have to contact the creditor directly. At this point, the credit bureau won't believe your claim, and won't correct the information in your credit report. However, the credit bureau WILL correct the information if your creditor requests the change. Therefore, you'll need to convince your creditor that the information is wrong.

To correct your credit report, then, you'll need to contact the credit bureaus and maybe your creditors too. How do you do that? That's right. Use the Write, Document, Track, Follow-Up process. Let's review it one more time.

Write Letters to the Credit Bureaus and Your Creditors

As you remember, the first step of the WDTF process is to WRITE letters to each credit bureau or creditor. In your letter, explain what the mistake is, and why it's wrong. To help you with this, I've included a sample letter, Diagram 9-2. Then, to show you how your completed letter might look, I've also included two letters by John Consumer. You'll find these completed letters in Diagrams 9-3 and 9-4. Notice that Diagram 9-4 provides more details about the dispute than does the sample letter in Diagram 9-3.

Document the Letters

When you've completed your letters, it's time to DOCUMENT them. As you remember, there are two steps to this part of the WDTF process. First, make photocopies of your letters, or save your computer files.

Then, when you're ready to mail your letters, take them to the post office and send them by Certified Mail - Return Receipt Requested. After a week or so, you should receive the Certified Mail receipts from the post office. These receipts will show when the credit bureaus received your letters. Keep these receipts for your files.

Track the Letters

The third step in the WDTF process is to track your letters. Remember, it's very important that you know when the credit bureaus receive your letters. Therefore, remember to record the relevant information about each letter on the Complaint Sheet, Diagram 9-1. This will help you to keep track of your credit repair efforts and prevent anything from getting lost.

You'll also want to complete the remaining portions of the Complaint Sheet at each step in this process. For example, complete the section labeled "Date Credit Bureau Received Your Letter" when you receive the Certified Mail receipts from the Postal Service.

Follow-Up

The final step in the WDTF process is to follow-up on your letters. Remember, persistence pays off. Therefore, you'll need to stay on top of everything. To help you with this, let's review how the credit bureaus or your creditors might respond, and what you should do to follow-up.

If You Receive a Preliminary Response from the Credit Bureaus or Creditors

The first response you receive from the credit bureaus or your creditors may be a preliminary response. This means that they've received your letter, but haven't yet finished their investigation. Generally, they want you to send them additional information. For example, they may want copies of your bankruptcy schedules or discharge order.

To follow-up on any initial response, just comply with their request. If they want additional information, send it to them. That's all you can do until they've completed their investigation.

If the Credit Bureaus or Creditors Correct the Mistakes

Eventually, you should receive some response from the credit bureaus or creditors. The best response is one that complies with your request and corrects the mistakes in your credit report. If you receive this response from the credit bureaus or creditors, congratulate yourself! You've just "repaired" your credit.

If the Credit Bureaus or Creditors Do Not Correct the Mistakes

However, if the credit bureaus or creditors deny your initial request, you've got more work to do. Unfortunately, this means that you'll probably need to contact your creditor to correct the mistake.

Remember, we talked about this problem in the first section. The credit bureaus have no way of directly verifying most of the information that they include in your credit report. Therefore, they must rely on your creditors to supply and maintain the correct information. If your creditors verify the disputed information, correct or not, the credit bureau will probably NOT change the information in your credit report.

So what should you do if the credit bureaus refuse to correct the mistakes in your credit reports? First, try to prove your claim to the credit bureau. Although I said they probably won't correct the information, you should try. To do this, send the credit bureaus copies of any bills, receipts, checks, etc. that prove your side of the story. If your proof is convincing, the credit bureau MAY correct your report.

The second step is to talk to the individual creditors directly. Do this by making an appointment with the credit manager, either by telephone or letter. Creditors are generally willing to work with you if you have a legitimate claim. If you can convince the creditor that your claim is valid, the creditor will contact the credit bureaus and have them correct your report.

If the Credit Bureau Fails to Respond Within 30 Days

At some point, the credit bureaus should respond to your initial letter. However, as you know, they must do this within a "reasonable period of time." An opinion by the Federal Trade Commission states that this period of time is 30 days. (We'll talk more about that in Section IV.) If the credit bureaus fail to respond to your request within this time, send them a second letter demanding that they respond to your initial request. To help you with this, I've included a sample letter, Diagram 9-7. As before, I've also included another letter, Diagram 9-8, to show you how a completed letter might look.

Final Words About Correcting Mistakes

You should be able to correct the mistakes in your credit report. If your credit information is wrong, the credit bureaus must remove it. However, you may have more difficulty with information that is technically correct, but misleading. I call this "inaccurate" information.

Unfortunately, several courts have taken a broad view of the term "inaccurate." These courts have held that credit bureaus don't need to provide all of the facts about a particular situation. Generally, this means that credit bureaus don't have to present information that favors your side of the story.

Therefore, credit bureaus can list information in your credit report that damages your credit rating, even if that information is misleading. If this happens to you, you really only have two options. Your first option is to wait out the statutory removal period. After a certain period of time, the credit bureau must then remove the disputed information from your credit report.

Your second option is to catch the credit bureau when it takes longer than a reasonable period of time to reinvestigate your complaint. Under section 1681i of the Fair Credit Reporting Act, the credit bureau must then remove the disputed credit information from your report. We'll talk more about both options in Section IV. For now though, let's look at the next step in the CARE system—ADD.

III. Add Favorable Information to Your Report

The second step in the CARE system is to ADD good credit information to your credit reports. When you add good information to your reports, it tends to neutralize the bad information. Therefore, a potential creditor is more likely to grant your credit request.

Add Missing Accounts

This good credit information will probably come from two sources. First, you may find that the credit bureaus aren't reporting some of your current accounts. If not, you'll want to add these good accounts to your reports. Second, you'll want to add in good accounts that you receive after your bankruptcy. (I'll tell you how to get these accounts in later chapters.)

You've probably noticed that I keep saying that YOU have to add the good information to your credit report. If so, you're probably wondering why YOU have to do this. After all, creditors automatically report all your accounts to the credit bureaus. Right?

Unfortunately, as we learned earlier—NO. Think back to our discussion about creditors and credit bureaus. If you remember, some creditors do report to each of the Big 3 credit bureaus. Therefore, these accounts will appear in all of your credit reports.

However, many creditors DON'T belong to all three credit bureaus. Some creditors may only subscribe, and report, to one or two of the credit bureaus. Therefore, the credit bureaus that your creditors don't subscribe to WON'T receive your credit information.

Additionally, some creditors don't report to ANY of the credit bureaus, unless they have some negative information to report. Therefore, NONE of the credit bureaus will have information about some of your accounts—probably the good accounts.

To get these good accounts listed in your credit reports, you'll have to take the initiative. To do this, figure out which of your good accounts don't appear in your credit reports. Then, send a letter to each credit bureau that has not reported the good information and ask them to include the information in your credit report. Some credit bureaus have a form for this. If not, draft a letter that outlines your request. To help you with this, I've included a sample letter, Diagram 9-14. I've also included a completed letter from John Consumer, Diagram 9-15, to show you how your completed letter may look.

Unfortunately, some credit bureaus may not accept account information from a creditor that doesn't subscribe—pay the fees—to that credit bureau. If this happens, there's probably not much that you can do about it. But, it doesn't hurt to try.

If the credit bureaus DO allow you to add good information to your reports, they may charge you for this service. However, the charge will be small, and it's money well spent. Anything you can do to downplay the bad information in your credit report takes you a step closer to repairing your credit.

Add New Accounts

Another way to add good information to your credit reports is to add NEW accounts. These accounts are those that you open after your bankruptcy. (I'm going to show you how to get these accounts in later chapters.)

This is a VERY important technique. If you can add several new accounts to your credit report, potential creditors will know that you've recovered financially, and that you're now willing and able to repay your debts. This new account information will tend to neutralize the negative information from your old accounts, and should make potential creditors more willing to lend to you.

You'll want to make sure that every credit bureau reports these new accounts. There are two ways to do this. First, ask your new creditors which credit bureaus they report to. If they don't report to all of the credit bureaus, then contact the neglected credit bureaus and have them include your new account information. You can use Diagrams 9-14 and 9-15 for this, just as above.

The second way to make sure that the credit bureaus report your new accounts is to review your credit reports shortly after opening the new accounts. You should wait for at least a month after opening any new account, however, to give the creditor a chance to report the information.

Then, contact any credit bureau that does not report the new account. As before, use the credit bureau's form to report the new account, or use Diagrams 9-14 and 9-15 to draft your own letter. As I mentioned earlier, the credit bureau may charge you a small fee to add the new account information to your credit report. But again, this is money well spent!

IV. Remove Bad Credit Information from Your Report

The third step in the CARE system is to REMOVE bad credit information from your credit reports, even if that information is correct. In this section, I'll show you three ways to do this.

First, I'll show you two ways to get the credit bureaus to remove the bad information. You'll do this by using the Fair Credit Reporting Act. Under the Fair Credit Reporting Act, the credit bureaus must remove information from your credit report for two reasons. First, they must remove information if it is "obsolete." This means that the credit bureau has reported the information for too long. Second, the credit bureaus must remove bad information if you request "reverification" of that information and they fail to respond within 30 days of your request. We'll talk about both methods in this section.

We'll also talk about a way to get your creditors to remove the bad credit information from your credit report. You'll do this by offering your former creditors a great deal—something for nothing. I'll tell you what I mean in a moment. For now, though, let's talk about getting the credit bureaus to remove your bad credit information.

Obsolete Information

When Congress passed the Fair Credit Reporting Act, they realized that they should limit the number of years that credit bureaus could report bad credit information. If they didn't, the credit bureaus would report your bad information FOREVER, and you'd never escape your past.

Therefore, they included section 1681c in the Fair Credit Reporting Act. Under section 1681c, credit bureaus can only report bad credit information for a certain number of years. After that period, they CANNOT report this information on your credit report.

However, as with most things, there are exceptions to these statutory time limits. We'll talk about these exceptions in a moment. But first, let's see how long the credit bureaus can report your bad credit information.

Statutory Time Limits for Reporting Bad Credit Information

Under section 1681c, credit bureaus can report MOST types of bad credit information for only seven years. However, there are two exceptions to this seven-year period. First, the credit bureaus can report bankruptcies for 10 years after the date of filing. (However, most credit bureaus will only report Chapter 13 bankruptcies for seven years.) Second, the credit bureaus can report suits and judgments for more than seven years if the governing statute of limitations is longer than seven years.

To give you a feel for this, let's look at each type of credit information and find out how long the credit bureaus can report it.

Bankruptcies

Under section 1681c(1), credit bureaus can report information about bankruptcies for 10 years after the date of filing. Let's look at an example of this. If you filed your bankruptcy petition on May 15, 1990, the credit bureaus could report information about your bankruptcy until May 14, 2000. (Notice, the starting date for this 10-year period is the date of filing, not the date of discharge.)

Suits and Judgments

Under section 1681c(2), credit bureaus can report information about any suits or judgments against you for seven years from the date of entry. However, if the governing statute of limitation is longer than seven years, the credit bureaus can report this information until the statute of limitation expires. (For you legal buffs, a statute of limitation prevents anyone from suing you after a certain amount of time.)

Unfortunately, some statute of limitations last for up to 20 years in some jurisdictions. Therefore, the credit bureaus could report this type of information for up to 20 years.

Paid Tax Liens

Under section 1681c(3), credit bureaus can report information about any paid tax lien for seven years after the date of payment.

Collection or Profit-and-Loss Accounts

Under Section 1681c(4), credit bureaus can report information about collection or profit-and-loss accounts for seven years. According to Federal Trade Commission rules, credit bureaus must count the seven-year period from the date of last activity for your account. Remember, the date of last activity is the date that something last happened in your account. It could be the date that you last paid your creditor, or the date that the creditor gave up its collection efforts on your account.

Let's look at an example for this one. Let's say that you last paid your creditor in January 1991. This COULD be the date of last activity for your account. However, your creditor probably took some further action on this account. For example, your creditor probably sent you several notices about your late payments over several months. Then, your creditor probably gave up and charged your account to profit-and-loss or assigned it to a collection company.

If your creditor took these further actions—and it probably did—then the date of last activity is the later date. In our example, the date of last activity would be the date when your creditor charged your account to profit-and-loss, or sent it to a collection company. The seven-year period would then run from that date—not the date that you last paid your creditor.

If your creditor has charged your account to profit-and-loss, or sent it for collection, the date of this action is the date of last activity. However, this date of last activity does NOT change if for some reason you later pay on the account. Your payment does NOT cause the statutory seven-year period to run from that date.

Arrest, Indictment, or Conviction of Crime

Under section 1681c(5), credit bureaus can report records of arrest, indictment, or conviction of crime for seven years from the date of disposition, release, or parole. However, the credit bureaus should NOT report this information if a court or jury finds that you're not guilty, or if your opponent drops the case against you.

Any Other Bad Information

Under section 1681c(6), credit bureaus can report any other bad credit information for seven years after the date of the report. This is the "catchall" phrase in the Fair Credit Reporting Act.

The Three Exceptions

We now know that credit bureaus must remove all bad credit information from your credit report after a certain number of years. However, as I told you earlier, the Fair Credit Reporting Act lists three exceptions to the statutory time periods. You'll find these exceptions in section 1681c(b). Let's talk about these exceptions now.

A Credit Transaction Involving More than $50,000 in Principal

Section 1681c(b)(1) lists the first exception to the statutory time periods. Under this exception, credit bureaus can report any bad credit information in your credit file—FOREVER. That's right. If you apply for a loan involving more than $50,000 in principal, your potential creditor can see ANY adverse credit information that has EVER been in your credit file. (However, your creditors won't see it if the credit bureaus have actually removed the information from your file. We'll talk more about that in a moment.) You see, the statutory time periods in section 1681c prevent the credit bureaus from REPORTING your bad credit information, they don't prevent the credit bureaus from KEEPING it.

How does this affect you? If you apply for a mortgage loan with a principal amount of more than $50,000, your potential lender gets to see EVERYTHING. Did you file bankruptcy 40 years ago? The credit bureaus could report this. Were you convicted of a crime 30 years ago? The credit bureaus can report this. I think you get the picture.

Just because the credit bureau reports this information, however, doesn't mean that you won't get the loan. Your potential creditor is bound only by its own lending standards. It can therefore use the reported information, or choose to ignore it. After all, how relevant is information about a 40-year old bankruptcy case?

A $50,000+ Life Insurance Policy

Section 1681c(b)(2) lists the second exception to the statutory time periods. Under this exception, credit bureaus can report bad credit information beyond the statutory time periods if you apply for a life insurance policy that has a face amount greater than $50,000. As before, this means that an insurance underwriter can see ALL of your bad credit information, even if it's obsolete.

Employment that Pays $20,000+ Annually

Section 1681c(b)(3) lists the final exception to the statutory time periods. Under this exception, credit bureaus can report ALL of your bad credit information beyond the statutory time periods if you apply for a job that pays $20,000 a year or more. You are VERY likely to run into this exception.

Congress probably thought that this exception would only affect executives. However, inflation since the passage of the Fair Credit Reporting Act has eroded the buying power of $20,000. Although $20,000 may have been a large salary at the time that of the Act's passage, it's not as large today. Therefore, MANY consumers will face this exception.

The Good News

Now that we've looked at the exceptions to the statutory time periods, let me tell you the good news. Most credit bureaus do NOT keep information that is statutorily obsolete. Once any information becomes obsolete, most credit bureaus simply delete the information from their files. This is great news for all of us!

Remove the Obsolete Information

O.K. Now that you know about obsolete information, let me tell you how to remove it from your credit reports. Let's do this step-by-step.

Determine the Beginning Date for the Statutory Time Periods

The first step in removing obsolete information from your credit reports is to figure out which information is obsolete. Unfortunately, this isn't as easy as it sounds. You see, it's sometimes very difficult to know when the statutory period starts to run.

As you now know, these statutory time periods begin on some specified date. For bankruptcies, that date is the date of filing. You should have that information, so figuring out the time period is easy.

But what if you DON'T have the information? For example, we know that the statutory period for collection and charge-off accounts starts on the date of last activity. However, you probably don't know when that occurred. You MAY know the date that you last paid on the account. But as we've already seen, that may not be the date of last activity.

Additionally, the credit bureaus may not report the date of last activity for your accounts. Trans Union and TRW do NOT report the date of last activity. TRW usually reports the date that the creditor closed the account and sometimes reports the date of last payment. Fortunately, Equifax DOES report the date of last activity for most of its reported accounts.

Therefore, the best thing to do for these accounts is to record them in Section II of your Credit Report Summary. Then, you can compare the information that each credit bureau reports about each account. For example, look back to Diagram 8-2(b)(1) in Chapter 8. You'll notice that Equifax is the only credit bureau that reports the date of last activity for the GMAK account. Trans Union and TRW don't even report the closing date for the account.

According to the Equifax credit report, the date of last activity for the GMAK account is May 1986. This means that this account information will be obsolete seven years later—May 1993. Therefore, John Consumer can force Equifax to remove his GMAK account information from his credit report on that date. In addition, John should use the date of last activity information from Equifax to force Trans Union and TRW to remove the GMAK information from their reports too.

If you've completed Section II of the Credit Report Summary for your credit reports, you should be able to use the Equifax information in the same manner. However, you may find that Equifax doesn't report a date of last activity or closing date for some accounts. If this happens, see if Trans Union or TRW report a closing date for these accounts. If so, try to get Equifax to use the same information, and report it as the date of last activity.

Write Letters to the Credit Bureaus

Once you've found the information that you want the credit bureaus to remove from your reports, it's time to start the WDTF process. As you remember, the first step is to write letters to the credit bureaus. In these letters, you should demand that the credit bureaus remove the obsolete information from your credit records. To help you with this, I've included a sample letter, Diagram 9-5. As before, I've also included another letter, Diagram 9-6, to show you how your completed letter might look.

Document Your Letters to the Credit Bureaus

The second step in the WDTF process is to document your letters. As you remember, this means you should make photocopies of your letters, or save your computer files. This also means that you should send your letters by Certified Mail - Return Receipt Requested.

Track Your Letters to the Credit Bureau

The third step in the WDTF process is to track your letters. As you remember, this means you should record the relevant information about these letters in your Credit Report Summary. This also means that you should continue to record information in the Complaint Sheet as you receive responses from the credit bureaus.

Follow-Up on Your Letters to the Credit Bureau

The final step in the WDTF process is to follow-up on your letters. As you remember, this means you should stay on top of your requests. If the credit bureaus want more information, send it to them. If they fail to respond within 30 days, send them another letter. You know the process by now. If you don't remember all the steps, look back to my step-by-step description in Section II.

Remove Bad Information That's Not Obsolete

Now that you know how to remove bad credit information that's obsolete, let's go to the next level. If you've just recently declared bankruptcy, most of your bad credit accounts are probably years away from becoming obsolete. If this information is correct, it will stay on your report until the statutory period runs out.

However, there is something you can do about this. In this next section, I'm going to tell you how to remove bad credit information from your credit report, even if that information is correct and not obsolete. As you can imagine, this is the most difficult type of information to remove from your credit report. Additionally, removing this type of information creates some ethical and moral problems.

Let's talk about these problems first. If we accept the idea that we need some type of credit reporting industry—maybe not—then we need to avoid anything that hurts that system. Unfortunately, if we allow people to remove correct credit information from their credit reports, it probably hurts that system. If we accept this, then you shouldn't attempt this credit repair technique and I shouldn't tell you how to do it. But I've decided against that idea for two reasons.

This Technique Prevents Credit Bureaus from Abusing the Credit Reporting System

First, I've decided to explain this technique to you because I believe it prevents the credit bureaus from abusing their power—at least in this area. Congress built a procedural safeguard into the Fair Credit Reporting Act to prevent credit bureaus from abusing their vast power. As you know, section 1681i of the Fair Credit Reporting Act requires that credit bureaus respond to consumer requests within "a reasonable period of time."

Without this safeguard, credit bureaus could take as long as they wanted to respond to consumer requests. If this happened, the credit reporting system would suffer. Creditors would receive credit reports that contained many mistakes. Innocent consumers would lose their ability to get credit. The list of problems could go on and on. Congress recognized this when it passed the "reasonable period of time" clause.

Therefore, under section 1681i, the credit bureaus must respond to your request within 30 days. If they don't, they must correct the information you complained about, or remove it from your credit report.

I know that some people might object to this "procedural" credit repair technique. However, you'll find similar procedural safeguards throughout many areas of the law. Legislators have designed these procedural safeguards with one purpose in mind—to prevent people from abusing the system.

I can give you many examples of these procedural safeguards. Let's say that a police officer charges into your house one night and searches every inch of it. Eventually, the officer finds a marijuana cigarette that your son left in a drawer. Then, the officer arrests you for possession of marijuana.

Later, you find out that the police officer didn't have a search warrant. As you know, police officers must generally have a search warrant to search your house. This is a procedural safeguard to prevent the police from abusing the criminal justice system.

When you go to trial, your lawyer tells the judge that the police officer didn't have a search warrant. Do you know what the judge will do? That's right. The judge won't even look at the evidence. That's the penalty for violating the procedural safeguard. Therefore, you'll probably go free.

Let me give you another example that we've already talked about. At the beginning of this chapter, I told you about a mortgage foreclosure that I was involved in. As you remember, I sent letters by Certified Mail to seven companies to let them know that we were foreclosing on their mortgage. I did this because the law allowed them 10 days to respond, and I wanted to make sure that they complied with the law.

This 10-day period is another procedural safeguard that legislators built into mortgage foreclosure law. (In fact, most defendants only have 10 days to respond to a complaint.) This 10-day procedural safeguard keeps defendants from stalling lawsuits forever, and therefore prevents abuse of the court system. Because these companies failed to respond to my complaint within the 10-day period, they lost. That was their penalty for violating the procedural safeguard.

Section 1681i is just another procedural safeguard. If the credit bureaus fail to comply with the procedural rule of section 1681i, they lose. That's their penalty for violating the procedural safeguard and abusing the credit reporting system.

Credit Repair Companies Use this Technique

I've also decided to explain this technique to you because I don't want unscrupulous "credit repair" companies to steal your money. These companies became popular in the 1980's by offering to repair bad credit reports. For a fee—often ranging from several hundreds to several thousands of dollars—these credit repair companies "guaranteed" to repair the credit records of their clients. As part of this guarantee, these companies promised to remove bad credit information, even if it was correct, and not obsolete.

Let me be clear about this. This credit repair technique DOES work. But, it is NOT 100% effective. You may be able to remove some of your bad credit information with this technique, but you probably won't be able to remove it all.

The credit repair companies, however, promised to remove ALL bad credit information from their client's credit reports. Unfortunately, the results were usually poor. Typically, these credit repair companies were "fly-by-night" operations, and disappeared after collecting the high fees from their clients. Of course, their clients never received any benefit from these services and never got their money back.

Occasionally, however, some credit repair companies did successfully remove bad credit information from their client's credit reports. In these rare cases, the companies succeeded because they used the techniques in this chapter. And because you know these same techniques (or will by the end of this chapter) you'll be able to remove bad credit information YOURSELF. You DON'T need these companies. We'll talk more about credit repair companies in Chapter 16.

The Technique

To remove bad credit information from your credit reports, if it's not obsolete, you must use the procedural safeguard that Congress included in section 1681i. This safeguard states that "the consumer reporting agency shall within a reasonable period of time reinvestigate and record the current status of that information." The important clause is "within a reasonable period of time."

I know, you were hoping for more than that. But that's it. The credit bureaus must respond to any dispute "within a reasonable period of time," or remove the disputed information from the credit report. But what is a "reasonable period of time?" Unfortunately, Congress failed to define this clause anywhere in the Fair Credit Reporting Act.

When Congress fails to define a term in some statute, another government entity must step in. Generally, the courts do this. However, I don't know of any court that has defined "a reasonable period of time" with a specific number of days. Fortunately for us, though, the Federal Trade Commission (the "FTC") has done this.

In MIB, Inc., 101 FTC 415, 423 (1983), the FTC sued a medical information agency that supplied its clients with the medical histories of consumers throughout the country. In this 1983 decision, the FTC ordered MIB, the medical information agency, to comply with section 1681i. Specifically, the FTC wanted MIB to reverify disputed information and respond to consumer requests within a reasonable period of time.

However, to enforce its order, the FTC had to define "a reasonable period of time." Therefore, the decision stated that "30 days shall be presumptively deemed a reasonable period of time, in the absence of unusual circumstances."

According to this FTC decision, then, 30 days is a reasonable period of time under section 1681i. If a credit bureau takes longer than 30 days to reverify disputed information, absent unusual circumstances, it should remove the disputed information from your credit report.

Until a court in your jurisdiction rules otherwise, the FTC's interpretation seems reliable. Courts often rely on agencies with expertise in a particular area to help them interpret statutes. Because the FTC is responsible for enforcing the Fair Credit Reporting Act, a court would probably rely on the FTC for guidance. Therefore, this 30-day reasonable time period should prevail.

How to Use the "Reasonable Period of Time Clause"

So how do you use the "reasonable time period" clause? If you've copied the sample letters in earlier sections of this book, then you've already used it. You've probably noticed that the earlier complaint letters included the following paragraph:

> Please respond as soon as possible to this request. I understand that your investigation must be completed within a "reasonable period of time" under 15 U.S.C. section 1681i(a), and that the Federal Trade Commission has stated that 30 days constitutes a "reasonable period of time" under this statute. Therefore, I look forward to your response within 30 days.

You may have wondered why this paragraph was in the earlier letters. Now you know. It's my attempt to remove the bad credit information from your credit report.

You might also have noticed that I've included this paragraph in all the sample letters (except the initial request for the credit report). If so, you're probably wondering why we need to include it when we complain about mistakes or obsolete information. After all, the credit bureaus will remove this information anyway. Right? Well, maybe not.

As we discussed before, you may have difficulty in getting the information corrected. If your creditor reports the wrong information to the credit bureaus, it may take many months to correct your credit report.

Additionally, your creditor or the credit bureaus may refuse to change the incorrect information. With the paragraph, you can force them to remove the bad information from your report— something they should have done anyway.

But there's another reason that you may want to include the paragraph in your letters. Some types of information will hurt your credit report even if you get the credit bureaus to correct it. For example, let's say you complain to the credit bureaus about one of your bankruptcy accounts because your credit reports list it as a charge-off account. If the credit bureaus comply with your request and report the account as a bankruptcy account, then you've "repaired" your credit—well a little bit anyway. BUT, the account information is still BAD. It's not going to help you get any new loans.

If, however, the credit bureaus fail to respond to your request within a reasonable period of time—30 days— they might remove the credit reference completely. Now you've really repaired your credit and you're one step closer to new loans. (Of course, they still might just correct the information according to your complaint. Therefore, it sometimes pays to be a little vague.)

How Credit Repair Companies Use It

Now let me tell you how some credit repair companies use this technique. They review their clients' credit reports very carefully, looking for ANY mistake at all. Then they flood the credit bureaus with complaint letters about every mistake. At some point, the process breaks down, and the credit bureaus fail to respond within a reasonable period of time. Then, the credit bureaus must remove the disputed information mentioned in the missed letters. Some credit repair companies have used this technique to successfully remove references about judgments, liens, criminal convictions, and yes ... even bankruptcies.

How You Can Use It

If you want to use this technique yourself, just review the Credit Report Summary. It will provide a great deal of information and will help you to spot a variety of errors. Then, send complaint letters to the credit bureaus that list your disputed information. Don't include too many complaints in one letter. If you do, the credit bureau will probably respond to some, but not all, of your demands. Then you'll have to start all over. Therefore, try to dispute only one item in each letter you send.

Remember to use the WDTF process when you communicate with the credit bureaus. Therefore, WRITE your letters to the credit bureaus.

Then, DOCUMENT your letters by photocopying them. And most important, make sure you send your letters by Certified Mail - Return Receipt Requested. That will prove the date that the credit bureau first received your letter.

After that, TRACK the information in the Complaint Sheet, especially the date information. The Complaint Sheet will help you to keep track of your letters and will tell you the date that each credit bureau should respond to each letter.

Finally, FOLLOW-UP on your complaints. If the credit bureaus don't respond within 30 days, send them a letter demanding that they remove the disputed information from your credit report. To help you with this, I've included a sample letter in Diagram 9-7. And as always, I've also included a letter from John Consumer to show you how a completed letter would look.

Problems With the Technique

Before you get too excited about this technique, I probably should mention two problems with it. First, you MAY not get the credit bureaus to remove your bad credit information, even if they do miss the 30-day deadline. As I said earlier, they may respond by correcting the information according to your complaint, even if they weren't able to verify it. To the credit bureaus, this is better than removing the information completely.

In this case, you'd have to take your complaint to the FTC or to the courts. Unfortunately, you may not find a friendly audience at either of those institutions. The likely response from a court or the FTC is that you got what you asked for—a corrected credit reference. I don't have any solid information to back up this prediction—it's just a hunch.

The second problem with this technique is something we've already discussed—the "frivolous or irrelevant" clause. This clause shares the sentence with the "reasonable period of time" clause. Here's the rest of the sentence from section 1681i:

> If the complete accuracy of any item of information contained in his file is disputed by a consumer, and such dispute is directly conveyed to the consumer reporting agency by the consumer, the consumer reporting agency shall within a reasonable period of time reinvestigate and record the current status of that information unless it has reasonable grounds to believe that the dispute by the consumer is frivolous or irrelevant.

Notice the "frivolous or irrelevant" clause that follows the "reasonable period of time" clause. This is a built-in loophole for the credit bureaus. If the credit bureaus think that you're playing games with the system, then they can refuse to investigate your dispute. And guess what? The credit bureaus have a very broad interpretation of this clause.

The credit bureaus abuse this loophole even though the FTC has warned them against this practice. So watch out. Don't start flooding the credit bureaus with hundreds of letters. If you do, the credit bureaus will probably cry "frivolous and irrelevant" and end your credit repair attempts.

The best way to avoid this is to be very patient with your credit repair efforts. Send the credit bureaus one letter at a time. Try to be vague about your specific complaint—but not so vague that the credit bureau thinks you're making something out of nothing. Remember—BE PATIENT. You'll eventually get what you want.

Get Your Creditors to Remove Bad Information

I told you at the beginning of this chapter that there were three ways to remove bad information from your credit reports. We've looked at the two ways to get the credit bureaus to remove this type of information. Now let's look at a way to get your creditors to remove it.

As you remember, credit bureaus get most of your credit information from your creditors. Your creditors report your payment history, current status, balance amounts, overdue amounts, etc. Unfortunately, the credit bureaus must hope that this information is correct. If not, the credit bureaus will only know it's wrong if your creditors tell them that it's wrong.

Now you're beginning to see how this technique works. You can repair your credit report if you can convince your creditors to "correct" the information that they have reported to the credit bureaus.

For example, let's say that one of your former creditors had previously reported your account as a profit-and-loss write-off. This is the type of bad credit information that you want to remove from your report. Unfortunately, you'd normally need to wait seven years before the credit bureaus would remove this account from your credit reports.

However, you could have the credit bureaus remove this bad information MUCH sooner if you can convince your creditor to report that your account is current. If your creditor did this, the credit bureaus would then revise the information on your credit report. Then, your account would go from bad to good.

But why would a creditor agree to help you? After all, you're probably not one of the creditor's most favored customers. The answer is simple—MONEY.

That's right. MONEY. Which means, unfortunately, that this technique is going to cost you something. A creditor may agree to change the reported status of your account in exchange for cold, hard cash—an amount equal to some percentage of your former balance. I'll show you how this works.

Let's say that you've reviewed your credit reports, and have found several bad accounts that you'd like to repair. Therefore, you contact the credit manager for one of these former accounts. For this example, let's say that you owed this creditor $1,000.

Because you included this account in your bankruptcy case, your discharge wiped out the $1,000 debt. Therefore, your creditor got nothing from you. Unfortunately, that's the most that this creditor could ever hope to get from you—nothing. But now, you offer the credit manager a deal that's hard to pass up—something for nothing.

You explain to the credit manager that you're trying to re-establish your credit following the unfortunate circumstances of your bankruptcy. You continue by explaining that you want to repay some portion of the debt you once owed this creditor—even though you don't have to do this. You then suggest some portion of the former balance—say $300 of the former $1,000 balance.

Let's stop for a moment and see what we have here. Before you called, this creditor was out $1,000. There was nothing this creditor could ever do to collect this amount from you. But suddenly, the credit manager has an opportunity to collect $300 from you—something for nothing. This will look very good to the credit manager's superiors.

But wait—is this really something for nothing? Before you agree to repay the $300, you'd like some small concessions in return. The first is very small—to allow you to repay the $300 over a period of time. This period may be over 6, 12, or 24 months, it's up to you and the credit manager to decide. The credit manager should not object to this, since most accounts are repaid over time.

Oh, and by the way—you don't want to pay interest on this amount either. Well, it's worth a try. After all, the creditor won't get anything without your cooperation.

And just one more small concession. You want the creditor to "update" your account information with any credit bureau that it reports to. The creditor can do this in one of two ways. First, your creditor can contact the credit bureaus and report that it can't verify your account information. Therefore, the credit bureaus must remove your account information from your credit reports.

Your creditor can also update your account information by reporting that your account is active and in good standing. If your creditor does this, you'll have a good account to balance any bad accounts in your report. This is the best result.

Will a creditor agree to all of this? Maybe. By entering into this arrangement with you, the creditor receives $300. This is found money for the creditor and a good business deal.

Unfortunately, some creditors would rather lose their money than work with you. (I guess they want to pay you back for defaulting.) These creditors may require that you repay 100% of the debt or may not be interested in negotiating with you at all. Oh well. At least give it a try. The results will probably excite you.

The MOST important part of this technique is to get your agreement in WRITING. Remember, people have a way of forgetting their obligations. If you get the agreement IN WRITING, no one will forget.

You'll also want to make sure that your creditor agrees to one of two things. First, try to get your creditor to contact the credit bureaus and report that your account is current and in good standing. This is the ideal result.

However, if your creditor won't agree to do this, get it to contact the credit bureaus and report that it can't verify your account information. If your creditor does this, the credit bureaus will remove your account from your credit reports.

If you can't get your creditors to agree to one of these two conditions, then DON'T make the deal. Remember, you're trying to repair your credit. You DON'T have to pay your creditor ANYTHING. If your creditor won't help you repair your credit, then you haven't gained anything by repaying your old debts. It's just wasted money.

To help you with your negotiations, I've included a sample settlement agreement, Diagram 9-9. In this agreement, I've included everything you could hope to get from your creditors. Therefore, it's best if you can get your creditors to agree to all sections of the agreement. However, you can use pieces of the agreement to create your own agreement if your creditor won't agree to everything. As always, I've also included a completed agreement to show you how your agreement might look when you're finished. You'll find this completed agreement in Diagram 9-10.

You may be asking yourself, "Can the creditor really do this?" That is, can the creditor report to the credit bureaus that your once delinquent and bankrupt account is now an account in good standing? The answer? ABSOLUTELY! Your creditors are the ONLY source of information for the credit history section of your credit report. Therefore, your creditors are the ONLY ones that can decide whether your accounts are good or bad.

To give you a concrete example of this, look at Diagram 9-11. This is a reproduction of a form that one of my former creditors accidentally sent to me during my credit repair efforts. This form is a "Universal Data Form" that many creditors use when updating credit information. You'll notice that the creditor supplies ALL of the information about the credit account, including status, delinquency amounts, and special comments or remarks.

What does this mean? It means that your former creditors can help you to repair your credit. It also means—don't give up. If the local credit manager of a former creditor is unwilling to negotiate with you, try to contact the regional or national credit manager. Eventually, you should find someone that recognizes a good business deal.

V. Explain Any Remaining Bad Credit Information in Your Report

The final part of the CARE system is to EXPLAIN your bad credit information. You'll need to do this only if you haven't corrected all of your bad credit information with the other three parts of the system. If you have completed the other parts, and you still have bad credit information on your reports, then you'll need to explain them to potential creditors.

Write a Personal Statement

You can do this in two ways. First, many creditors are willing to look beyond the bankruptcy notation on your credit report. However, before they'll do this, they'll want you to explain why you filed your bankruptcy case. If you have a good reason, they may be willing to work with you.

Creditors are generally willing to work with you if you had high medical bills, lost your job, or experienced some other disaster. The main thing that creditors look for is that some event beyond your control forced you into bankruptcy. They DON'T want to see that you charged trips to Bermuda and bought expensive jewelry.

Therefore, you need to show your creditors that you weren't the sole cause of your bankruptcy. The best way to do this is to write a statement about your bankruptcy. In this statement, explain why you filed your bankruptcy case. (I mean, explain why some event beyond your control FORCED you into bankruptcy.)

Try to be as persuasive as possible in your statement. Include the reasons that you would want to see if you were a creditor, and leave out those things that might offend you. For example, you'd probably want to play up your high medical bills or unemployment. But, you'd probably want to leave out that your creditors lied to you. I think you get the idea.

Once you've completed your statement, you'll be ready if a creditor ever asks you about your bankruptcy. If so, you can give the creditor your written statement, or just use it to focus your thoughts during your conversation.

If you don't have a completed statement about your bankruptcy, a creditor might catch you off guard. If that happens, you might blurt out the wrong information, like "My creditors lied to me!" If you do, say good-by to your loan.

Write a Consumer Statement

Creating a statement that explains the reasons behind your bankruptcy is one way to explain your bad credit information to potential creditors. Unfortunately, this is a one-on-one approach. You'll only offer your explanation if a potential creditor asks you for it.

However, there's another way to explain your bad credit information to anyone who sees your credit reports. Under section 1681i(b) of the Fair Credit Reporting Act, you can explain any disputed information in your credit reports. To do this, section 1681i(b) allows you to place a statement, or statements, in your credit report.

For example, let's say that you bought a television on credit, but it didn't work when you took it home. Therefore, you called the dealer and asked it to give you another television. Unfortunately, the dealer refused to exchange the television, or let you return it. So, you refused to pay the dealer when it sent you a bill. Eventually, the dealer sent your account to a collection agency, and reported to the credit bureaus that your account was in collection.

If this happened to you, you'd have a mess on your credit report. You'd probably first try to convince the credit bureaus to remove the information. However, as we've already seen, the credit bureaus are really at the mercy of your creditors. Therefore, you probably wouldn't have much success with the credit bureau. After that, you'd probably try to talk to the creditor again. But, considering your earlier encounters, you probably wouldn't get very far with this approach either.

Therefore, you'd have to try the final approach, and explain the dispute in your credit reports. By including a statement in your credit report, other creditors will at least see your explanation, and your side of the story. Sometimes, this is the only way to fight these problems.

Section 1681i(b), allows you to add a statement about your dispute to your credit reports. However, you can only do this if two things have happened. First, you must have already complained to each credit bureau about the particular information involved. Second, the credit bureaus' investigations must not have resolved the dispute.

Additionally, although your statement can be any length, the credit bureaus may limit it to 100 words or less. However, to do this, they must help you to write a clear summary of your dispute. Therefore, try to draft your original statement with fewer than 100 words, if possible.

Once you've satisfied these conditions, you can send your statement to the credit bureaus. Under section 1681i(c), the credit bureaus must then include your statement, or a clear codification of it, whenever they print your report.

To help you create your consumer statement, I've included two sample statements, Diagrams 9-12 and 9-13. These sample statements should give you an idea of how your consumer statement might look.

Your Updated Credit Report

Before we end our discussion on credit repair, I want to tell you about one more thing. Section 1681i(d) requires that the credit bureaus send out updated versions of your credit reports if they correct or remove information from your credit reports. They must also do this if you add a consumer statement to your reports.

The credit bureaus will send your updated report to anyone who received the old report, for any reason, within the previous six months. They'll also send your updated report to anyone who received the old report for employment purposes within the previous two years. However, they'll only send out your updated credit reports if you request it.

Whether you choose to take advantage of this provision will depend upon your circumstances. For example, let's say that a creditor denied your credit request several months ago because you had some bad credit information on your credit reports. However, the credit bureaus have subsequently deleted this bad information. If this happens, you may want the credit bureaus to send this creditor your corrected credit report.

But, you probably don't want to take advantage of this provision every time you correct your credit report. If you still have several bad credit references on your credit report, you may want to wait until you've completed more of your credit repair efforts. Then a creditor will be more likely to change its mind and grant your credit request.

Final Words

Congratulations! You've finished the most difficult parts of this book. And soon, if you use the CARE system, you'll also be finished with the most difficult parts of your life after bankruptcy.

Diagram 9-1

The Complaint Sheet			
	Complaint 1	Complaint 2	Complaint 3
Specific request or complaint			
Name of credit bureau			
Date that credit bureau received your letter			
Date 30 days from the Date that credit bureau received your letter			
Date that you received credit bureau's response			
Contents of response			
Date that credit bureau received your second letter			
Date that you received credit bureau's response to second letter			
Contents of response			

Complaint Sheet Instructions

You should only complete the final three sections of the Complaint Sheet if the credit bureau doesn't respond to your letter within 30 days. If it doesn't, you should send the credit bureau another letter and demand that it remove the disputed information from your report. Then, complete the remaining sections of the Complaint Sheet.

Date Credit Bureau Received Your 2nd letter

In this section, list when the credit bureau received your second letter. As before, you'll find this date on the Certified Mail receipt.

Date that You Received Credit Bureau's Response to Your Second Letter

In this section, list when you received the credit bureau's response to your second letter.

Contents of Response

In this section, list the credit bureau's response to your second letter.

Complaint Sheet Instructions

Whenever you send a request or complaint to any credit bureau or creditor, record the following information on your Complaint Sheet:

Specific Request or Complaint

In this section, list the reason that you've written the credit bureau or your creditor. For example, let's say that one of your bankruptcy accounts lists a $15,000 balance amount. (Remember, you shouldn't have any balance on your bankruptcy accounts.) Therefore, you want the credit bureau to correct the balance amount to "$0." In this section, write "Balance Amount is $15,000, should be $0."

Name of Credit Bureau or Creditor

In this section, list the name of the credit bureau or creditor that received your letter.

Date that Credit Bureau or Creditor Received Your Letter

In this section, list the date that the credit bureau or creditor received your letter. You'll find this date on the Certified Mail receipt. This date starts the beginning of the "reasonable time" period for the credit bureau to respond to your complaint. (Unfortunately, your creditors don't have to respond to your requests at all! Therefore, you can't force them to correct your credit information if they fail to respond to your request within 30 days.)

Date 30 days from the Date that Credit Bureau Received Your Letter

In this section, list the date that is 30 days from the Date listed on the Certified Mail receipt. (This is 30 days from the date you listed in the "Date that Credit Bureau or Creditor Received Your Letter" section.) The credit bureaus must respond to your request by this date. If they don't, they must remove the information from your credit report.

Date You Received the Credit Bureau's Response

In this section, list when you received the credit bureau's response to your letter. This date will show whether the credit bureau responded to your request within a "reasonable period."

Contents of Response

In this section, list what the credit bureau or creditor had to say about your letter. Record whether the credit bureau or creditor corrected all, some, or none of the information you disputed. For example, write "Corrected" if the credit bureau or creditor corrected all of the incorrect information that you complained about in your letter. Or write "Corrected ______, but not ______," if they only corrected some of the information.

Diagram 9-2
[Sample Letter Objecting to Credit Information]

Your Address
City, State Zip

Date

Credit Bureau Name
Credit Bureau Address
City, State Zip

Dear Sirs:

I requested a copy of my credit report from your company on _______, and received this report on ________. After carefully reviewing the information contained within this report, I have discovered an [or "one" or "several" or "some"] error [or "errors"]. Specifically, the credit report indicates ____________________________ ____.

This information is incorrect. Please reinvestigate the information and promptly delete it from my credit report.

I understand that your investigation must be completed within a "reasonable period of time" under 15 U.S.C. § 1681i(a), and that the Federal Trade Commission has stated that 30 days constitutes a "reasonable period of time" under this statute. Therefore, I look forward to your response within 30 days.

Thank you for your assistance in this matter.

Sincerely,

Your Name

Diagram 9-3

5825 Red Wood Drive
Colonia, FL 32331

February 20, 1993

Equifax Information Service Center
P.O. Box 740241
Atlanta, GA 30375

Dear Sirs:

I requested a copy of my credit report from your company on February 1, 1993, and received this report on February 18, 1993. After carefully reviewing the information contained within this report, I have discovered an error. Specifically, the credit report indicates that I owe $15,000 to GMAK on account #20043748.

This information is incorrect. Please reinvestigate the information and promptly delete it from my credit report.

I understand that your investigation must be completed within a "reasonable period of time" under 15 U.S.C. §§ 1681i(a), and that the Federal Trade Commission has stated that 30 days constitutes a "reasonable period of time" under this statute. Therefore, I look forward to your response within 30 days.

Thank you for your assistance in this matter.

Sincerely,

John Consumer

Diagram 9-4

5825 Red Wood Drive
Colonia, FL 32331

February 20, 1993

Trans Union Corporation
P.O. Box 7000
North Olmstead, OH 44070

Dear Sirs:

I requested a copy of my credit report from your company on February 1, 1993, and received this report on February 18, 1993. After carefully reviewing the information contained within this report, I have discovered two errors. First, the credit report indicates that I owe $1,500 to Househeld Finance on account #25-2872-34572. Second, the report indicates the current status as "PROFIT-AND-LOSS WRITEOFF."

This information is incorrect. The Househeld Finance debt was discharged in my bankruptcy case and I am no longer obligated to repay this debt. Therefore, the "Balance" section of my credit report should indicate "$0," and the "Remarks" section should indicate that this debt was included in my bankruptcy case. Please reinvestigate this information and promptly delete it from my credit report.

I understand that your investigation must be completed within a "reasonable period of time" under 15 U.S.C. § 1681i(a), and that the Federal Trade Commission has stated that 30 days constitutes a "reasonable period of time" under this statutes. Therefore, I look forward to your response within 30 days.

Thank you for your assistance in this matter.

Sincerely,

John Consumer

Diagram 9-5
[Sample Letter Requesting Removal of Obsolete Information]

Your Address
City, State Zip

Date

Credit Bureau Name
Credit Bureau Address
City, State Zip

Dear Sirs:

I requested a copy of my credit report from your company on ________, and received this report on _________. After carefully reviewing the information contained within this report, I have discovered that __________________________ reference is greater than __ years old. Therefore, under section 1681c of the Fair Credit Reporting Act, this reference is obsolete and you must remove it from my credit report.

Please respond as soon as possible to this request. I understand that your investigation must be completed within a "reasonable time" under 15 U.S.C. §§ 1681i(a), and that the Federal Trade Commission has stated that 30 days constitutes a "reasonable time" under this statute. Therefore, I look forward to your response within 30 days.

Thank you for your assistance in this matter.

Sincerely,

Your Name

Diagram 9-6

5825 Red Wood Drive
Colonia, FL 32331

May 15, 1993

Equifax Information Service Center
P.O. Box 740241
Atlanta, GA 30375

Dear Sirs:

I requested a copy of my credit report from your company on April 15, 1993, and received this report on April 20, 1993. After carefully reviewing the information contained within this report, I have discovered that the GMAK account reference is greater than 7 years old. Therefore, under section 1681c of the Fair Credit Reporting Act, this reference is obsolete and you must remove it from my credit report.

Please respond as soon as possible to this request. I understand that your investigation must be completed within a "reasonable time" under 15 U.S.C. §§ 1681i(a), and that the Federal Trade Commission has stated that 30 days constitutes a "reasonable time" under this statute. Therefore, I look forward to your response within 30 days.

Thank you for your assistance in this matter.

Sincerely,

John Consumer

Diagram 9-7
[Sample Letter Demanding Removal of Erroneous Information Following the Expiration of a "Reasonable Period of Time"]

Your Address
City, State Zip

Date

Credit Bureau Name
Credit Bureau Address
City, State Zip

Dear Sirs:

On _____________, I wrote to your company about some erroneous information contained in my credit report. You received this letter on ___________, as evidenced by your employee's signature on the certified mail receipt.

In my _____________, I requested that you respond to my request within 30 days. As you know, under 15 U.S.C. § 1681i(a), you are required to respond to my complaint within a "reasonable period of time." As you also know, the Federal Trade Commission has defined this period of time to be 30 days. Additionally, because you did not immediately contact me to request additional time, you implicitly accepted the 30 day time limit.

I have not received a reply from you within this 30 day period. I must assume this is because the disputed information was inaccurate or because you were unable to reverify the information. Regardless, you must now comply with section 1681i(a) and "promptly delete such information" from my credit report.

Please respond immediately, as I do not wish to pursue this matter further. However, I will take full advantage of my rights under the Fair Credit Reporting Act if you do not comply.

Sincerely,

Your Name

Diagram 9-8

5825 Red Wood Drive
Colonia, FL 32331

May 15, 1993

Trans Union Corporation
P.O. Box 7000
North Olmstead, OH 44070

Dear Sirs:

On April 5, 1993, I wrote to your company about some erroneous information contained in my credit report. You received this letter on April 8, 1993, as evidenced by your employee's signature on the certified mail receipt.

In my April 5 letter, I requested that you respond to my request within 30 days. As you know, under 15 U.S.C. § 1681i(a), you are required to respond to my complaint within a "reasonable period of time." As you also know, the Federal Trade Commission has defined this period of time to be 30 days. Additionally, because you did not immediately contact me to request additional time, you implicitly accepted the 30 day time limit.

I have not received a reply from you within this 30 day period. I must assume this is because the disputed information was inaccurate or because you were unable to reverify the information. Regardless, you must now comply with section 1681i(a) and "promptly delete such information" from my credit report.

Please respond immediately, as I do not wish to pursue this matter further. However, I will take full advantage of my rights under the Fair Credit Reporting Act if you do not comply.

Sincerely,

John Consumer

Diagram 9-9
[Letter Agreement]

Letter Agreement

Name of Creditor
Address
City, State, Zip

Dear Sirs:

This letter agreement (this "Agreement") confirms our agreement regarding the settlement of a debt that I previously owed to your company. The terms of the Agreement are as follows:

1. "I," __________, agree to pay ________________ ("You") $______ in full satisfaction of all amounts that I owe to You and You agree to accept $____ from me in full satisfaction of all amounts that I previously owed to You.

2. I agree to pay the $____ in __ monthly installments of $____, without interest. I will pay the first payment on ______, 199_ and every remaining payment on the ______ of each following month. I will make these payments by mail to Your main office, located at

____.

3. If I do not pay the full amount of each payment when it is due, I will be in default. If I am in default, You may send me a written notice telling me that if I do not pay the overdue amount by a certain date, You will require me to immediately pay the full amount of the $____ which has not been paid. That date must be at least 30 days after the date on which the notice is delivered or mailed to me.

4. You agree to notify each credit bureau to which You report credit information that any adverse credit information regarding my account with You is no longer verifiable and should be deleted from my credit report.

If You agree to the foregoing terms and conditions, please sign the Agreement and the enclosed copy in the places provided and return the documents to me.

Date: ________, 199_

____
Name of Debtor

Accepted and Agreed to this
__ day of ______, 1992.

By:______________________

Name:__________________
Title: __________________

Diagram 9-10

Letter Agreement

Househeld Finance Company
P.O. Box 1404
Atlee, GA 10527

Dear Sirs:

This letter agreement (this "Agreement") confirms our agreement regarding the settlement of a debt that I previously owed to your company. The terms of the Agreement are as follows:

1. "I," John Consumer, agree to pay Househeld Finance ("You") $300 in full satisfaction of all amounts that I owe to You, and You agree to accept $300 from me in full satisfaction of all amounts that I previously owed to You.

3. I agree to pay the $300 in 10 monthly installments of $30.00, without interest. I will pay the first payment on May 1, 1993 and every remaining payment on the first of each following month. I will make these payments by mail to Your main office located at P.O. Box 1404, Atlee, Georgia, 10527.

4. If I do not pay the full amount of each payment when it is due, I will be in default. If I am in default, You may send me a written notice telling me that if I do not pay the overdue amount by a certain date, You will require me to immediately pay the full amount of the $300 which has not been paid. That date must be at least 30 days after the date on which the notice is delivered or mailed to me.

5. You agree to notify each credit bureau to which You report credit information that any adverse credit information regarding my account with You is no longer verifiable and should be deleted from my credit report.

If You agree to the foregoing terms and conditions, please sign the Agreement and the enclosed copy in the places provided, and return the documents to me.

Date: April 15, 1993

____
John Consumer

Accepted and Agreed to this
__ day of ______, 1993.

By:___________________________
Name:________________

Diagram 9-11

UNIVERSAL DATA FORM

This form has been approved for reporting or updating account information.

☐ New ☐ Change If Change makes trade current, is previous delinquent history
☐ Delete to be deleted? ☐ Yes ☐ No

(Do not include security passwords with codes below.)

Subscriber Name: ______________ CCA Subscriber Code: ______________

EQUIFAX Subscriber Code: ______________

Subscriber Address: ______________ TRW Subscriber Code: ______________

TU Subscriber Code: ______________

CONSUMER INFORMATION

Name	First	M.I.	Suffix	SSN	DOB/Age

Current Address	City	State	Zip

Previous Address	City	State	Zip	Telephone, if available

Current Employer Name	Occupation	City	State

Spouse's Surname	First	M.I.	Suffix	SSN	DOB/Age

Additional Spouse Information (Complete only if joint account)

Current Address (If different)	City	State	Zip

Current Employer Name	Occupation	City	State

Terms/Amount

CURRENT/HISTORICAL ACCOUNT INFORMATION (See tables on reverse side for codes.)

Account Number	Date Open	Present Status			High Credit	Payment History	Type Acct MOP
		Date	Balance	Amount Past Due			

Metro Status Code	Credit Limit	Terms/Amount	Date Last Payment	Maximum Delinquency			Status/ Closed Date	ECOA
				Date	Amount	MOP		

Type of Loan/Collateral	Special Comments/Remarks	Historical Status			
		No. of Months	30 days	60 days	90 days

Must be present when reporting a chargeoff or repossession. ☐ Automated ☐ Manual

When you sign this form, you certify that your computer and/or manual records have been adjusted to reflect any changes made.

Reason for deletion or status change from adverse to favorable: ______________

Authorized Signature: ______________ Date: ______________

Please Print Name: ______________ Telephone: ______________

Diagram 9-12
[Sample Consumer Statement]

Your Address
City, State Zip

Date

Credit Bureau Name
Credit Bureau Address
City, State Zip

Dear Sirs:

On ______, I sent you a letter disputing information in my credit report regarding ________, one of my former [present] creditors. On ____________, I received notification from you that you would not alter the reported information because _________ had verified the accuracy of that information. Because this information is incorrect, I now demand that you include the following consumer statement in my credit report:

I understand that under 15 U.S.C. § 1681i(b), you must include my statement in any subsequent consumer report that includes the disputed information. Additionally, because my statement contains less than 100 words, I demand that you include the full text of the statement in my report, without changes.

Thank you for your assistance in this matter.

Sincerely,

Your Name

Diagram 9-13

5825 Red Wood Drive
Colonia, FL 32331

March 25, 1993

Equifax Information Service Center
P.O. Box 740241
Atlanta, GA 30375

Dear Sirs:

On February 20, 1993, I sent you a letter disputing information in my credit report regarding GMAK, one of my former creditors. On March 20, 1993, I received notification from you that you would not alter the reported information because GMAK had verified the accuracy of that information. Because this information is incorrect, I now demand that you include the following consumer statement in my credit report:

> On April 13, 1985, I purchased a car at a GM dealer and received financing from GMAK. The GM manager promised that I could return the car within 30 days. I returned the car 14 days later after experiencing a variety of mechanical difficulties. The dealer wouldn't accept the car, however, and said I couldn't enforce any verbal promises in court. At this point, I left the car at the dealership, and never made any payments on the loan from GMAK. After some time, the dealership resold the car. However, GMAK continues to report my account as a repossession account.

I understand that under 15 U.S.C. § 1681i(b), you must include this statement in any subsequent consumer report that includes the disputed GMAK information. Additionally, because this statement contains less than 100 words, I demand that you include the full text of the statement in my report, without changes.

Thank you for your assistance in this matter.

Sincerely,

John Consumer

Diagram 9-14
[Sample Letter Requesting Addition of Credit Information]

Your Address
City, State Zip

Date

Credit Bureau Name
Credit Bureau Address
City, State Zip

Dear Sirs:

I requested a copy of my credit report from your company on ____________, and received this report on ______________. After carefully reviewing the information contained within this report, I have discovered that you do not list one [several] of my current credit accounts. I therefore request that you add the following information to my credit report:

Creditor
Address

Type of Account
Account #
Date Opened
Credit Limit
Balance

Please let me know if there is any fee for adding this information to my credit report, or if you require any additional information about this account.

Thank you for your assistance in this matter.

Sincerely,

Your Name

Diagram 9-15

5825 Red Wood Drive
Colonia, FL 32331

February 20, 1993

Equifax Information Service Center
P.O. Box 740241
Atlanta, GA 30375

Dear Sirs:

I requested a copy of my credit report from your company on February 1, 1993, and received this report on February 18, 1993. After carefully reviewing the information contained within this report, I have discovered that you do not list one of my current credit accounts. I therefore request that you add the following information to my credit report:

Creditor	Dunhill's
Address	1705 N. Hampton Street Atlanta, GA 30375
Type of Account	Revolving - Individual
Account #	251571992
Date Opened	6/22/90
Credit Limit	$2000
Balance	$500

Please let me know if there is any fee for adding this information to my credit report, or if you require any additional information about this account.

Thank you for your assistance in this matter.

Sincerely,

John Consumer

Chapter 10

Handling Problems With Credit Bureaus

The best victory is when the opponent surrenders of its own accord before there are any actual hostilities.

Sun-tzu

In the last chapter, you learned that you can repair your credit if you complain to the credit bureaus and your creditors. But what happens if they refuse to comply with your requests? Unfortunately, if your creditors refuse, there's not much that you can do about it. The Fair Credit Reporting Act does NOT apply to your creditors.

However, if the credit bureaus won't help you, there are two things you can do. The first is to lodge complaints with any agency that may regulate, oversee, or in some way affect the credit bureaus. This means that you should contact the Federal Trade Commission, your state agency that investigates unfair or illegal business practices, and the Better Business Bureau. Complaints made to these organizations may convince the credit bureaus to comply with your requests. In this chapter, I'll show you how to do this.

I'll also tell you about your second course of action—suing the credit bureau. You can sue any credit bureau that violates the Fair Credit Reporting Act. Additionally, you may have some private right to sue the credit bureau under your state's law. We'll discuss your right to sue the credit bureaus at the end of this chapter. We'll also examine why you may not want to take advantage of these rights.

Complaining About Credit Bureaus

The Federal Trade Commission

Under 15 U.S.C. § 1681s, the Federal Trade Commission (the "FTC") is responsible for enforcing the requirements of the Fair Credit Reporting Act. Therefore, if you're having problems with the credit bureaus, you should contact the FTC. The FTC can sue the credit bureaus if necessary, and it has occasionally done so.

When you send your letter to the FTC, make sure that you also send a copy of your letter to the particular credit bureau that you're complaining about. That may convince the credit bureau to quickly correct the problem before the FTC has a chance to contact it. Also, as always, keep a copy of your letter for your files.

To make this easy for you, I've included a sample complaint letter in Diagram 10-1. You can use this letter as a guide in drafting your own. I've also included a completed complaint letter by John Consumer, Diagram 10-2, to show you how your completed letter might look.

Send your complaint letter to the FTC at one of the addresses below. I've included the addresses and telephone numbers for the FTC's national and regional offices. You should probably first contact the regional FTC office closest to you. Then, contact the national office if you aren't satisfied with the results obtained by the regional office.

FTC Regional Offices	
1718 Peachtree Street, NW, Room 1000 Atlanta, GA 30367 (404) 347-4836	1405 Curtis Street, Suite 2900 Denver, CO 80202 (303) 844-2271
10 Causeway Street, Room 1184 Boston, MA 02222-1073 (617) 656-7240	11000 Wilshire Boulevard, Suite 13209 Los Angeles, CA 90024 (213) 209-7890
55 East Monroe Street, Suite 1437 Chicago, IL 60603 (312) 353-4423	150 William Street, 13th Floor New York, NY 10038 (212) 264-1207
668 Euclid Avenue, Suite 520-A Cleveland, OH 44114 (216) 522-4210	901 Market Street, Suite 570 San Francisco, CA 94103 (415) 744-7920
100 N. Central Expressway, Suite 500 Dallas, TX 75247 (214) 767-5501	2806 Federal Building 915 Second Avenue Seattle, WA 98174 (206) 442-4656

National Office

6th & Pennsylvania Avenue, NW
Washington, DC 20580
(202) 362-2222

State Agencies

Besides the FTC, you should contact your State Attorney General's office or other office responsible for consumer protection. These state agencies investigate illegal or unethical conduct by businesses, and can bring charges against credit bureaus operating within your state.

For your convenience, I've listed the names, addresses, and telephone numbers for these state agencies in Appendix 2. Therefore, just find your state in Appendix 2, and send a complaint letter to the listed agency.

Your complaint letter should resemble your letter to the FTC, and should at least contain the same complaint. As before, I've included a sample letter, Diagram 10-3, to help you with this. I've also included a completed letter by John Consumer, Diagram 10-4, to show you how your completed letter might look.

The Better Business Bureau

Besides the FTC and your state agency, you should complain to your local Better Business Bureau. Consult the white pages of your telephone book for the telephone number and address of your local Better Business Bureau office.

To draft your complaint letter to the Better Business Bureau, use the sample letter in Diagram 10-3. Just substitute the name and address of your Better Business Bureau.

Suing the Credit Bureau

If you're really harmed by the conduct of the credit bureau, you may want to consider taking legal action against it. Under section 1681n of the Fair Credit Reporting Act, you can sue a credit bureau for willful noncompliance. (This means that the credit bureau KNOWS it's breaking the law, but does it anyway.) If the credit bureau does this, it might have to pay your litigation costs, and any actual damages you suffered because of the credit bureau's conduct. The credit bureau might also have to pay you punitive damages. (Punitive damages punish the credit bureau for its conduct and are above and beyond any actual damages.)

Under section 1681o, you can sue a credit bureau for negligent noncompliance. (This means that the credit bureau DOESN'T KNOW that its breaking the law, but does it anyway.) If the credit bureau does this, it still has to pay your litigation costs and actual damages. However, it doesn't have to pay you any punitive damages.

Problems With Suing the Credit Bureaus

Before you get too excited about suing the credit bureaus, let me tell you about the problems you may encounter. First, if you're suing one of the Big 3 credit bureaus, remember that they have extensive resources and can afford to fight your lawsuit. Unfortunately, you probably don't have a great deal of money to spare for your battle. Therefore, you'll need to either bring the action in small claims court—where you don't really need a lawyer—or hire a lawyer on a contingency basis.

Another problem with suing the credit bureaus is that you might lose. Before you decide to sue a credit bureau, make sure that your claim has merit. Courts have ruled that truth is an absolute defense to any action brought under the Fair Credit Reporting Act. Therefore, even if a credit bureau fails to respond within a "reasonable period of time," you may not be able to recover any damages.

You might also lose your lawsuit if you can't prove that the credit bureau's conduct damaged your credit rating. If your bankruptcy appears on your credit report, a court may find that only some horrendous conduct by the credit bureau could hurt you. If so, you might not be able to prove damages. (Remember, if you lose your lawsuit, you'll have to pay your litigation costs.)

Therefore, don't rush into a lawsuit against the credit bureaus. Try to get the government agencies and the Better Business Bureau to pressure them. This is generally enough.

Diagram 10-1
[Sample FTC Complaint Letter]

Your Address
City, State, Zip

Date

Federal Trade Commission
6th & Pennsylvania Avenue, NW
Washington, DC 20580

Dear Sirs:

I understand that you have enforcement powers against credit bureaus under 15 U.S.C. §1681s. Therefore, I wish to lodge a complaint with you against the following credit bureau:

This credit bureau has refused to comply with its obligations under the Fair Credit Reporting Act. The substance of my complaint is as follows:

Please investigate this matter and inform me of the results. For your convenience, I have attached the ________, and ______ letters. Thank you in advance for your assistance in this matter.

Sincerely,

Your Name

Diagram 10-2

5825 Red Wood Drive
Colonia, FL 32331

May 30, 1993

Federal Trade Commission
6th & Pennsylvania Avenue, NW
Washington, DC 20580

Dear Sirs:

I understand that you have enforcement powers against credit bureaus under 15 U.S.C. §1681s. Therefore, I wish to lodge a complaint with you against the following credit bureau:

TRW's Pet Credit Bureau
1805 S. Carolina Street
Colonia, FL 32351

This credit bureau has refused to comply with its obligations under the Fair Credit Reporting Act. The substance of my complaint is as follows:

On April 5, 1993, I wrote to TRW's Pet Credit Bureau to inform them of some erroneous information in my credit report. They received this letter on April 8, 1993, as evidenced by the signature of an employee on the certified mail receipt. In my letter, I requested that the credit bureau respond as quickly as possible to my request, and reminded the credit bureau of it's obligation to reinvestigate disputed information within a reasonable period of time.

On May 15, 1993, I wrote the credit bureau another letter demanding that they respond to my request. The credit bureau received this letter on May 18, 1993, again evidenced by its employee's signature on the certified mail receipt. It is now May 30, and the credit bureau has still not responded to my request. The amount of time that has passed since the credit bureau received my first letter does not seem to be "a reasonable period of time."

Please investigate this matter and inform me of the results. For your convenience, I have attached the April 5, and May 15 letters. Thank you in advance for your assistance in this matter.

Sincerely,

John Consumer

Diagram 10-3
[Sample State Agency Complaint Letter]

Your Address
City, State Zip

Date

Name of Your State's Agency
Address
City, State Zip

Dear Sirs:

I wish to lodge a complaint with you against the following credit bureau for engaging in illegal and unfair business practices:

This credit bureau has refused to comply with its obligations under the Fair Credit Reporting Act. The substance of my complaint is as follows:

Please investigate this matter and inform me of the results. For your convenience, I have attached the _______, and _______ letters. Thank you in advance for your assistance in this matter.

Sincerely,

Your Name

Diagram 10-4

5825 Red Wood Drive
Colonia, FL 32331

May 30, 1993

Division of Consumer Services,
Dept. of Agriculture and Consumer Services
218 Mayo Bldg.
Tallahassee, FL 32399

Dear Sirs:

I wish to lodge a complaint with you against the following credit bureau for engaging in illegal and unfair business practices:

TRW's Pet Credit Bureau
1805 S. Carolina Street
Colonia, FL 32351

This credit bureau has refused to comply with its obligations under the Fair Credit Reporting Act. The substance of my complaint is as follows:

On April 5, 1993, I wrote to TRW's Pet Credit Bureau to inform them of some erroneous information in my credit report. They received this letter on April 8, 1993, as evidenced by the signature of an employee on the certified mail receipt. In my letter, I requested that the credit bureau respond as quickly as possible to my request, and reminded the credit bureau of it's obligation to reinvestigate disputed information within a reasonable period of time.

On May 15, 1993, I wrote the credit bureau another letter demanding that they respond to my request. The credit bureau received this letter on May 18, 1993, again evidenced by its employee's signature on the certified mail receipt. It is now May 30, and the credit bureau has still not responded to my request. The amount of time that has passed since the credit bureau received my first letter does not seem to be "a reasonable period of time."

Please investigate this matter and inform me of the results. For your convenience, I have attached the April 5, and May 15 letters. Thank you in advance for your assistance in this matter.

Sincerely,

John Consumer

Chapter 11

Rebuilding Your Credit

He that has lost his credit is dead to the world.

George Herbert

In the last several chapters, we talked about repairing your credit reports. We did this, of course, so that you can begin to rebuild your credit. In this chapter, I'll tell you how to do that.

First, in Section I, I'll tell you what creditors want to see on your credit applications. Then, in Section II, I'll tell you how to "beef up" your credit applications so that creditors will want to lend to you. Finally, in Section III, I'll show you several specific techniques that you can use to rebuild your credit. When you've completed these techniques, you should be well on your way to establishing new credit.

I. What Creditors Want to See in Your Credit Application

First, let's talk about credit applications. Before you can rebuild your credit, you'll need to complete at least one of these monsters. In it, you'll need to reveal your identification information, list your credit accounts, and generally bare your sole to your creditors. But don't worry. I'm going to show you how to slay these beasts.

To do this, you'll need to know what your creditors WANT TO SEE in your credit application. So, let me tell you. Creditors generally want to see three things—Capacity, Collateral, and Character. These three C's show creditors whether you have the money to repay the loan, the assets to back it up, and the willingness to make regular payments on time. Let's talk about each of these.

Capacity

The first thing that creditors want to know is that you can repay the loan. If you don't make enough money to meet the monthly payments, then your creditors probably won't lend you any money. Creditors call this ability to repay your loan "capacity."

To decide whether you have the capacity to repay the loan, creditors primarily look at your job and your other debts. These are the things that will allow you to, or prevent you from, repaying the loan. Let's look at these two areas and see why they're important.

Your Job

First, creditors want you to have a stable job that pays you enough money to meet the monthly loan payments. Therefore, they look at the type of job you have, how long you've been there, and how much money you make.

Creditors generally prefer to lend to high-paid professionals who have worked at the same job for many years. This means that they might be reluctant to lend to you if you're self-employed, temporarily employed, or in a "high-risk" job. The common thread is stability.

Remember, some jobs are more stable than others. Whether your job is stable depends upon the type of job. For example, if you're a construction worker, your job might depend on the weather or the housing market. However, if you're a lawyer, these things probably won't affect you. Therefore, the lawyer's job is more stable than the construction worker's job.

However, the stability of your job also depends upon how long you've worked for your employer. Employers generally release newer workers before they release older workers. Therefore, the senior employee's job is more stable than the junior employee's job.

Because creditors would rather lend to people who have stable jobs, your credit application should reflect these concerns. It's better if you have a "professional" job. It's even better if you've worked for the same employer for more than one year. (Don't worry if you can't list either of these things on your application. I'll show you how to get around them in Section II.)

Your Income

Creditors look at your income because they want you to have enough money to pay the loan. Generally, if you have a high income, you'll have more money to repay the loan. (This isn't always true of course.) Therefore, your chances of receiving loans increase with your income level. (Again, don't worry if your income isn't very high. I'll show you how to increase it in Section II.)

Your Other Debts

Although creditors are mostly interested in your job, they're also very interested in how many other debts you have. If you have too many other debts, you might not be able to repay the loan. This is why someone with a high-paying professional job might not receive a loan.

Different creditors have different standards about your other debts. Some are more lenient than others. However, let me give you a general guideline for what creditors look for.

Most creditors generally don't want your monthly debt payments—not including your mortgage payments—to exceed 10-20% of your gross income. Therefore, if your non-mortgage debt payments are greater than 20% of your income, a lender might be reluctant to lend to you. Let me give you an example.

Let's say that you gross $4,000 per month. That's more than most people earn, and most lenders would be anxious to lend to you. However, if your other debt payments are $1,200 per month (30% of your gross income), you might be out of luck. Therefore, try to keep your other debts low.

Collateral

The second thing that creditors look for on your credit application is "collateral." Remember, creditors are very conservative and don't like risk. Therefore, they like to protect themselves against default.

One way that they can do this is to take your property if you don't repay the loan. We've already talked about this. Your creditors will be more likely to lend you the money if you have other assets that they can take from you if you default.

Therefore, you'll improve your chances of receiving the loan with each new asset that you list on your credit application. Many creditors will lend you money even if your credit is bad, IF you have enough assets to back up your loan.

Character

The final thing that creditors look for on your credit application is character. Character refers to your willingness to repay your debts. This is the area that we've been working on throughout this book.

The main tool that creditors use to judge your character is your credit report. Most creditors believe that your past credit history will predict your future credit patterns. Therefore, if your credit report still contains several bad credit notations, you might be out of luck.

However, creditors don't only rely on your credit report. There are other things that they look at to judge your character. Perhaps the most important thing, however, is stability. Creditors want to know that you're going to stay in town and repay your loan.

Therefore, they look at whether you own or rent your home. If you own your home, you're more likely to remain there. They also look at whether you have checking and savings accounts. If you do, you're probably more stable than someone who cashes checks at the grocery store. Remember, they're looking for stability.

II. How to Improve Your Credit Application

Now you know what creditors are looking for in your credit application. In this section, I'm going to tell you how to use that knowledge to "beef up" your credit application. Let's do that according to the three C's—Capacity, Collateral, and Character.

Capacity

As you remember, creditors look at several things to decide whether you have the capacity to repay the loan. However, they mainly look at the type of job you have, how long you've been there, how much money you make, and how many other debts you have. Therefore, I'll focus on these things now.

Type of Job

Creditors prefer to lend money to people with "professional" jobs. Therefore, make your job sound "professional." The key is how you describe it.

For example, if you're a construction worker, don't just list "manual laborer" or "construction worker" for your job description. These titles probably don't even accurately describe your job duties. It's better to be more precise. If you're a carpenter, it may be more accurate to describe your position as "master carpenter" or "skilled carpenter."

Let me give you another example. If you're a clerical worker, you might list "secretary" on your credit applications. However, this probably doesn't reflect the true nature of your job. You can probably think of titles that are more descriptive, like "Executive Assistant" or "Office Manager."

I think you get the point. Try to list the most accurate description of your job on your credit applications. If these more accurate descriptions sound more "professional" than your old description, then that's even better. Think about this. If you were a loan officer, would you prefer to lend to a "construction worker," or a "master carpenter"?

Length of Time at Your Job

Creditors also look at how long you've been with your present employer. As you remember, your job generally becomes more stable the longer you've been there. Therefore, your credit application will be more persuasive if you've been with the same employer for more than one year.

Try to apply for credit when you've been with the same employer for more than one year. If you think you might change employers in the near future, complete your applications before you change jobs. Then, you'll get the benefit of your job stability.

However, there's not much that you can do if you've only been with your employer for a short time. DON'T misstate any facts. If you haven't been with an employer for more than a year, write a note next to the employment section of the application. (You can do this as an appendix to your application. For example, you might write a note that says "See Appendix A for explanation.")

In your note, explain the reason for your short time on the job. For example, you might have taken this job as a career-enhancing move. Maybe you received more responsibility and a higher position with the company than with your former employer. A lender will understand this. Remember, think like your lender thinks. Would you think that your reason is good if you were the lender?

Income

Creditors prefer to lend to people with high incomes. If you don't make very much money, then there's probably not much you can do about that. Of course, you may be able to find a higher-paying job, but that's easier said than done.

However, don't give up that easily. You may have forgotten several extra sources of income that you should list on your application. For example, let's say that you earn $8.00 per hour at your job. If you work a normal 40-hour week, you make $320 each week, or $16,640 each year. Therefore, you might list $16,640 as your annual income on your credit application.

But is that the true amount? Do you ALWAYS work 40-hour work weeks? Don't you sometimes put in extra hours? If so, you should list the extra income you earn from overtime hours. It could be a large amount.

You might also have forgotten to include any annual bonuses. Doesn't your employer give you extra pay during the holidays? If so, you should include this amount in your annual income.

Finally, you may have forgotten to include any raises that you might earn over the next year. If your employer plans to give you a 10% raise next month, make sure you include this amount in your annual income. I think you get the point. You probably make a lot more money than you give yourself credit for. Make sure that your creditor knows how much money you'll REALLY make during the year. It should increase your chances of receiving the loan.

Besides these legitimate techniques, some people try to increase their chances of receiving a loan by "inflating" their salary on the credit application. To do this, they just list a salary that's greater than what they really make. Many creditors won't verify your annual income with your employer. And, even when they do, many employers verify whatever amount the employee has listed. However, I don't suggest that you do this. It's fraudulent and possibly illegal.

Other Debts

Besides your job and income, creditors are also interested in how many other debts you have. Remember, if you have too many other debts, a creditor will be reluctant to lend to you. Therefore, you don't want to list too many debts on your credit application.

Now this doesn't mean that you should withhold information from your creditors. I've seen people "leave out" one or two of their credit accounts from their credit application. Unfortunately, this is generally a waste of time. Remember, your creditors WILL review your credit reports. Therefore, your creditor will know about any credit accounts that appear in them. (IF you're planning to do this, at least review your credit reports to see which of your accounts appear in them. Then, don't list any accounts that don't appear.)

However, this doesn't mean you should list every debt you have. You probably don't need to go in to any great detail about money you've borrowed from your family or friends. Just use your best judgment.

Collateral

Besides your ability to repay the loan, creditors are interested in any assets that you can use as collateral. Therefore, you'll improve your chances of receiving the loan if you list many assets on your credit application. As with your income, you probably don't give yourself enough credit for your personal worth.

Creditors are mainly interested in high-valued assets like your house. However, they're also very interested in cash and assets that you can convert into cash. For example, many banks will lend you money if you offer them your savings account as collateral. Or, a creditor might lend money to you if you can offer stocks or bonds as collateral for the loan.

However, you're not out of luck if you don't have lots of cash or stocks and bonds. You probably have many other valuable assets that you can use to secure the loan. For example, you may have many pieces of valuable jewelry. Or, you might have some expensive paintings, sculptures, or antiques. If you have any of these things, list them on your credit application.

Character

Finally, creditors look at your character. As you know, this is what we've been working on throughout this book. When you apply for a loan, the creditor will review your credit reports to see if you're a good risk. If you've followed the techniques in this book, your credit reports should be in good shape.

However, even if you couldn't repair your reports, don't worry. There are still some things that you can do to increase your chances of receiving the loan.

As I said before, creditors are mainly interested in stability. They want to know that you'll be around to repay the loan. Therefore, you'll improve your chances of receiving the loan if you prove your stability to the creditor.

For example, most creditors prefer to lend to homeowners. Therefore, you'll improve your chances for loan approval if you become a homeowner. (I'll show you how to do that in Chapter 13.)

Now I'm not saying that you should go out and buy a house so that you can receive a $1,000 loan. Buying a house is one of life's major decisions. But, if you think you'd like to settle down for a while, you should consider it. There are many advantages to homeownership—equity build-up, tax savings, security, etc.—that make this a good option.

However, if you don't own your home, you're still not out of luck. Remember, the word is stability. You can also prove your stability if you've rented the same house or apartment for several years. To creditors, this is much better than if you've lived in four different apartments over the last three years. Therefore, if possible, try to stay at the same location.

You can also prove your stability by opening a checking and savings account. I've talked with many lenders over the years about rebuilding credit. And one thing ALWAYS comes up in the discussion. These creditors say that the best thing you can do for yourself after bankruptcy is to open a checking and savings account. Then, you should make regular deposits into your savings account, preferably through a payroll deduction program.

Creditors want you to have checking and savings accounts because they show that you have financial responsibility. If you make regular deposits into your savings account, you show that you can save money.

Finally, many creditors want you to have a phone in your name. This doesn't seem very important, but many creditors have suggested this. I guess they want to make sure that they can contact you if you don't repay the loan. Probably most important, though, it shows that you have some stability.

III. Techniques You Can Use to Rebuild Your Credit

In this section, I'm going to show you several specific techniques that you can use to get new credit. Best of all, these techniques will work even if your credit reports still contain bad information. The secret to these techniques is to use collateral or another person's good credit to secure your loans.

Collateral

First, let's talk about collateral. As you remember, we talked about collateral in Chapter 2. In that discussion, I told you about "secured creditors" and "unsecured creditors." Secured creditors are creditors that have something more than your word. Besides your word, these creditors have collateral. The collateral could be anything you own that has value. The most common examples of collateral are real estate, automobiles, cash, stocks, bonds, paintings, etc.

When you offer your property as collateral for a loan, the loan becomes "secured" by your property. Then, if you don't repay the loan, your lender can seize your collateral. Because this is a safe investment, most lenders will be happy to lend you money, even if your credit reports contain bad information.

Secured debt, then, is a powerful technique that you can use to rebuild your credit. Creditors may not offer you an unsecured loan for several years after your bankruptcy. However, MANY creditors WILL lend you money if you can offer them something in return—money or property. With that in mind, let me show you some ways that you can use collateral and secured debt to rebuild your credit.

Passbook Loan

The first way to rebuild your credit is to use your savings account as collateral for a loan. Lenders call this a "passbook loan." Let me tell you how it works.

First, you need to open a savings account with your bank or credit union. As you remember, many creditors say that this is a very important step toward rebuilding your credit, because it shows your stability.

Once you've opened your savings account, try to make regular contributions to it. Probably the best way to do this is to have your employer automatically deduct some money from your payroll checks. Continue to deposit money into your savings account until you have enough to secure a loan. The amount of the loan depends on you. If you want a $1,000 loan, then you'll need at least $1,000.

If you're really in a hurry, you could skip the regular contributions and just deposit a lump sum in your savings account. The point is to have enough money in your account to adequately secure a loan. However, whatever amount you choose, remember that you can't touch the money once you use it to secure a loan. Therefore, make sure you won't need the money in the near future.

Next, make an appointment with the loan officer at the bank or credit union. Be very candid with the loan officer and explain your financial picture and the details of your bankruptcy. Continue by explaining that you want to rebuild your credit record and wish to receive a secured loan. Tell the loan officer that you have a savings account and are willing to fully secure the loan with its contents. Because the bank or credit union has no risk in making this loan, they should be very willing to extend this loan to you.

Make sure that the bank or credit union reports the loan and payment history to the credit bureaus. As we talked about before, not all banks and credit unions report consumer loans to the credit bureaus. Remember—the whole point in taking out this loan is to begin rebuilding your credit report. If your bank or credit union doesn't report the loan to the credit bureaus, there's no point in receiving the loan.

Although it's best if your selected bank or credit union reports to all of the Big 3 credit bureaus, it's not essential. You can probably have the neglected credit bureaus include the loan information anyway. To do this, just use Diagram 9-14 - Sample Letter Requesting Addition of Credit Information. As we discussed earlier, you may have to pay a small fee for this, but it will be worth the expense.

You can increase the effectiveness of this technique by opening several accounts in different financial institutions and getting several loans. To do this, you begin as before—open a savings account, approach a loan officer, and request a secured loan. BUT THEN, take the loaned money and open a savings account in a different financial institution. Now approach the loan officer at this financial institution and request a secured loan. When you receive the loan proceeds from this financial institution, open a savings account in yet another institution and begin the process again.

BE CAREFUL though. You MUST be able to meet the monthly payments on all of the loans. And remember, you're paying interest on each loan—this technique costs money. BUT, if each financial institution reports your payment history to the credit bureaus, your good credit history will begin to grow.

Secured Bankcards

You can also use collateral to obtain a VISA or MasterCard. This is VERY important. Having a bankcard is essential to your credit rebuilding plan. In many states, you must have a bankcard to rent a car or as additional identification. Additionally, bankcards are wonderful for guaranteeing hotel reservations, etc.

But, how do you get a bankcard with a poor credit history? Again, the answer is COLLATERAL. This technique is very similar to the passbook savings loan technique. However, with this technique, you deposit your money with a bank that will give you a line of credit through a bankcard—VISA or MasterCard.

Depending on the bank that issues the card, you may get a credit line that equals up to 150% of your deposit. For example, if you send the bank a $500 deposit, the bank will send you a VISA or MasterCard with a $750 line of credit. You can then use the VISA or MasterCard like any unsecured bankcard to buy gifts, rent cars, etc.

The biggest problem with secured bankcards is that they're expensive. Generally, the banks charge an application fee to receive the card initially and an annual fee each year you use the card. Additionally, although most banks pay you interest on your deposit, the interest is generally less than you would get with other investments. (Some banks don't pay ANY interest on your deposit!)

Finally, the annual percentage rate on secured cards is higher than that on most unsecured cards. This seems strange since you secure the entire credit line with your deposit. Unfortunately, the reason is simple—greed. Secured bankcard lenders know that people with poor credit histories will pay most any price for these bankcards.

However, even with these drawbacks, you MUST get at least one secured bankcard. The bank will report your payment history to the credit bureaus and this will rebuild your credit record. Additionally, after some period (usually one year), several banks will extend you some amount of UNSECURED credit. They may do this by returning some or all of your deposit, or by increasing your credit line without asking for an additional deposit.

Finally, some banks will issue you a completely UNSECURED bankcard once you've proven your ability and willingness to repay your debts. This will allow you to receive a normal, unsecured bankcard much sooner than you would otherwise. So—get a secured bankcard.

I've listed the names and addresses of banks that issue secured Visa and MasterCard bankcards in Appendix 3. You won't find any specific terms, such as interest rates and annual fees, because these things change so rapidly. If you'd like additional information on these cards, contact each bank and request literature on its secured bankcard program.

You can also write to RAM Research Corporation. This company tracks a variety of credit cards nationwide, and major newspapers often quote its reports. One of many publications that RAM Research produces is the Secured Credit Card Report. This Report currently costs $10. It lists all of the banks nationwide that issue secured bankcards and includes extensive information about interest rates, annual fees, etc. You can contact them as follows:

RAM Research Corp. Consumer Services
Box 1700 (College Estates)
Frederick, MD 21702

BEWARE: DON'T lose your money to middlemen offering you secured cards. You've probably seen their ads in newspapers, magazines, and on late night television. These ads look something like this:

DENIED CREDIT?
WE CAN GET YOU THE CREDIT YOU DESERVE
CALL 1-900-123-4567
GUARANTEED VISA AND MASTERCARD
NO ONE REFUSED!

This call will probably cost you $30-40, and will result in an application for ONE secured card from ONE bank. Don't do it! Instead, use Appendix 3 or the Secured Credit Card Report and apply to these banks yourself. For more information on secured card scams, see Chapter 16 on Credit Scams.

Another Person's Good Credit

Another way to rebuild your credit history and receive credit is by using the good credit of a friend or family member. This technique is useful if you don't have the money to fully secure a loan or line of credit. Remember—a creditor wants to make sure that you will repay the loan.

Unfortunately, if your credit report still contains bad information, and you don't have enough collateral to secure a loan, the creditor will deny your request. That is, unless you can offer the creditor another type of security. That security can be the good credit of another person.

Co-Signers

If you can get another person to "co-sign" your loan, your lender may be willing to go along with your request. When another person co-signs a loan with you, they become jointly responsible with you for the entire debt. Creditors call this "Joint Credit."

Creditors are more willing to lend to you when you have a co-signer because if you don't repay the loan, they can go after your co-signer for repayment. And, because your co-signer has a good credit history, creditors are reasonably sure that your co-signer WILL repay the loan if you don't.

To use this technique, find a friend or family member with good credit that trusts you enough to be jointly responsible for the debt. Then, approach a lender and explain that you want to apply for joint credit. Then, the lender will check your credit history and the credit history of your co-signer.

If your co-signer's credit report is good enough, the creditor will give you the loan or line of credit. Then, as you repay the loan, your creditor will report your payment history to the credit bureaus. Therefore, as you repay the loan, you'll rebuild a good credit history.

BE CAREFUL—Don't abuse the confidence that your co-signer has given you by defaulting on the loan. Remember—if you don't pay the loan or credit line, the creditor will come after your co-signer. Unfortunately, if your co-signer doesn't have enough money, the co-signer might also default on the loan. This will hurt your co-signer's credit history.

Authorized User Accounts

Another technique you can use to rebuild your credit history again relies on a friend or family member. With this technique, you become an "Authorized User" on the account of another person. As an authorized user of the account, you can use the credit line, BUT, you are NOT responsible for repaying the loan.

To become an authorized user of an account, the holder of the account must request that the creditor add your name to the account as an authorized user. You may or may not receive a credit card imprinted with your name. You may become an authorized user of a bankcard or of a department store account. Then, the credit bureaus will probably list the account in your credit reports as an authorized user account. (However, the credit bureaus may also list the account as "unknown." Therefore, other creditors will think that the account is your individual account.)

This is a good technique for adding favorable credit history to your credit report without any large risk or cost. However, if the holder of the account fails to repay the loan, this information will appear on your credit reports as well.

Non-Bankruptcy Accounts

Another technique that you can use to rebuild your credit is to use any accounts that you did NOT include in your bankruptcy. These accounts are probably accounts that had a zero balance at the time of your bankruptcy. If you did have any accounts with a zero balance, you probably didn't list them on your bankruptcy schedules. Therefore, the creditors probably didn't find out about your bankruptcy.

Because these creditors didn't find out about your bankruptcy, you should be able to use the accounts without any problem. This is how I first started my credit repair efforts. I had one department store account that had a zero balance at the time of my bankruptcy. During the Christmas following my bankruptcy, I was short on cash and wanted to buy some Christmas presents. So, I took a chance and asked the credit department about my account.

They told me that I had a $300 credit limit, but that they would be happy to raise that limit to $1,000 so that I could buy Christmas presents. What a deal! They never checked my credit reports. Why should they? All they knew was that I hadn't used my account for some time. They were very happy to help me use it again.

To find these accounts, look through your old credit records and compare them against your bankruptcy schedules. Then, if you find one or more accounts that you didn't include in your bankruptcy, check with the creditor to see what your credit line is. Then, start rebuilding your credit.

Of course, you can only do this if you had a good payment history with these creditors. It won't matter that you didn't include the accounts in your bankruptcy if you had bad relations with the creditors in the past.

Reaffirmed Accounts

The final way to rebuild your credit is to use any accounts that you DID include in your bankruptcy, but agreed to pay anyway. This happens when you "reaffirm" a debt with a creditor. If you reaffirm a debt, you agree to continue making payments on the debt, even after the bankruptcy. You may have done this to keep secured property, such as your car, or because you wanted to maintain good relations with a particular creditor.

If you do have reaffirmed debts, you may be able to use these accounts. Many creditors will allow this if you continue to repay your loan. I guess this is your reward for repaying the loan.

You probably know if you have any reaffirmed accounts. If not, look through your bankruptcy file for any reaffirmation agreements.

Final Words

I hope this chapter has given you some good ideas. You CAN rebuild your credit after bankruptcy. In fact, if you use the techniques in this chapter, you can start to rebuild your credit on the day you walk away from the bankruptcy court. So, get to it, and good luck!

Chapter 12

Transportation

Necessity never made a good bargain.

Benjamin Franklin

We're now ready to take a new direction in our quest for survival and prosperity after bankruptcy. Until now, we've primarily focused on rebuilding your credit. But there's more to life after bankruptcy than getting new credit accounts. You also need to get on with your life. You need transportation, shelter, and a job or education.

Unfortunately, you may find it difficult to do this. It's true that Congress designed the bankruptcy laws to give you a fresh start. However, your bankruptcy may continue to stand in your way for years to come. You may find it difficult to rent a car, buy a house, or start a new job.

Therefore, in the next several chapters, I'll tell you how to do all these things—and more—even if you never repair your credit reports. In this chapter, I'll tell you everything you need to know about transportation. Then, in the following chapters, I'll tell you how to buy or rent a house or apartment, how to avoid employment discrimination, and how to finance your education. These things will help you to survive and prosper after bankruptcy, and really get a fresh start in life.

Transportation

In our mobile society, the ability to get from place to place is really a necessity. You need to get to work, school, stores, etc. To do this, you can rely on public transportation, or friends and family. However, life is really a lot easier when you have your own transportation.

Unfortunately, your bankruptcy may prevent you from buying, renting, or leasing this transportation. Lenders and rental companies may be reluctant to finance your purchase or extend credit to you. Therefore, many people just give up and buy cheap cars for cash.

But, YOU don't need to do that. In this chapter, I'll show you many ways to buy, lease, or rent the vehicle of your dreams. In Section I, I'll teach you several techniques that you can use to buy a new or used car. Then, in Section II, I'll tell you all about leasing, and show you how to take advantage of it. Finally, in Section III, I'll show you how to rent a car, even if you don't have a bankcard. By the time you've completed this chapter, you should be on the road again!

I. Buying Your Dream Car

Let's start with the techniques that you can use to buy your own car or other vehicle. (For the rest of this chapter, I'm going to use the term "car" as a catchall phrase. I know that you may want a truck, motorcycle, or other vehicle. When I say "car," I mean to include all other vehicles as well.)

Traditional Financing

The first way to buy your dream car is with traditional financing. With this type of financing, a lender generally requires that you pay some portion of the car's purchase price. If you have good credit, the lender might want you to put down 10-20% of the car's purchase price. Then, it would finance the remaining amount over several years.

Lenders are generally unwilling to lend the full amount of a car's purchase price because cars depreciate (lose their value) so quickly. A new car's value declines by 20% the moment you drive it out of the dealer's parking lot. After that, a car may depreciate by 20-40% each year—not a very safe investment for a lender.

However, even with depreciation, lenders are willing to finance a large portion of the car's value for people with good credit. They do this for two reasons. First, the car does provide some security for the loan. Second, and perhaps most important, they're fairly certain that someone with good credit will repay the loan.

Unfortunately, if a bankruptcy notation appears on your credit reports, you'll probably need to put down a much larger portion of the car's purchase price. That is, IF you can find a lender willing to make the loan at all.

Financing Sources

So how do you get traditional financing? First, you need to consider your source for financing. You can approach traditional lenders like banks or credit unions, or you can focus on the lending companies associated with the major car manufacturers.

Banks

Banks may be the toughest source for your car financing needs. They are traditionally conservative in their lending policies, and generally won't look beyond the bankruptcy notation on your credit report. And, if you can persuade them to finance your car, they'll probably require a high down payment. This could be as high as 20-50% of the car's purchase price. Therefore, unless you have a good relationship with a particular bank—or lots of money—it's probably best to approach other lenders.

Credit Unions

Credit unions are generally more willing to look beyond your bankruptcy. Unlike many banks, credit unions will focus on the cause of your original financial problems and your current financial status. Therefore, if you've had a clean credit history since your bankruptcy, a credit union is more likely to finance your car.

I can personally vouch for the progressive lending approach of some credit unions. I purchased a brand new car several years ago with the help of my credit union. They offered me a flat $10,000 financing for any car I wanted. Therefore, if the car cost $10,000, they would finance 100% of the purchase price—and that was at the prevailing market interest rate. Now that was a great deal.

Can you guess how the commercial banks treated my loan request? That's right. At least three banks refused to finance any portion of the deal, even though I had repaired most of my credit reports and had a fairly high income. These banks just closed their eyes—and their pocketbooks—when they saw the bankruptcy notation on my credit report.

Car Dealer Finance Companies

You should also consider the financial affiliates of major car manufacturers. These financial affiliates, like General Motors Acceptance Corporation ("GMAC") and Ford Motor Credit, allow car dealers to offer financing for the cars they sell.

For example, you can go to a Ford dealership, purchase a car from the lot, and finance your purchase through Ford Motor Credit. It's so easy, you can do it all in one afternoon. And that's what they want—the Ford dealer, the Ford Motor Company, and Ford Motor Credit. They're all in business to sell you a car, and they want to make that as easy as possible.

When they provide the financing, you don't need to battle commercial banks for your loan. Besides, the commercial banks might slow the buying process—or even worse—prevent the buying process. Therefore, you should take advantage of their desire to sell you a car. How? Let's see.

The Technique

The first step in this technique is to find the car dealer with the greatest sales volume in your area. In fact, the dealership doesn't even have to be in your area. The key is to make sure that it's a high volume dealership.

You'll want to do this because high volume dealerships have the best chance of financing your purchase. They provide big sales for the manufacturer and many "high quality" loans for the finance companies. Therefore, they also have more leverage with the financing companies than low volume dealerships.

The credit managers at these high volume dealerships can slide a "weak" loan application in with several "strong" applications. Then they call up the finance companies and say,"Hey, look at all the good credit applications we're sending you—we think you should also take this 'poor credit' application."

And guess what? The finance companies DO take these weak loan applications, and everyone benefits. The manufacturer sells a car, the dealer sells a car, the finance company makes money, and you get your dream car. It's a no-lose situation. Therefore, go to a high volume dealership.

The next step is to pick out your dream car, and negotiate for the lowest price. (Remember, you CAN negotiate on the price of most cars.) Of course, make sure that the car is within your price range—you don't want to add ANY negative credit information to your credit report after the bankruptcy. Remember, we're trying to go forward in life—any bad credit at this point will really hurt your chances of getting new credit.

Next, ask to speak with the dealership's credit manager. Explain your financial situation to the credit manager, and the circumstances of your bankruptcy. Then, tell the credit manager that you're interested in receiving financing from the company's financial affiliate, and ask what the down payment and interest rate will be.

The Financing Game

This is where the financing game begins. The credit manager probably knows what the financing company will require for a down payment, and what the interest rate will probably be. However, he probably won't tell you at this time. He'll tell you later, when he's heard back from the financing company. Meanwhile, he'll transmit your credit report information and credit application to the financing company. If they approve your application, they'll specify the terms and conditions for the loan.

And what will those terms and conditions be? Well, it depends. Most of the major car financing affiliates use a classification system to "rate" your credit risk and to specify the terms available to you.

For example, Ford Motor Credit uses a five-tier classification system to rate credit applicants. A "zero" is the best rating. If Ford Motor Credit places you in the "zero" category, then you'll probably receive the best interest rate available. Additionally, you probably won't need to make any down payment on your purchase.

However, as you move further from the perfect "zero" rating—from "one" to "four" under Ford's system—the interest rate and down payment requirements become less favorable to you. With a recent bankruptcy on your record, you'll probably be in the "four" category, and receive the most unfavorable loan rates and terms.

So what happens if the financing company places you in a high risk category? The financing company will probably tell the credit manager to "write" (make) the loan. However, it will probably also place conditions on the loan.

For example, the financing company might specify a certain down payment amount and interest rate, or a range of down payment amounts and interest rates. If it specifies a certain down payment and interest rate, that's it. Either you come up with the down payment amount and accept the interest rate, or you don't get the loan. (Well, that may not be it. You may be able to have someone co-sign the loan. But we'll talk about that in a minute.)

However, the financing company may also specify a range of acceptable down payment amounts or interest rates. If so, the credit manager will probably try to hit you at the high end of the ranges. Therefore, he'll want you to make the largest down payment, and accept the highest interest rate authorized by the financing company. Basically, he's trying to bargain for the highest interest rate.

That's right, I said BARGAIN on the interest rate. What? He can do this? Absolutely. This is the biggest secret in car financing. Car dealers make a LOT of money by getting you to pay the highest possible interest rate. Let's see how this works.

Let's say that you've just negotiated for your new dream car. You explain to the credit manager that you filed bankruptcy, but that you're actively seeking to rebuild your credit. You're willing to put down a sizeable deposit and do anything necessary to obtain the loan.

Now the credit manager will obtain a copy of your credit report from one or more of the credit bureaus, and submit your application to the manufacturer's finance company. (The credit manager might also try to locate another financial institution that will lend you the money for that dream car.)

If the credit manager is successful, the finance company or bank will probably tell the credit manager what "range" of interest rates are acceptable for the loan. This means that the credit manager can write the loan with more than one interest rate, depending on what he or she can talk you into.

This probably surprises you. I bet you didn't know that you can negotiate on the interest rate, just as you can on the price of the car. Surprisingly, this can often be the most profitable part of the car sale for the dealership. The dealership may be willing to sell a car at a rock bottom price, if it can earn more profit on the "back end"—financing portion—of the deal.

So how does the dealership make money by pushing a higher interest rate on you? Let me give you an example. Among my many careers, I once sold new and used import cars. During this short car-selling career, I once had a customer that had recently declared bankruptcy. This customer was a very good negotiator and was able to secure a bargain price on a used car. But, he lost out completely when he walked into the credit manager's office.

A local bank informed this credit manager that he could write the loan with an interest rate that could range from 18 to 25%. (You have to remember that this was during a time of high interest rates generally. But this was still an outrageously expensive loan.) Because this customer didn't realize that he could negotiate on the interest rate, the credit manager was able to write the loan at the top of the range—25%. And guess what? The dealership got to keep most of the "spread"—difference—between the 18% interest rate and the 25% interest rate.

Guess how much money the dealership made on this one transaction? As I remember, I received several hundred dollars on the financing portion of this sale, and I only received one-fourth of the profit! (Incidentally, the credit manager also convinced this unsuspecting man to purchase credit life insurance. This increased the profit on the deal. We'll talk about credit life insurance in a minute.)

What's the bottom line? TRY to avoid getting caught with a very high interest rate. If the credit manager proposes a loan with a high interest rate, you may consider declining the offer temporarily, and going to your bank or credit union. They may be able to offer you a better deal.

Additionally, you may want to START with your bank or credit union and see if, and under what terms, they will make a car loan to you. This will give you some advance knowledge when dealing with the dealership's credit manager. REMEMBER—Interest rates are generally negotiable.

Avoid Credit Life Insurance

Credit life insurance is VERY expensive term life insurance that will repay your car loan if you die. Besides making money on the "spread" of high interest rate loans, credit managers make their money by getting consumers to purchase credit life insurance. However, most finance experts agree that you should probably refuse this coverage.

Unfortunately, many unethical credit managers will imply that you must purchase credit life insurance as a condition for loan approval. Don't fall for this argument. It's against the law for credit managers to insist on credit life insurance as a condition for loan approval.

Why is credit life insurance such a bad deal? Generally because it's just too expensive. Dealerships get a very large commission for selling the credit life policy to you—perhaps as high as 50% of the total premiums. Therefore, you might pay twice as much as you should for the insurance coverage.

If you're really concerned that you might die before you repay the loan, purchase a term life insurance policy from an insurance company. This will be MUCH less expensive than the policy that the credit manager offers you.

Final Words on Traditional Financing

You CAN obtain financing for your new or used car from traditional sources. These sources may include banks, credit unions, and the financing affiliates of the major car manufacturers. Unfortunately, cars don't provide lenders with very stable security because they depreciate so quickly. Therefore, car lenders are more concerned about your ability and willingness to repay the loan than are many mortgage lenders. This means that you'll probably have to compensate a lender for the added risk of making a loan to you. And how will you compensate the lender? You'll probably have to put down a larger amount of money up-front, and pay a higher interest rate than someone with a perfect credit record.

But don't worry. There are other ways to finance your dream car that may allow you to lock in a low down payment or market interest rate. One of those techniques is co-signing, and we'll talk about it now.

Co-Signing

Another technique that you may use to obtain a car loan through traditional sources is to find a friend or family member willing to co-sign the loan with you. A lender will be more willing to finance your purchase if you can find someone with good credit to co-sign your loan. Additionally, the lender is more likely to offer you favorable terms and conditions as well.

Why would lenders be so agreeable when you provide a co-signer? Because with a co-signer, lenders have additional security. When someone co-signs a loan with you, they become jointly responsible for that loan's repayment. Therefore, besides the value of the car, the lender can look to your co-signer to repay the loan if you don't. If you fail to make the payments as scheduled, the lender will come after your co-signer for payment.

Let me caution you about this. Even if the lender repossesses your car, there may be a deficiency that your co-signer can't pay. This will damage your co-signer's credit history. So be careful. Don't abuse your co-signer's trust and confidence.

With all of that said, how do you use this technique? Well, it depends. You may start the process yourself, if you don't think a bank or finance company will lend you the money. To do this, find a friend or family member with good credit, and ask them if they would be willing to co-sign your car loan. (You may want to take out some term life insurance to cover the loan amount. That way, your co-signer won't be stuck with the loan if anything should happen to you before you repay it.)

Next, follow the steps we talked about earlier. That is, find your dream car, negotiate the best price, and ask to speak with the credit manager. But now, once you're with the credit manager, explain your financial situation, and mention that you're willing to provide a co-signer who has excellent credit. In fact, you may even want to bring your co-signer with you. This will speed up the process. Otherwise, the credit manager will need to give you a credit application for your co-signer to complete.

Yes, that's right. Your co-signer will need to complete a credit application. After all, your co-signer IS applying for a loan. (This may prevent some people from co-signing your loan. Therefore, it's best to be up-front about this from the beginning. That way, if your co-signer refuses, you'll have the opportunity to find another co-signer before you approach a credit manager.)

If your co-signer's credit is strong enough, the credit manager will proceed as if you'd received the loan yourself. Now, however, you and your co-signer will sign on all the dotted lines. After that, YOU are responsible for making the monthly payments, and your co-signer should never hear about the loan again—at least until it's paid off. If your co-signer DOES hear from the lender, it's probably because you have failed to make the scheduled monthly payments. DON'T let this happen.

Another way that you might become involved with a co-signer is if the credit manager or lender suggests that you get a co-signer. They will often do this when a credit applicant has poor credit or limited income. However, the technique and results are the same whether you suggest a co-signer or the credit manager or lender suggests one.

In each case, you increase the lender's security by bringing in someone with good credit. The lender makes a safer loan, the dealer sells a car, and you get your dream car. Therefore, everybody wins. This can be a very effective way to purchase your dream car.

Straw Purchase

Another technique, although I don't recommend it, is the "straw man purchase." To use this technique, you'll need to find someone who's willing to purchase your car under his or her name and using his or her credit report. However, once this person purchases the car, they give it to you. Then, you make payments to the purchaser or directly to the lender.

There are some problems with this technique, though. First, the purchaser is solely responsible for repaying the debt. Therefore, you may damage the purchaser's credit reports if you don't make the monthly payments. Second, your repayment history for the loan won't appear on your credit reports. Therefore, it won't help you to rebuild your credit history. (It's usually better to get a co-signer for your car loan. That way, you'll rebuild your credit rating as you repay the loan.)

An alternative to this is to have someone purchase the car as above, but then sell or lease the car to you. Then, the purchaser may be able to deduct the car's depreciation and make some money in the process. BE CAREFUL though. The terms of the loan may prohibit the purchaser from selling or leasing the car without prior approval from the lender.

Recourse Loan

Another technique is to have the dealership "co-sign" the loan. Credit managers call this a "recourse loan." With this technique, the dealership sells your loan to the bank, but promises to buy the loan back from the bank if you default. The bank doesn't risk anything by purchasing the loan, and is glad to have you make payments to them.

To use this technique, ask to speak with the dealership's credit manager. Tell the credit manager that you've had credit problems and would like to re-establish credit. Therefore, you want to purchase a car "on recourse." Your best chance for success with this technique is to approach a large dealership. They will have the financial ability and desire to make this type of loan.

Now let me tell you the bad news about recourse loans. Although they were popular many years ago, most car dealers now refuse to use them. Therefore, you may not find a dealer willing to finance your car on recourse. But, give it a try—you never know.

Buy Here - Pay Here

One final way to finance your car purchase is the "Buy Here—Pay Here" technique. With this technique, you purchase a car at the dealership, and the dealership finances the purchase price. This leaves the banks out of the entire process.

Why would a dealership want to finance your purchase? That's right. The dealership wants to sell you a car. This is the same strategy that the major car dealers use. If you remember, the major car dealers use affiliated finance companies to help them sell cars. The buy here—pay here dealerships do the same thing. They just operate on a much smaller scale.

Unfortunately, buy here-pay here financing is expensive. The dealer will probably require a high down payment and charge a high interest rate. (Some buy here-pay here dealerships claim that payments are interest-free. But, that's just not true. To cover the cost of these "interest-free payments," the dealers just raise the price of the car.)

Another problem with buy here—pay here dealerships is that they generally only offer used cars in fair condition. In fact, they often break even on their cars when they receive the down payment. The remaining payments are all profit. Let me tell you how this works.

I have a friend who owns a buy here—pay here dealership. It's a small operation with 20 to 30 cars on the lot at any one time. He's owned this dealership for many years and has always managed to make a good living from it. Now let me tell you what I've learned from him.

My friend buys his cars at car auctions or from people who need quick cash. Either way, he never pays more—and generally pays less—than the wholesale price for his cars. And do you know how much he pays for these cars? He generally pays between $300 and $500 for them. He can buy them this cheaply because he looks for cars that are eight to fifteen years old.

Then, he cleans them up, puts them on his lot, and places a big sign in their windows that advertises the low down payment. Guess what the down payment amount is? That's right. It's between $300 and $500. He recovers his investment before the cars leave his lot. He can't lose.

Then, he sells the cars for between $1,500 and $2,000. And, because he's a true gentleman, he allows his customers to make WEEKLY payments WITHOUT interest. He's really a gentleman.

Now let's look at the deal. First, he has no risk because he's already recovered his investment. Then, he makes a profit that ranges from 400 to 500 percent. He doesn't NEED to charge interest. (Of course, this is what I talked about earlier. Is this really an interest-free loan? Or is it only a grossly inflated purchase price? Does it matter?)

Then there's one final thing. Because he receives WEEKLY payments, he knows very quickly if someone can't repay the loan. If his customers miss a payment, even one payment, he repossesses their cars. If this happens, they lose any money that they've already paid him. Then, to top it all off, he puts these repossessed cars on his lots and resells them—starting the process all over again. (Maybe I should think about this friendship.)

Now I'm not saying that all buy here—pay here dealerships operate like my friend does. But many of them do. Therefore, you need to be very careful if you approach these dealerships. To protect yourself, have a mechanic carefully inspect your dream car. Then consult a car valuation book, such as the BLUE BOOK, to make sure you don't pay too much. You can find these publications in your local library or by contacting your bank or credit union.

II. Leasing - The Purchase Alternative

What about leasing? Or maybe a more basic question should be—what is leasing? When you lease a car, you only pay for the USE of that car for a certain period—generally two to five years.

During this time, you get to use the car as if you owned it. You can go anywhere and do anything you want. However, you're not supposed to exceed a certain number of miles—generally 15,000 miles each year—and you're supposed to keep the car in good condition. Then, after the specified period, you either return the car to the leasing company, or purchase it.

Why would you want to do all of this? You'd do this because the monthly payments on a lease are generally lower than monthly payments on a loan. Lease payments are lower because you're only paying for the portion of the car that you "use up." Although I've greatly simplified this, let me tell you how leases work.

Leasing companies figure out what the value of your dream car will be at the end of the specified period. As we talked about before, cars depreciate, or lose their value, over time. Therefore, your car will be worth 30 to 70% less at the end of the lease term. That's the secret of leases—you only pay for the depreciation. Let's see an example of this.

Let's say that you find a car with a purchase price of $10,000. You'd like to lease the car for five years. Therefore, the leasing company calculates what your car will be worth at the end of this five-year period.

Let's say for this example that the leasing company thinks your car will be worth only 25% of its present value in five years. That means that it will depreciate 75% in five years. On our $10,000 car, the depreciation amount will be $7,500. Therefore, the leasing company will want you to pay $7,500 over five years, plus interest. At the end of the lease period, you may have the option to purchase the car for $2,500, or return it to the leasing company.

Now can you see why you'll have lower monthly payments with a lease versus a traditional loan? If you purchased the $10,000 car outright with a traditional loan, you'd have to repay the entire $10,000 plus interest over the term of the loan. If you leased that same car, you'd only have to pay $7,500 plus interest over the term of the lease. Taking interest into account, your payments would be more than 25% less with a lease than with a traditional loan. And, your savings could be even greater if your dream car didn't depreciate as fast as in our example. Remember, you only pay for the depreciation. If the car doesn't depreciate very much, then you don't have to pay very much.

Problems With Leasing

So what's the problem with leases? They sound too good to be true, right? Well, there are several problems. First, as I mentioned earlier, most leases restrict the number of miles that you can drive over the course of the lease. This is generally about 15,000 miles each year. If you drive more than this, as I do, then you'll have to pay a mileage penalty at the end of your lease. And this can be substantial. The typical mileage penalty is usually 15 to 20 cents per mile. Even if you only drive an extra 1,000 miles each year during a five-year lease, your penalty at 20 cents per mile would be $1,000. You'd have to hand that over with the keys.

Another problem with leases is that you may not know how the leasing company calculated your payments. If you don't know the important figures, like you car's estimated future market value, or your interest rate, the leasing company and the dealership can make out like bandits. Let me tell you how this works.

Returning now to my car selling days, I remember a very strong example of the power of leases. I had worked for weeks to sell a brand new Nissan 300ZX 2+2 sports car to a postman. It was loaded with every gadget that Nissan had at the time, and was therefore the most expensive car on the lot. This postman, unfortunately for me, was a very shrewd negotiator. Over the course of those several weeks, he managed to bring the price of that profit-laden car down to a virtual break-even deal. However, because it was just about the end of the year, my sales manager authorized this puny deal.

Therefore, I sadly proceeded to take care of all the paperwork. After that, I ushered the postman into the credit manager's office and hoped that the postman wasn't as shrewd at negotiating interest rates as he was at negotiating price. (After all, it was nearly Christmas, and I had gifts to buy.)

To my horror, the postman left very suddenly. It seems that he hadn't considered how much this decked-out sports car was going to cost him each month. Although he had negotiated the lowest possible price that we could sell it for, he just couldn't afford the payments.

Well, I wasn't about to let several weeks of work go down the drain, so I followed him and tried to switch him to a lower priced car. But he'd already caught the fever. He was set on that sports car, and nothing else would do.

So, did I give up? Of course I didn't. I remembered the training I'd received some time earlier about leases. The trainers advised me to switch a customer off a traditional loan and onto a lease if the customer complained about the monthly payment amount. At the time, I wasn't really sure why lease payments were less than loan payments. But I thought I'd give it a try.

I suggested to the postman that he lease the sports car rather than purchase it. That way, he'd get his lower payments, and the dream car. And you know what? It worked. He leased that car for five years and drove away as happy as you could ever imagine.

At the time, I didn't think very much more about this. I made a sale, and I was happy with that. I knew it wasn't a very profitable deal, but at least I had another "unit" sold. That is, until I received my paycheck the next week.

I made perhaps the biggest commission I ever received for selling one car. As I remember, it was somewhere between $800 and $1,000 for that one sale. (And remember, I only made 25% of what the dealership made.) I was expecting to make about $50. So what had happened in the credit manager's office that made me so much money?

When the credit manager switched the postman from the loan to the lease, he DIDN'T use the price that the postman had negotiated for the loan. He used the FULL purchase price of the sports car to calculate the lease payments. In addition, the lease interest rate was higher than the postman would have paid under a traditional loan.

This postman, who had been such a shrewd negotiator on the purchase price, was totally duped by the lease. He NEVER questioned the figures that the credit manager or leasing company used to calculate his lease payments. Had he done so, his lease payments would have been much lower than they were. But he didn't know this. The result? He was happily ignorant, and I made a lot of money.

So what's the point of this very long example? Don't be happily ignorant and let some car salesman or credit manager make a lot of money at your expense. Ask to see, and make sure that you understand, the figures that the credit manager and leasing company have used to compute your lease payments.

There's one final problem with leases. Historically, creditors have required a higher credit standard with leases than with traditional loans. This would take most leases out of the reach of anyone having a bankruptcy notation on their credit report. Fortunately, things are changing.

Because of the current weak economy and poor car sales, some car manufacturers have become aggressive in their marketing techniques. They want to sell cars—as many as they can. One way of doing this is with leases. In fact, you may find it easier to get a short-term lease from a manufacturer's financing company than a traditional car loan.

For example, Ford Motor Credit is pushing a two-year lease on many Ford cars. Ford credit managers have told me that it's easier right now to get approval for this two-year lease than other financing forms. This is especially true for anyone with a bankruptcy listed on their credit report. Therefore, give it a shot. Just remember my little story when you're talking to the sales person or credit manager.

Other Leasing Opportunities

Besides receiving a traditional lease, you may be able to "take over" the payments of someone who is already leasing a car and wants to get out of it. You may find these individuals in the classified section of your newspaper. Be aware, however, that the leasing company may not allow this transaction without its approval. If you agree to take over the payments, and the leasing company finds out, it may declare the lease in default and take the car from you. So be careful.

Another way to find people who want to get out of their leases is to use companies that act as "go-betweens." (You'll probably find these companies in the classified section of the newspaper as well.) These companies find people that have leased cars, but don't want them, and match them with people that want cars, but can't get them.

Be careful with these companies, though, and carefully review any contracts or agreements they ask you to sign. Generally, the former lessee (the person leasing the car) is still responsible for making the lease payments, and you may or may not be. (You will be responsible for making the payments according to your contract with the middleman company. However, the original lease will probably not apply to you.) Therefore, the lease payments may or may not appear on your credit reports.

Additionally, you may have the same problem with the leasing company that we talked about earlier. The leasing company may not want another person to take over the lease payments, and probably prohibits this in the lease agreement. If it finds out about your arrangement, it may declare the lease agreement in default and take the car from you. Again, the bottom line? Be careful.

III. Renting Cars and Other Vehicles

Without a credit card, you may find it difficult to rent a car. Therefore, if you haven't already done so, apply for a secured bankcard. (Remember, you'll find a list of secured bankcards in Appendix 3, and in the special reports on secured credit cards.) Then you shouldn't have any problems with renting a car.

However, if you don't have a secured bankcard, you may be able to convince the rental agency to rent you a car with a cash deposit. Several rental companies have procedures that will allow you to rent a car without a credit card. However, they all require that you contact them before the desired rental date, and complete an application. Here's a run-down on the rental policies of some major rental companies.

Avis

Avis does have a program—they call it "cash qualifying"—that allows you to rent cars without a major credit card. To take advantage of this program, you must complete an application before the desired rental date. Unfortunately, a bankruptcy notation on your credit report will automatically disqualify you from consideration for this program.

In some cities, however, Avis will allow you to use the credit card of another person. Avis will list this person as the primary driver, and you as an additional driver. Unfortunately, many Avis locations will also require a major credit card from the additional driver, which leaves you out in the cold again.

Enterprise

Enterprise will NOT rent you a car unless you have a major credit card. (Are you starting to see why you should get a secured credit card, or become an authorized user on another person's account?)

Hertz

Hertz is more progressive than some other rental car companies. You can rent a car from Hertz, without a credit card, by using one of two methods. First, like some other companies, you can "cash qualify" at specific rental locations. For Hertz, this means that you must complete an application before the desired rental date.

To qualify, you must meet several requirements. First, you must be at least 25 years old. Second, you must have held the same job for at least one year. Finally, you must put down a cash deposit equal to the estimated rental amount, plus the greater of an additional 50% or $100.

The second method for renting a car from Hertz without a credit card is to obtain a Hertz Cash Deposit Card. To obtain this card, request an application from Hertz. Once Hertz approves you, you can rent a car from any Hertz location without having to prequalify each time you want to rent a car.

National

National also has a cash qualifying program. As with the other rental companies, you must contact a specific National rental location before the rental date, and complete an application. National will charge you a $10 application fee for this, and will check your current credit, business references, and phone number. Additionally, you must put down a $100 cash deposit when you rent the car.

Thrifty

Thrifty does not have a national policy regarding rentals without credit cards. Many Thrifty locations will allow you to cash qualify, but the terms and conditions vary from location to location. To rent a car from Thrifty, contact the specific location before the desired rental date, and ask them about their policies.

Final Words on Renting

So you see that you CAN rent a car from several of the major rental companies without a credit card. But, it's a LOT easier if you have a credit card. Think about applying for a secured credit card, or asking a family member to list you as an authorized user on their credit card account.

Another rental option you may consider is a "Rent-a-Wreck" type company that specializes in renting older cars. These cars may or may not be in poor condition, but will probably get you where you want to go. These companies generally don't require a credit card, and have fewer requirements for their non-credit card rentals.

Final Words on Transportation

You CAN obtain transportation, even if you have a bankruptcy notation on your credit report. By using any of the methods described in this chapter, you should be able get that dream car. (Well, you can get decent transportation anyway.) If a specific lender or company rejects your application, try another. Or, if one technique doesn't work, try another. In the end, you WILL have transportation, and be on the road again!

Chapter 13

Housing

The house of everyone is to him as his castle and fortress, as well for his defense against injury and violence as for his repose.

Sir Edward Coke

If you survived your bankruptcy with the home of your dreams—and you plan to live there for the rest of your life—then you can skip this chapter. But, if you're looking for something more, then keep on reading. I've got some good news for you.

Contrary to popular belief, you CAN buy a house, even if your bankruptcy is just one year old. (In fact, I'll show you a way to buy a house on the day you walk away from the bankruptcy court.) In addition, if you prefer to rent a house or apartment, you should be able to do so without too much aggravation.

In this chapter, I'll tell you everything you need to know about housing. In Section I, I'll show you how to rent a house or apartment. Then, in Section II, I'll show you several specific techniques that you can use to buy your dream home.

After reading this chapter, you may think of other techniques that we haven't discussed. If so, give it a shot. (Also, make sure you write and tell me about your ideas—other people could benefit from your experiences.) The worst that can happen is that someone will say no to your offer. If that happens, just go on to the next offer or try someone else. You WILL find someone to rent or sell you a home!

I. Renting

Let's start our housing discussion with the basics of renting. If you want to rent a house or apartment, there are several steps you should take.

First, locate the house or apartment you're interested in renting. Then, make sure the rental payments are within your budget and that you can afford any security deposits. Also find out about the terms of the lease—how long it lasts, your repair obligations, etc. Throughout this process, try to build a rapport with your potential landlord.

If you decide that you've found your next home, the landlord will want several things from you. For example, the landlord will probably ask you to complete a rental application and to leave a deposit to hold the unit. These are standard requests.

Unfortunately, the landlord will probably also have another request. Most landlords will ask you to complete a credit application. This gives the landlord the right to check your credit report.

As you remember, a potential landlord may legally check your credit report under the Fair Credit Reporting Act. Therefore, if a bankruptcy notation still appears on your credit reports, your potential landlord WILL find out about your bankruptcy. (That is, of course, if the landlord checks your credit report. Some landlords may not check. However, you should assume that they will.)

If the landlord does ask you to complete a credit application, you've got to a decision to make—whether you'll say anything about your bankruptcy. Although you may be uncomfortable with this approach, the best strategy at this point is to be up-front and truthful with your potential landlord BEFORE the landlord sees your credit report. Then, if the landlord isn't going to rent you a home, you'll know right away.

Generally, however, landlords understand and appreciate your honesty. Although the landlord may require a larger security deposit than normal (probably not), you should be able to rent a house or apartment with little difficulty. Remember—be honest.

II. Buying

Unfortunately, buying a house is more difficult than renting one. Many lenders still refuse to give mortgage loans to anyone who's been through bankruptcy. Therefore, a mortgage lender may not lend you money to buy a house, even if the value of your house completely secures the loan.

Although lenders can foreclose on your home if you stop paying your mortgage, they DON'T want to do this for several reasons. First, because housing laws generally favor homeowners, it will take your lender several months and a fair amount of expense to foreclose on your home.

Second, lenders don't want to lose money. If your lender does foreclose, it must sell your house to recover the money it lent you. Unfortunately, if the housing market is in a slump when your lender forecloses, it may not recover the full mortgage amount when it sells the house. Therefore, the lender DOESN'T want to foreclose. It wants YOU to repay the mortgage.

Because of these problems, some traditional mortgage lenders won't want to take a chance on you. These lenders would rather lose the opportunity to earn interest from you, than face the problems with foreclosure. Remember, lenders are traditionally very conservative. They DON'T want to lose money.

But, I told you I had GOOD news for you. And I do. There are many ways to finance your dream home. In the next several sections, I'll show you some of them. Let's start with the traditional mortgage loan.

Traditional Mortgages

The first way to finance your dream home is with a traditional mortgage. With this type of loan, a lender will require you to pay some portion of the purchase price—usually 10-20%. Then, the lender will finance the rest. This is the way that most people finance their homes. Unfortunately, this may be the most difficult way for YOU to finance your home.

Conservative Lenders

Whether it's difficult for you will depend on the lender's policies and what the lender does with your mortgage loan. Many traditional mortgage lenders have very strict lending policies, and are usually reluctant to make mortgage loans to people with bad credit. They're just not willing to take a chance and lose money.

Therefore, you probably won't receive a mortgage loan from these conservative lenders. That is, of course, unless the lender SELLS your mortgage to an investor that IS willing to take a chance on you. Let me explain this.

When you receive a mortgage loan, your lender can either keep the mortgage as an investment, or sell it to another financial institution or investor. If a conservative lender keeps your mortgage as an investment, it will want to make sure that you don't default. If you do, the lender loses money. Therefore, it probably won't lend you the money.

However, a conservative lender can SELL your mortgage to another investor that IS willing to take a greater risk on its investment. If the lender does this, it doesn't take any risk in lending you the money. All the risk shifts to the new investor. Therefore, you only need to satisfy the less conservative lending requirements of the new investor.

So what's the point of this long explanation? You CAN get a traditional mortgage loan, even from a conservative lender. But, to find out, you'll have to ask. Don't worry, the worst thing that the lender can do is say no.

Progressive Lenders

O.K. That takes care of the conservative lenders. What about the progressive lenders? Let's talk about them now.

Not all lenders will refuse your mortgage application just because you have bad credit. These lenders, I call them "progressive lenders," look at other information as well.

The most important thing that lenders look for is that you're willing and able to repay the mortgage. If you've re-established some credit, have a stable income, and can contribute some money toward the purchase price, you'll probably find traditional financing. Let me tell you how to do this.

First, approach the financial institution where you regularly bank, and ask to speak with a loan officer. By this point, you should have already established some credit with it, by taking out and successfully repaying a secured loan. (If you haven't done this, review Chapter 11.)

Then when you meet with the loan officer, point out the positive account history that you've established with the lender. You'll also want to explain any bad credit references that remain on your credit reports. If you're persuasive, your financial institution may be willing to lend you the money you need. Let me give you a real-life example of this.

In the last chapter, I told you that my credit union lent me the money to purchase a car. As you remember, they did this even though the bankruptcy notation still appeared on my credit report. But, my credit union was willing to do even more for me.

When I received the car loan, the loan officer mentioned that the credit union would also be happy to lend me the money for a new house. They would offer me a 30-year fixed rate mortgage at market interest rates, if I made a 20% down payment. Now that wasn't the lowest down payment requirement around. However, traditional mortgage lenders often require a 20% down payment, even for people with good credit reports.

So you see then, you CAN get traditional mortgage financing through traditional lenders. If your financial institution won't lend you the new money for a new home, go to another lender. Don't give up on traditional mortgages—yet.

Government Mortgage Programs

Fortunately, traditional mortgages aren't the only way to finance a home. Because home ownership is the "American Dream," the government has created various programs to help you buy your dream. In this section, I'll tell you about two of these programs.

The FHA Mortgage Program

The Federal Housing Authority (the "FHA") administers the first government mortgage program that we'll talk about. Under the FHA program, you may obtain a loan with as little as 5% down. And best of all, this is at market interest rates.

The FHA isn't really in the mortgage lending business, however. Under the most common program, the FHA "insures" that you'll repay the loan. If you fail to pay your mortgage, the FHA will step in and pay it. Therefore, the lender can't lose any money if you default, and is happy to give you the loan.

Best of all, you can get an FHA loan within ONE year after your bankruptcy discharge. That's right. You get the low down payment and the market interest rate within one year of your bankruptcy. Now that's good news!

Of course, you'll still have to meet the FHA income and debt qualifications before they'll approve you for the program. At the time of this writing, your mortgage and other debt payments can't exceed 55% of your monthly net income. (I've greatly simplified the qualifications' formula for this explanation. Your loan officer can tell you all about the qualifications process when you apply for the loan.)

To apply for an FHA mortgage, contact your local lending institution or talk to your real estate broker. They will help you obtain application forms, or guide you to the proper institution.

The VA Mortgage Program

The Veterans Administration (the "VA") also administers a government mortgage program that you may be eligible to participate in. Like the FHA program, the VA will pay a bank if you default on the mortgage. However, this program is different from the FHA program in many ways.

The first difference between the two programs concerns eligibility. Unlike the FHA program, only "qualifying veterans" can participate in the VA program. (However, you can still take advantage of the program by "assuming" a VA mortgage. I'll tell you about that in a moment.)

Another difference between the two programs concerns the repayment amount. While the FHA "insures" the payment of your loan, the VA only "guarantees" a certain portion of it. The VA calls this amount the "veteran's entitlement."

At the time of this writing, the VA entitlement is $36,000 to $46,000, depending upon the size of the mortgage. This means that the VA will guarantee payment of up to $46,000 of the mortgage. Although this doesn't cover the full amount of the mortgage, like the FHA program, it will probably be enough to protect the lender against any default. Therefore, the lender is still without risk and is happy to extend the loan.

O.K. So how do you become a qualifying veteran? At the time of this writing, you must satisfy one of the following:

1. You served on active duty for at least 90 days during World War II, the Korean War, or the Vietnam War.
2. You served on continuous active duty during peacetime for at least 180 days and all of this duty was before September 7, 1980.
3. You served on active duty for at least 24 months after September 7, 1980.

Because these qualifications change from time to time, you'll want to contact your local VA office for the current requirements. In addition, you'll need to obtain a Certificate of Eligibility from the VA to qualify for your mortgage loan.

If you're a qualifying veteran, what do you get? First, you get a guarantee from the VA that they'll repay your loan, up to a maximum of $46,000.

What else do you get? You get the possibility of making a ZERO down payment. That's right, you can get a VA mortgage without making ANY down payment. That's great news. (However, you may still be responsible for closing and other administrative costs.)

What else? You get the opportunity to take your entitlement with you when you sell your house. If you sell your house, and repay the VA mortgage, you may reapply for your entitlement and use it to purchase another house.

Finally, and perhaps most important for our purposes, you get some flexibility from the VA. The VA doesn't have any strict qualification guidelines. You must be able to afford the monthly payments of course. But from there, the VA decides each case individually. The VA will generally allow you to obtain a VA mortgage within two years of your bankruptcy discharge. Again, good news!

To apply for a VA mortgage loan, contact your local VA office. They'll get the process rolling by issuing you a Certificate of Eligibility. From there, you may want to contact your local lending institution or real estate broker. They can help you with the application process, or direct you to someone that can help you.

Mortgage Brokers

The techniques we've just discussed for the VA, FHA, and traditional financing programs generally require that you seek out a specific financial institution to apply for your mortgage. This shouldn't be a problem if you can find a progressive lender that's willing to look beyond your bankruptcy. However, you may not have the knowledge and resources to locate a progressive lender in your area.

Therefore, you may want to consider using the services of a mortgage broker. A mortgage broker specializes in bringing together people or organizations with money and people that need money. These sources of money may include traditional banks and savings and loans and may also include private individuals or groups of investors.

The mortgage brokerage business has become very large in the last few years. The main reasons for this growth are the increasing complexity of mortgages and the collapse of many savings and loans. The National Association of Mortgage Brokers, a mortgage broker trade group, estimates that mortgage brokers today place more than 50% of all home mortgages. That number is probably much higher for people with poor credit histories.

Mortgage brokers can be very helpful in locating lenders that are willing to give you a mortgage loan. Although you could probably call several banks in your area, most mortgage brokers have an extensive network of banks and other lenders that they work with every day. A good mortgage broker can estimate your chances of receiving a loan, and the probable interest charges, down payment requirements, and other terms. But be prepared!

Depending on your financial situation, you might need to offer a sizeable down payment and pay a higher interest rate than would someone with a good credit report. Additionally, you may have to pay a fee to the mortgage broker for finding you the loan. Although most mortgage brokers receive a great portion of their fee from the lender, some brokers require an advance payment from the borrower. Review the chapter on Credit Scams before giving ANYONE an advance fee. If the mortgage broker is reputable, you MAY want to make this advance payment.

To use this technique, refer to your local telephone directory and contact several mortgage brokers. Explain your financial situation and question them about their ability to locate financing for you. They'll want to know what price range you're interested in and how much money you can put down on the house. To be safe, you should ask them some questions too. For example, ask the mortgage brokers about the number of banks they represent. A good mortgage broker should represent at least 10 lenders. And, these lenders should be in different parts of the country so that you can get the best deal.

You should also ask the mortgage brokers about their closing ratios. A closing ratio shows how many of the broker's clients have received mortgage loans, versus the number of times the broker has arranged financing. (This shows you how successful the broker is.) The percentage for normal transactions is 70% and above. However, the ratio may be lower if the broker has many clients with bad credit histories.

Another important point is to ask the mortgage brokers for references. These references should be from banks and real estate agents and brokers in the area. Call these references and ask questions about the mortgage broker. Some mortgage brokers have very good reputations in the community, while others don't. You'll know which you have after some phone calls.

Finally, you should make sure that the mortgage broker tells you about ALL of the charges you will encounter for the broker's services, and for the lender's services. Don't wait until closing to discover that you owe several thousands of dollars in unanticipated fees. Therefore, make sure that you get everything in writing before you commit to anything.

This technique can be very powerful. But remember to compare rates among the various mortgage brokers. You should include ALL costs in your comparison. Then you'll be an informed buyer. Don't let the mortgage broker or the lender scare you into something that you don't want to do. There are always other brokers and other lenders. As always, be careful!

Non-Qualifying Assumable Mortgages

Another way to buy your dream home is to "take over" the mortgage payments of another person. Some mortgage lenders allow this. If so, their loans are "assumable."

Generally, the best sources for assumable loans are our now familiar friends—the Veterans Administration (the "VA") or the Federal Housing Authority (the "FHA"). (Although some private mortgage lenders issue assumable mortgages, most do not. Most private mortgage lenders include a "due-on-sale" clause in their mortgages. This prevents another person from assuming the mortgage payments.)

As we talked about before, the VA and FHA offer government mortgage programs to people who qualify. But, even if you can't qualify for either program, you may still be able to assume mortgages that they have guaranteed or insured.

When you assume a VA or FHA loan, you agree to continue making payments on the present loan, and you don't have to get another loan. This sounds good, doesn't it? Well, it gets better. You may be able to assume a VA or FHA loan even if you would not qualify for the loan yourself.

There are two types of assumable loans—qualifying and non-qualifying. With a qualifying assumable mortgage, you must meet certain VA and FHA requirements. Generally, these are the same requirements that most lenders use to determine your eligibility.

Although the VA and FHA are probably more liberal than traditional mortgage lenders, they still ask the same questions. Do you have the income to repay the loan? Do you have too many other debts? Does your credit report show your willingness and ability to repay the mortgage? Therefore, if your bankruptcy appears on your credit report, you may face difficulty in qualifying for this type of mortgage.

However, with a NON-QUALIFYING assumable mortgage, you DON'T need to satisfy ANY requirements. If you can make the monthly payments, then you can assume the mortgage from the present homeowners. This is a great deal and will allow you to purchase a house, even if your bankruptcy and other bad credit information appear on your credit reports. In fact, you could assume a non-qualifying mortgage on the day you receive your bankruptcy discharge! Now that's a powerful technique!

There are several ways to find a non-qualifying assumable mortgage. First, try scanning the classified section of your local newspaper. Look for advertisements in the housing section that identify the mortgage as a non-qualifying assumable mortgage. Generally, the advertiser will place this information in bold letters at the top of the advertisement. (It's a strong selling point for the house!)

You should also check with local real estate magazines. These are generally free publications carried by convenience stores. These publications generally list many homes with non-qualifying assumable mortgages.

Finally, you might want to check with a real estate agent or broker. They'll probably know about hundreds of homes with non-qualifying assumable mortgages. In addition, real estate agents and brokers are used to working with people with bad credit. Therefore, they should be a great asset to you.

Just remember, most agents and brokers represent the seller in a real estate transaction. They will know your credit situation and the difficulty you may have in purchasing a home. DON'T let them use this information to your disadvantage. If you're uncomfortable with the deal, don't hesitate to negotiate. If the seller refuses to budge, just walk away. You WILL find another opportunity.

Problems with Non-Qualifying Assumable Mortgages

Although non-qualifying assumable mortgages may help you to purchase a house, there are some problems with them. First, the FHA STOPPED issuing non-qualifying assumable mortgages after 1987. Therefore, only older houses will have non-qualifying assumable mortgages. To assume a mortgage that the FHA issued after 1987, you'll need to qualify for the loan. However, there are still MANY good houses for sale with non-qualifying assumable mortgages.

Second, the FHA will only insure mortgages up to a certain amount. Therefore, only modestly priced homes will have non-qualifying assumable mortgages. Unfortunately, in areas of the country with high housing costs, you may find that you can't find a suitable home with a non-qualifying assumable mortgage.

Owner Financing

Another way to buy your own home is to let the present owner finance some, or all, of the purchase price. To use this technique, you would give the seller a first or second mortgage on your home. Let's talk about both types now.

First Mortgages

If the seller agrees to finance the entire purchase price, you'll need to give the owner a "first mortgage" on your home. Then, if you default on the loan, the seller can foreclose. But why would a seller want to finance your purchase?

First, a seller might agree to do this so that you'll buy the house. With today's weak real estate market, it may take several months or more to sell a house. This could be a problem if the seller has already purchased another house.

A seller might also finance your purchase as an investment. If the seller has a large equity in the house, or owns it completely, your mortgage payments can be a guaranteed source of income. As with any creditor, the seller can foreclose on the house and evict you if you fail to make your scheduled payments. This is a safe and attractive investment for many homeowners.

To find homes with owner financing, check with the same sources as before. First, scan the classified section of your local newspaper and the real estate magazines. Look for the words "Owner Financing" or "Owner Holds Second" or something similar. These are your clues to owner financing.

In addition, look for publications that advertise homes for sale by their owners, like "For Sale By Owner." Unlike other real estate magazines, these publications only list houses where the homeowner is handling the sale, instead of a real estate agent or broker. You may find several owner financing offers in these publications.

Finally, as before, check with a local real estate agent or broker. They can find homeowners who are willing to finance your purchase.

Second Mortgages

In the last discussion, we focused on the seller as the primary lender. However, the seller can also finance part of your purchase with a "second mortgage." You might need the seller to do this on assumable loans if the seller has built up a large "equity" in the house.

For example, let's say you found the house of your dreams. It has a selling price of $75,000 and a $40,000 non-qualifying assumable first mortgage. So far so good, except that you don't have $35,000 to put down on the house to account for the difference. The $35,000 difference is the seller's "equity" in the property. This is the amount that the seller actually owns, and comes from a combination of payments on the mortgage and an increase in the value of the house.

If you really want that house, and can't finance the remaining $35,000 of seller's equity, you should ask the seller to "take back" a second mortgage. As above, the seller may be willing to do this to sell the house or to make a secure investment. If the seller agrees, then you assume the seller's payments under the first mortgage AND make payments to the seller under the second mortgage.

Try to have the term of the second mortgage as long as possible. The seller will probably be looking for a short term—three years or less—but should be willing to negotiate. If you want your dream house bad enough, this may be a great way to get it.

Equity Sharing

Another way to finance your home purchase is to use "equity sharing." With this technique, you find an investor willing to lend money, good credit, or both to the deal. Then, you agree to live in, and maintain, the house for a certain number of years. You also agree to pay your portion of the mortgage and other expenses and to pay the investor a fair rental amount for the house. At the end of the specified period, you sell the house. Then you repay the investor for any amounts that the investor initially contributed, and split the remaining profits.

Investors like equity sharing deals because they're a safe investment and generally provide a good profit. And, although an investor could probably find an investment house that's just as desirable as your dream house, you add one very desirable element to the deal—YOU.

It's not just that you're a good person. The most important part of this deal is that you will live in, take care of, and pay rent on, the house. If you weren't in the house, the investor would have to find a suitable tenant for the house and hope that the tenant stayed for a while. When the tenant left, the investor would have to pay more money to clean and repair the house, and hope to find another tenant.

However, with you in the deal, the investor has a built-in tenant for the duration of the equity sharing agreement. The investor doesn't have to worry about finding a new tenant every time the lease expires. And most important, because you have an interest in the house, you're going to take great care of it. These are strong inducements for any investor. To help you understand this, let's look at how a typical equity sharing deal might work.

Let's say you have $5,000 that you can apply to the purchase price of your dream house. After an exhaustive search, you find your dream house. Your dream house is in good condition, in a desirable neighborhood, and sure to increase in value over the years. Unfortunately, your dream house also has a selling price of $100,000.

To purchase this house with a traditional mortgage, you'd have to come up with 20% of the selling price as a down payment. In this example, you'd have to put down $20,000. Even if you had that much money to contribute to the deal, you'd still run into another problem—your credit rating. A mortgage lender would probably be unwilling to lend you the remaining $80,000 to purchase the house if the bankruptcy notation still appeared on your credit reports. At this point, the average person would either leave the housing market entirely, or set their sights on something less costly.

But, you start thinking creatively. You can purchase your dream home if someone will contribute $15,000 toward the down payment and lend good credit to the deal. Therefore, you approach a likely candidate and explain your plan.

First, you need to work out the down payment. You tell your investor that you'll contribute $5,000 toward the down payment and your investor will contribute $15,000. Then, when you sell the house at the end of the agreement, you'll each receive your initial contribution.

Now you need to work out the mortgage payments. Let's say that you find a 30-year mortgage with a 10% interest rate. Therefore, your monthly payments on the $80,000 mortgage will be about $700. You tell your investor that each of you will pay half the monthly mortgage payment—$350 in this example.

You also agree to split the cost of insurance, property taxes, etc., and to pay the investor half the fair market rental rate for the house. If the house would rent for $850 per month, then you'll pay the investor $425 per month, besides your portion of the monthly mortgage payment. Therefore, your total expenses each month will be $775, plus your share of other expenses.

You can deduct your interest portion of the mortgage payments, and your share of property taxes, from federal and state income taxes. Your investor can also deduct interest payments and property taxes, and may also depreciate half the house under the applicable depreciation schedule. Therefore, you both win.

At the end of the specified period, let's say five years, you sell the house and split the proceeds. To do this, you must first refund the investor's $15,000 down payment and you must take your $5,000. Then, you may split the proceeds in whatever proportion you agree upon. If you had originally agreed to split the proceeds evenly, then you take half the remainder, and the investor takes the other half.

For our example, let's say that you sold the house for $135,000 after the five years. Your remaining balance on the original $80,000 mortgage would be approximately $77,000. (Not a big decrease, is it?) After paying off the $77,000 mortgage, there would be $58,000 left. Your investor takes $15,000 as the original down payment and you take your $5,000. That leaves $38,000 left over. You and your investor split the $38,000 evenly, so that you each get $19,000.

Remember, your investor has also had the benefit of a secured cash flow of $425 each month for five years -your rent payment. Almost all of this would be tax free because the investor was paying half the mortgage—most of which was deductible mortgage interest. Therefore, your investor received more than twice his original $15,000 investment. That works out to more than a 35% return on the investor's money—an amount most investors would be happy to receive.

And what did you get from the deal? You lived in a great house for five years and deducted about $4,000 each year as mortgage interest payments. Best of all, though, you made $19,000 on your original investment of $5,000. You almost quadrupled your investment—receiving a 76% return on your investment every year. With the $24,000 that you now have, and five years of mortgage payment history, you can buy your next dream house—a bigger one— without another investor.

Although I've simplified this example, equity sharing CAN work. But, you need to find an investor. The best way to do this is to contact several local real estate agents or brokers. Explain your interest in equity sharing and your plan. They should be able to help you.

You might also review the classified section of your local newspaper. Look under the general real estate headings, and under columns labeled "Money to Lend" or something similar. If you're still unable to find an equity sharing investor, you might want to place an ad in the "Money Wanted" section. Explain your interest in equity sharing and your suggested terms. You'll probably get someone to respond to this if your terms look interesting.

Final Words about Equity Sharing

If you decide to try equity sharing, you should probably hire an attorney to draft an equity sharing agreement for you. Or, at the very least, hire an attorney to review your proposed contract. However, make sure that the attorney knows something about equity sharing.

Co-Signers

As we discussed in the section on secured credit, one of your most valuable assets is your family and friends. If you find yourself with a poor credit record after filing for bankruptcy, and no where else to turn, you'll always have your friends and family. You may find that friends or family members are willing to lend you their good credit toward the purchase of your new home. If they're willing, you could have a friend or family member co-sign the mortgage with you.

If you remember, when someone co-signs a loan, they become jointly liable under the loan with you. This also means that if you fail to make the required loan payments on the loan, then your co-signer is responsible for paying the full amount of the loan. And, if your co-signer can't make the payments, your lender will foreclose on the property.

If your lender forecloses, it may also go after you and your co-signer for any deficiency. In addition, the foreclosure will damage your co-signers good credit history, and will probably end your relationship with the co-signer. Therefore, if you decide to pursue a mortgage with a co-signer, do everything in your power to avoid defaulting on the loan. Meanwhile, you'll live in your dream house and rebuild good credit by paying monthly mortgage payments to the lender.

Before you approach a friend or family member about co-signing, check with several lenders about their policies regarding co-signers. Most banks are happy to have more people to pursue if you stop making the payments. Other banks, however, may be suspicious of this arrangement.

Final Words on Home Financing

You CAN finance your dream home, even with a bankruptcy notation on your credit report. You may have to do a bit more research than someone with a perfect credit history. However, you'll probably find a mortgage with the same terms and conditions that a lender would offer to even the good credit risk.

Therefore, don't give up! If one lender refuses your application, try another. If one technique doesn't work, try another. But, I think you'll find that it's not as hard to obtain home financing as many people believe. Good luck!

Chapter 14

Employment

> *No poor, rural, weak, or black person should ever again have to bear the additional burden of being deprived of the opportunity for an education, a job, or simple justice.*
>
> *Jimmy [James Earl, Jr.] Carter*

You may be wondering whether your bankruptcy will affect your present job, or your search for a new job. This is a common concern of people following bankruptcy. Unfortunately, your bankruptcy MAY affect your employment.

Employer Access to Your Credit File

As we talked about before, employers CAN check your credit report if they do so for "employment purposes." Because this allowance is so broad, your present or potential employer can easily access your credit report.

Unfortunately, the news gets even worse. If your present or potential job pays $20,000 per year or more, the credit bureaus can report ALL the bad information that has EVER appeared on your credit reports. If you remember, this is an exception to reporting obsolete information.

Therefore, your current or potential employer will see everything, even obsolete information. If it's been more than 10 years since your bankruptcy discharge, the credit bureaus can still report your bankruptcy to employers. This applies to all other types of bad credit information as well—bad accounts, charge-offs, judgments, etc.

Therefore, technically, you will NEVER be free of your credit history. Fortunately, however, most credit bureaus will remove this information from your credit report at the statutorily prescribed times—seven years for most bad information, and 10 years for bankruptcy.

Discrimination by Public Employers

Now let me tell you some good news. It's against federal law for public employers to discriminate against you. 11 U.S.C. § 525(a) prohibits all federal, state, and local governmental units from discriminating against you just because you filed for bankruptcy.

To give you a feel for this, let me show you the relevant part of the statute.

> A governmental unit may not ... deny employment to, terminate the employment of, or discriminate with respect to employment against, a person that is or has been a debtor under this title or a bankrupt or a debtor under the Bankruptcy Act, or another person with whom such bankrupt or debtor has been associated, solely because such bankrupt or debtor is or has been a debtor under the Bankruptcy Act.

In the employment area, this means that a public employer CANNOT fire you or refuse to hire you BECAUSE of your bankruptcy. However, a public employer can still fire you for other reasons. Therefore, don't give anyone an excuse to fire you. (I'll tell you more about this anti-discrimination law in Chapter 15.)

Discrimination by Private Employers

Private employers also CANNOT fire you or refuse to hire you. 11 U.S.C. § 525(b) prohibits private employers from discriminating against you just because you filed for bankruptcy.

As before, let me give you a feel for this with the relevant part of the statute.

> (b) No private employer may terminate the employment of, or discriminate with respect to employment against, an individual who is or has been a debtor under this title, a debtor or bankrupt under the Bankruptcy Act, or an individual associated with such bankrupt, solely because such debtor or bankrupt -
>
> (1) is or has been a debtor under this title or a debtor or bankrupt under the Bankruptcy Act;
>
> (2) has been insolvent before the commencement of a case under this title or during the case but before the grant or denial of a discharge; or
>
> (3) has not paid a debt that is dischargeable in a case under this title or that was discharged under the Bankruptcy Act.

Unfortunately, however, a private employer can probably refuse to hire you based on other information, like your otherwise bad credit report. It's often difficult to know whether an employer has refused to hire you BECAUSE of your bankruptcy or for another reason. Similarly, an employer may cite another reason for firing you.

You might want to talk to an attorney if you think that an employer—public or private—has discriminated against you because of your bankruptcy. Or, you might want to tell the employer about this anti-discrimination law. That might be enough to correct the problem.

Chapter 15

Education & Discrimination

Education is the best provision for old age.

Aristotle

As part of your quest to survive and prosper after bankruptcy, you may want to continue your education. However, you might think that your bankruptcy will prevent you from getting government student loans or other financial assistance. Fortunately, you should find that your bankruptcy will not prevent you from pursuing your higher education goals. In Section I, I'll tell you about your many options for education finance.

You might also think that you bankruptcy will prevent you from getting government benefits or privileges. In the past, governmental agencies have denied public housing, welfare benefits, and drivers' licenses to people who filed for bankruptcy. Fortunately, things have changed. In Section II, I'll tell you about the federal law that protects you from these kinds of discrimination.

I. Education

One way to survive and prosper after bankruptcy is to continue your education. That's what I did. However, it costs a lot of money to go to school, even if you go to a state-supported school. Therefore, unless you have the funds, you'll need to receive loans or grants. Let's talk about the most common loans and grants.

Government Education Loans

The most common form of government-supported educational assistance is the Stafford Loan (formerly called the Guaranteed Student Loan). With this loan program, you apply to a private lender for the educational loan, and the government guarantees to repay the creditor if you default on the loan. Additionally, the government subsidizes the interest payments while you attend school. Therefore, you don't have to make ANY payments on the loan while you're in school. Even better, you NEVER have to repay the interest that accumulated while you were in school. This is a great program for students.

Because the government guarantees your loan, creditors have little to lose if they lend you the money. Therefore, it shouldn't be hard to find a lender. Your best bet is to speak with your school's financial aid department. Explain your financial situation to them. They'll know which lenders will work with you.

Can you really get these loans if a bankruptcy notation appears on your credit report? ABSOLUTELY! I received $7,500 in Guaranteed Student Loans for each of the three years that I attended law school. And that was only one year after I received my bankruptcy discharge. With the help of the Guaranteed Student Loan program, I turned my life around. Now I'm really surviving and prospering after bankruptcy. You can too!

CAUTION—I want to warn you about government-subsidized student loans. Congress has increased the enforcement and collection of student loans. It's very difficult to avoid repaying student loans. You can't even discharge them in bankruptcy unless they become due seven years before you file for bankruptcy. So be careful—repay your student loans. This will help to rebuild your credit history and get you back on your feet again.

Private Education Loans

Another way to finance your education is to borrow the money from a private lender. Several private lenders offer educational loans to students. However, these loans are similar to regular consumer loans. Therefore, the lender will review your credit report before it lends you any money.

If the bankruptcy notation or other bad credit information still appears on your credit reports, these lenders will probably reject your application. If this happens, you might want to find someone to co-sign the loan with you. If your co-signer's credit history is good enough, the lender may lend you the money. Then, the lender will report your repayment history on your credit reports. What a deal! You get to rebuild your credit history as you increase your education.

Remember—these commercial loans don't offer the generous terms found with the Stafford loan. The interest rate will probably approach the rate charged on other types of consumer loans. Additionally, your lender might not allow you to defer the interest payments while you attend school. Even if you can defer the payments, they'll accrue (add up) while you attend school. Then, when you start to repay your loan, you'll need to repay this interest with the rest of your loan.

Grants and Scholarships

Your bankruptcy filing should not prevent you from getting grants or scholarships. There should be no reason for a sponsoring agency to check your credit history when deciding whether to award you a grant or scholarship. Since you generally don't need to repay grants and scholarships, no one is concerned about your willingness and ability to repay the money.

II. Governmental Discrimination

In the last chapter, I told you about 11 U.S.C. section 525. If you remember, that's the federal law that prohibits public employers from discriminating against you. But section 525 does more than just protect you from employment discrimination. It also prevents governmental agencies from discriminating against you in other ways. Let me give you some examples.

Governmental agencies CANNOT deny you public housing, or evict you from public housing just because you filed for bankruptcy. Governmental agencies also CANNOT deny or cancel any public benefits, like welfare. Additionally, governmental agencies CANNOT withhold your college transcript or deny you a driver's license. The list goes on and on. Just remember, governmental agencies CANNOT discriminate against you just because you filed for bankruptcy.

To help you understand this law, let me give you the relevant portion of it. (It's long and boring. I'm only including it here for you legal buffs!)

> A governmental unit may not deny, revoke, suspend, or refuse to renew a license, permit, charter, franchise, or other similar grant to, condition such a grant to, discriminate with respect to such a grant against, ... a person that is or has been a debtor under this title or a bankrupt or a debtor under the Bankruptcy Act.

You must always remember—you are NOT a criminal because you filed for bankruptcy. If a governmental agency does discriminate against you in any of these ways, or in another way based solely on your bankruptcy, you should consult an attorney for assistance.

Chapter 16

Avoiding Credit Scams

The world wants to be deceived.

Sebastian Brant

BEWARE! You'll attract con artists of all colors and shades for many years to come. They'll try to take advantage of your need for credit and your willingness to pay handsomely for it. In this chapter, I'm going to tell you about several credit scams and tricks, and how to avoid them. But remember—con artists come up with new scams everyday. So be careful when you receive an offer from someone for some credit-related product or advice. Remember the old saying—if it sounds too good to be true—then it probably is.

Catalog Credit Cards (Wolves Posing as Bankcards)

One scam that you're almost certain to run across is the catalog credit card. Catalog credit cards are credit cards that allow you to buy merchandise from one company's catalog of merchandise. The typical "hook" to attract your interest is a high credit line—up to $5,000—with NO credit check. That's right, no credit check. So you're thinking to yourself that this is too good to be true. Well, read on.

First, to use your new credit line, you must purchase goods from the company's catalog. The type and value of these goods vary, but include such items as perfume, glassware, appliances, etc. Unfortunately, there are many problems with purchasing goods with a catalog credit card. First, these goods usually cost more than similar goods in regular retail establishments. Therefore, you're paying a big cost for this credit from the very beginning.

Second, many of these cards require that you make a large down payment for your purchase. This down payment typically ranges from 40% to 85% of the already inflated purchase price. (Are you starting to see how these companies can offer such high credit lines with no credit check?)

Because of the inflated purchase price, and the large down payment, these companies break-even when you buy the goods. Remember, they paid wholesale prices for their goods. With your large down payment, you've probably paid more than the wholesale cost of the merchandise up front. So the company has nothing to lose by offering you credit. Everything they collect from you is pure profit, with no risk to them at all.

Third, these companies make money by charging you for application fees, annual membership dues, and order processing. These fees can range up to $50 for each category. Again, a very expensive way to get credit.

Finally, many of these companies try to make money by promoting other credit-related offers to you. These offers include promotions for secured bankcards, other catalog credit cards, and books on "easy credit." And of course, these credit cards have high "processing" fees, high annual interest rates, and other charges that make them less than desirable. As for the books on "easy credit," just beware.

Examples of Catalog Credit Cards

I've listed the following cards to give you an idea of the offers you might receive for catalog credit cards. I obtained this information, with permission, from RAM Research' Cardsearch. Cardsearch is a wonderful publication that reports on every type of credit card you can imagine, including several excellent chapters on credit scams. If you'd like your own copy of Cardsearch, contact RAM Research. I've listed their address in Chapter 11.

I don't offer any opinion regarding the value of these particular cards. I'm only listing them here to give you an idea of what's out there. If you're interested in these cards, investigate ALL the terms and make sure that you're willing to pay the price for this credit.

Card Name: American Consumer Express
Issued From: Pompano, Florida
Cost: $20 **Charges:** No Interest
Payment History Reported: NO—However, they will write a reference letter for you.

You may only use the card to purchase items from a 32-page gift catalog. Items offered: perfumes, porcelain figures, glassware, etc. Cardholders must make a 50% down payment and pay 10% per month on the balance. For example, if you order item #2270 Desk Pen Set, it will cost you $20.40 ($16.95 plus $3.45 shipping) requiring a $10.20 down payment. (The same item sells locally for $7 - $9.)

The company also offers cardholders the chance to become AMERICAN CONSUMER EXPRESS card agents, and earn large commissions.

Card Name: NATIONAL CREDIT SAVERS GOLD CARD
Issued From: Ozark, Alabama
Cost: $39.95 **Charges:** No Interest
Payment History Reported: NO—However, they will write a reference letter for you.

You may only use the card to purchase items from the Consumer Specialty Company's 100-page "VISTA" catalog under the "MAXAM" brand name. Down payments vary from 40% to 85% depending on the item you order. Minimum down payment is $50. For example: if you order item #CF52AB 52" Ceiling Fan, it will cost you $112.20 ($102 plus $10.20 shipping) requiring a $50. down payment. (The same ceiling fan sells nationally for $50.)

Cardholders receive a credit repair manual written by Sam Pitts, the founder of **National Credit Savers.** You'll also receive an invitation for another catalog gold card called: **Family Shoppers Union Gold Card** for $49.95. Finally, you'll also receive offers for two higher-priced, secured VISA and MasterCards from **New Era Bank** and **First Interstate Bank** and book offers from "easy credit experts."

Promoting the Catalog Credit Cards

Besides offering you high credit lines with no credit check, the people and companies behind catalog credit cards usually promote them in one of two ways. First, they advertise them as credit rebuilding cards. Under this promotion, they say that you'll rebuild your credit history if you purchase items through the catalog and repay the purchase price over time. That sounds like a good offer. After all, that's what we're trying to do, right?

With these cards, unfortunately, the answer is usually—WRONG. Remember, to rebuild your credit history, you need to get the good credit history recorded with the major credit bureaus. Then, any creditor can see that you're becoming a better credit risk.

However, most of the catalog credit card issuers don't subscribe or report to the major credit bureaus. Therefore, no one other than the promoters of the card know about your repayment record. You WILL NOT rebuild your credit history if they don't report to the credit bureaus!

If you want to receive one of these cards, even after reading this section, then at least make sure that they report to the major credit bureaus. If they don't—and they probably don't—then it's better to pass on the offer.

The second way that catalog credit card issuers promote their cards is by making it sound like you're going to receive a bankcard. And usually, they'll push these cards as gold or platinum cards. That sounds like a good deal. If you believe their offers, you can get a gold card with a $5,000 credit line and no credit check. Remember, though, if it sounds too good to be true, then it probably is.

Unfortunately, most of these gold or platinum catalog credit card offers just aren't true. As we saw before, you may get a $5,000 credit line with no credit check. But, you must buy overpriced goods and make a large down payment. These cards are generally not worth your consideration.

To give you an idea of what to look for, I've listed a small sample of nationally-advertised catalog credit cards. The promoters of these cards generally offer them to people with bad credit:

Gold Cards	Platinum Cards
VISTA GOLD	PLATINUM PLUS
USA GOLD CARD	AMERICAN PLATINUM PLUS
UNIVERSITY GOLD CARD	
UNIVERSAL GOLD CARD	

Notice the use of "gold" and "platinum" in their names. They sound very good, don't they? Remember, I'm not expressing any opinion about the value of the cards listed above. I've only listed them to show you the many names and common use of "gold" and "platinum" in catalog credit cards. You must make your own decision about any of these cards. Just be careful, and investigate them fully before making any purchases or committing yourself in any way.

Final Words on Catalog Credit Cards

If you want to rebuild your credit history, it's probably better to obtain a secured bankcard. Unlike catalog credit card programs, most of the banks offering secured bankcard programs will report your repayment history to the major credit bureaus. Therefore, other creditors will know about your good credit history.

Although you must make an initial down payment with secured credit cards, they're still better than catalog credit cards. Remember, catalog credit cards require high down payments for your purchases—generally more than the cost of the product. Additionally, catalog credit cards DON'T report your credit history. Therefore, avoid catalog credit cards.

900 and 976 Numbers

Now let's talk about telephone scams. Con artists have found a new way to steal your money—pay-per-call telephone numbers. Most of these numbers have 900 and 976 prefixes. (It's NOT fraudulent to use 900 and 976 numbers. However, many scam artists use these numbers to promote credit-related scams. That's why I've included them in this section.)

900 and 976 numbers are special telephone numbers that the telephone companies have created for pay-per-call service. Companies lease these numbers from the telephone company, and then offer products or services to the public. Then, customers call the 900 or 976 number to receive the company's product or service.

While this may seem like the normal procedure for telephone service, there's a twist with 900 and 976 numbers. Instead of simply charging you for the cost of placing the telephone call, the telephone company also bills you for an additional amount. The additional amount is the charge for the product or service that you received when you called the 900 or 976 telephone number. Then, the telephone company and the company that leased the 900 or 976 number split the money.

Let me show you how this works. Let's say that you want to know your future. Therefore, you call a 900 or 976 number that promises to reveal your future—for the low price of $3.95 per minute. That's right, this service costs you $3.95 for every minute that you're on the phone.

If you're on the phone for five minutes, then you pay $19.75 for the call. The charge for this $19.75 appears on your telephone statement. Then, you pay the telephone company, the telephone company takes its share, and then the telephone company pays the fortune-telling business the remainder.

900 and 976 numbers have become very popular. You can spend your money on just about anything you can imagine. Common services available through these numbers are horoscopes, betting lines, sports information, and dating services.

However, there's another type of service that we need to talk about. Scam artists love to use 900 and 976 numbers for credit-related come-ons, generally for secured bankcards and catalog credit cards. You've probably seen the advertisements for them.

> $5,000 credit line guaranteed! ... No credit check! ... Everyone approved! ...

All you have to do is call the 900 or 976 number to order your card and the rest is history.

Unfortunately, if you do this, so is your money! These calls can cost you as much as $50 each—by the minute, or by the call. Therefore, a charge for $50 might appear on your telephone bill even if you were on the phone for less than a minute!

And what do you get for your money? You generally get an application for ONE secured bankcard from ONE bank, or ONE catalog credit card. You could find this out for yourself by doing some research. Besides, the costs will probably go up from there. The bank or processing company might want more money for "processing fees" or some other made-up cost.

Therefore, try to avoid 900 and 976 numbers for credit-related information and offers. Although recent legislation has allowed authorities to crack down on the worst abuses, scams still abound. You'll be better off if you do your own research and stick with known authorities in this area.

Advance-fee Loan Scams

Perhaps the most dangerous scam in the credit-related area is the advance-fee loan scam. With this scam, a company or individual offers to find you a loan, even if you have bad credit. However, to get this loan, you must pay the "loan broker" an advance fee. Let me tell you how this scam works.

Advance-fee loan brokers usually offer their services in the classified sections of newspapers and magazines. The advertisement promises that the loan broker will find you a loan, even if you have bad credit. However, to receive this loan, you must send an advance fee to the loan broker for arranging the loan.

For example, a loan broker may offer to find you $15,000 loan. To compensate the loan broker for this service, you must pay the broker a $400 fee. However, this isn't a normal arrangement where you pay for services when the broker completes them. Here, you must pay the loan broker BEFORE the broker finds the loan for you.

And, guess what happens? The loan broker NEVER finds anyone willing to lend you the money, and generally disappears with your money before the authorities catch on to the scam.

State and federal authorities are working on legislation to crack down on the abuses in this area. However, people continue to lose large sums of money to fly-by-night operations. According to the Council of Better Business Bureaus, more than 300,000 people complained about advance-fee loan scams in 1992.

Therefore, avoid anyone that offers to find you a loan if you prepay them for their services. You don't need to do this. Any reputable loan broker will recover for services from the loan amount. And remember, this scam comes in many forms and appears in several different media types.

For example, they might appear on cable television urging you to respond to an 800, 900, or 976 number. If you call the 900 or 976 number, you'll probably lose your money right away—or at least when the charge appears on your telephone bill. If you call the 800 number, the loan broker might ask you to charge the advance-fee to a credit card, or to send a check or money order. Either way, you've probably lost your money.

Final Words on Advance-Fee Loans

As always, I can't say that EVERY advance-fee loan offer is illegal or fails to deliver the promised loan. But BE CAREFUL! Check with your local Better Business Bureau or state consumer protection agency. You may also want to check with the Federal Trade Commission.

Even if these agencies haven't received bad information about the loan broker, proceed with caution. And if you DO lose your money, report the loan broker to these agencies right away. You may not get your money back, but at least you'll prevent other people from losing their money.

Credit Repair Companies

We've already talked about this scam, but it's worth revisiting. As you remember, a credit repair company is one that promises to repair your credit for a fee. The problem with this is that they often charge a great deal of money for their services, and usually don't accomplish what they promise. In addition, many of these credit repair companies are fly-by-night operations that disappear shortly after collecting money from unsuspecting consumers.

Because of the rampant abuse in this area, many states have enacted legislation to regulate credit repair companies. Today, most credit repair companies must meet several requirements BEFORE they can take your money. In this section, I want to tell you about these requirements.

However, before we get started, let me make one suggestion. I strongly urge you to repair your own credit. You can do EVERYTHING that the credit repair companies can do. In fact, you've already learned all of the techniques in this book. Therefore, don't pay a credit repair company several hundreds of dollars for something that you can easily do yourself.

O.K. I know some of you out there are going to want someone else to do this for you. Therefore, IF you really don't want to repair your own credit, at least let me tell you how to avoid the rip-offs.

Requirements on Credit Repair Companies

As I mentioned a moment ago, most states have enacted legislation to regulate credit repair companies. You'll find that most of these state laws are very similar. Therefore, to give you an idea of the requirements that credit repair companies must meet, I've included the full text of Florida's credit repair law in Appendix 4.

It would require too much space to include every state's credit repair law. However, you'll find that Florida's law contains the requirements that most other states use. Besides, I've also listed the remaining states that regulate credit repair companies and noted any differences from Florida's credit repair law. I've also listed the statute sections so that you can find the full text of your state law. You'll find all of this information in Appendix 4.

With knowledge of your state's credit repair law, you can wisely select a credit repair company. You may find, however, that NO company can comply with the law. If this happens, don't waste your money. Repair your credit yourself. You CAN do it!

Sample Credit Repair Statute

To help you understand these credit repair statutes, let's go over the most important sections of Florida's credit repair statute.

Bonding Requirements

Most states require credit repair companies to obtain a bond before they can accept any money for uncompleted services. In Florida, a credit repair company must obtain a $10,000 bond before it can accept payment. (Remember, this is for services that the credit repair company has NOT yet completed. If the credit repair company HAS completed the service, and you're happy with it, then it can collect your money.) Then, if the company fails to deliver the promised services, and won't return your money, you can recover your money from the bonding company.

Now how can you use this information? First, review Appendix 4 to see if your state has a credit repair statute. (Remember, these are the states that had credit repair laws at the time of publication. Your state might have passed legislation since then.) If it does, see if the law requires credit repair companies to obtain a bond. If so, you'll know what to ask when talking to the credit repair company.

If you ask them if they have a bond, and they say no, watch out! Under most state laws, they can bypass the bonding requirement, but only if they complete the services before they take your money. Therefore, if they don't have the required bond, DON'T give them any money until they finish the job to your satisfaction.

Explanation of Your Rights

Most state laws also require that the credit repair companies explain your rights under the Fair Credit Reporting Act and any state laws. Your rights include everything that we talked about in this book. For example, you know that you have the right to obtain your credit reports, and to contest any mistakes in your credit reports. Generally, the credit repair companies must explain your rights in writing, and must have you sign a paper that says you know about your rights.

We need these laws because most people DON'T know their rights under federal and state law. Credit repair companies take advantage of this, and suggest that they can manipulate the law to your advantage—for a small fee, of course. But remember—YOU can do anything that the credit repair companies can do.

However, remember these laws if you do want a credit repair company to help you. If the credit repair company doesn't explain your rights, ask them to do so. If they're reluctant, you should probably not risk your money with that company.

Clear Explanation of Services and Written Contract

Most states also require that the credit repair company explain, in detail, every service they intend to do for you. Additionally, most states require that they give you an estimate of how long it will take to complete these services. Generally, they must also explain these things to you in writing.

Most states require a written explanation because many credit repair companies describe their services in vague terms. When you first meet, they tell you that they'll remove all the bad information from your credit reports. But later, when they can't remove everything, they change their earlier statements. They say, "We never promised to remove that information, just this and that." However, if you have their promises and explanations in writing, they can't do this.

Three to Five Days to Cancel the Contract

The last requirement that we'll review is the cancellation clause. Most states allow you to cancel the contract with the credit repair company within three to five days after you sign it. This allows you time to change your mind, and prevents aggressive sales agents from tricking you during your first meeting.

This is a great requirement. Don't forget it! If you do hire a credit repair company, remember that in most states with credit repair legislation, you can cancel the contract within three to five days. Don't be bullied or tricked by an aggressive sales pitch!

Final Words on Credit Scams

Remember—if it sounds too good to be true, then it probably is. Be a careful and informed consumer. If you run across a suspicious credit offer, be careful. If possible, you should investigate the background of the company behind the offer. You can do this by checking with your local Better Business Bureau, or the Attorney General or Consumer Protection office for your state. They can tell you if anyone has complained about the offer or its promoters.

Chapter 17

Starting a New Life

We should be careful to get out of an experience only the wisdom that is in it - and stop there; lest we be like the cat that sits down on a hot stove-lid. She will never sit down on a hot stove lid again - and that is well; but also she will never sit down on a cold one any more.

Mark Twain [Samuel Langhorne Clemens]

You took a bold step toward survival and prosperity when you filed for bankruptcy. Sure, many people still don't understand bankruptcy, or why you needed to use it. However, more people than ever understand and accept what you've been through. YOU must also learn to accept your bankruptcy. IT HAPPENED! Now move on.

However, before you get too far, let's make a promise to one another. Let's promise that we'll NEVER again need to use bankruptcy. NEVER! EVER! It's just not worth it.

To keep our promise, though, we'll need to avoid the problems of the past, and learn from our mistakes. If you filed for bankruptcy because you had major medical expenses and didn't have medical insurance, then get insurance. (I know you've already done this.) If you filed for bankruptcy because you lost your job, then develop a plan for surviving a future job loss.

These are hard lessons. But you've probably learned them well. I know that I have.

BUT, there's another lesson than many people never learn, even people that have experienced the pains of bankruptcy. What lesson? You're probably ahead of me on this one. That's right—MONEY MANAGEMENT!

Many people face bankruptcy because they lose control of their finances. You may be one of those people. Do you struggle at the end of each month to meet everyday living expenses? Are you becoming deeper in debt to friends or family? Are you getting back into the same credit trap that brought you down before?

If so, you may be a problem spender. There are many reasons to spend money—some good, some not so good. You may be spending money for the wrong reasons—or spending too much money for the right reasons. Whatever! The point is this—you MUST get control of your money. Where does it come from? Where does it go? These are questions we'll try to answer together in this chapter.

Creating a Budget

Probably the best thing that you can do for yourself after bankruptcy is to create a budget. Yuck! There's that word. Well, call it what you like—a plan, strategy, etc. The point is that you need something to help you control impulse buying and overspending. That something is a budget—or (insert your word.)

You say you've never made a budget before? Well, it's really very simple, and we're going to do it step-by-step together. Ready?

The first step in making your budget is to figure out how much money you're spending every month. Do you know? Most people don't. They just know that they don't have any money left over at the end of the month. But we're going to put a stop to that right now. To get a clear picture of where YOUR money goes each month, we're going to keep track of EVERY expenditure you make for the next month.

That's right. We're going to record everything. Just bought lunch? Write it down. Picked up some groceries on the way home from work? Record that too. Yes, even track the quarters you plug into game machines. Write down every expense for the next month—to the penny.

But we're going to make this very easy. Let's just start this for one week. Buy a small notebook and record every expense you incur for one week. (It's probably best to start this at the beginning of the month, then you'll have an accurate count for one full month.) I carry a pocket "Daytimer" notebook that includes a section for daily expenses. But, a pocket notebook or even a piece of paper will work as well. This is how your daily record might look:

March 18

Toll	.75
Lunch	5.82
Magazine	3.50
Toll	.75
Groceries	16.52
Dinner	11.79

That's all there is to it. Just remember to write down EVERYTHING. It won't take you very long to get used to this.

Creating Your Weekly Expense Record

After faithfully recording your daily expenses for one week, it's time for the next step. You now need to transfer your daily records into categories and total the amounts. This begins the process of totaling your expenditures for the month, which is our ultimate goal. But here, we're only concerned with the expenses for one week—the week you've just recorded.

To total your expenses for the week, you'll need to create a record that includes various expense categories. These categories can be anything you choose—it's your record. To give you an idea of what your weekly expense record might look like, look at the sample record below.

Rent	$
Groceries	
Eating Out	
Entertainment	
Magazines	
Gasoline	
Taxi	
Tolls	
Electric	
Phone	
Total	

The various expense categories in this weekly record came from the expenses I had during a particular week. That's how you'll create your categories as well. Did you spend money last week on chewing gum? You might need to include a category for chewing gum. Did you take a trip to the mountains last month? Then you'll probably need a category for travel in the weekly expense record. You get the idea.

Repeat this process for the remaining three weeks in the month. Write down every daily expense and then create a weekly expense record to total the expenses for that week into categories. Remember—the last week in the month may have more that seven days. It could have as many as 10 days. That's O.K.

Creating a Monthly Expense Report

Now that you've recorded your expenses for the entire month, you can create your monthly expense report. This is nothing more than the compilation of your four weekly expense reports. Let's look at an example.

Look at Diagram 17-1. This is a sample monthly report that John Consumer prepared. It was easy for him to do this. The four weekly expense reports provided the categories for the monthly report and the totals for each category. All John had to do was add them up.

And you can do the same thing. Use your weekly expense reports to create your monthly report. Do this by transferring each category from your weekly reports to the monthly report. Then, transfer the totals from each category for each week to the monthly report.

When you've completed this process, you can see at one glance where your money went. The monthly expense report shows you what you spent your money on that month and how much you spent for each category. This is the first step to gaining control of your finances. You're almost there! But there's one more step.

Creating Your Budget

At the end of the month, look at your expenses. It may surprise you! Do you spend $6 every day on lunch? $2 on tolls? You may find that you can save money here and there by eliminating unnecessary expenditures. For example, do you need to eat lunch out every day? Can't you occasionally bring your lunch to work? Do you need to take the toll road into town, or are there other roads without tolls that you can take? These are personal decisions, but probably ones you can easily make.

And now it's time to make those decisions. That's right—it's budget time. How do you do it? It's easy. Just work with what you already have—the monthly expense report. Examine each of your categories and look closely at the monthly totals. Do you like what you see? Or, do you think that you could cut back in some places? Make these decisions, one by one, on your monthly expense report. Then, record your "goal" on your budget. Let me show you what I mean.

Look at Diagram 17-2. You'll notice that the budget looks a lot like the monthly expense report. In fact, it IS the monthly expense report—with two additions. I've added a column called "Goal" and another called "+ or -." The "Goal" column is your budget for each category. In the sample budget above, John decided that he could cut back on some of his monthly expenses in April.

For example, the electric expense for March was $125. It was still a little cool in March and John ran the heater quite often. But, John expects that April will be more moderate, and he plans to be a bit more frugal. Therefore, he thinks he can keep the electric bill down to $100 in April. To record this goal, John writes "$100" as his "Goal" for April's electric expense. You'll notice other reductions as well.

Now look at the "+ or -" column. This is where you record the difference between your actual expenses and your goal. For example, John's April goal for electric expense was $100. But April was cooler than John had imagined and he wasn't as frugal as he'd planned. Therefore, his actual electric expense for April was $115. This was $15 more than John's goal for April. In the "+ or -" column, then, John should record +15. This lets him know that he was over his goal by $15.

With that information, John could do one of two things. First, he could promise to do better next month and again shoot for the $100 goal. If so, John would have $100 as his goal for May.

John's second option is to revise his goal. Maybe $100 was too optimistic. Perhaps $115 is a more realistic goal. It's up to John to decide.

And it's up to you to decide your own goals. Making a budget doesn't mean that you have to deprive yourself of all the luxuries in life. In fact, you don't have to deprive yourself at all. It's up to you. Your goal should be to meet your monthly expenses and have extra money to put away for emergencies and investments.

To construct your own budget, do what John did. Use your monthly expense report as a guide. Then draw in the two additional columns for the "Goal" and the "+ or -." In the "Goal" column, record your goal for each budget category. Then, you can record your weekly totals right on the budget. At the end of the month, total each category and figure out whether you were above or below your goal. Then, record that amount, and show whether you were above or below the goal with a "+" or "-."

In no time at all, you'll have a good feel for your finances. You'll know exactly where your money goes each month, and what expenses are unnecessary. With that information, you should never lose control of your finances again. Therefore, you'll also NEVER AGAIN face bankruptcy!

For your convenience, I've included a sample budget form that you can copy and use for your budget. I've left all of the spaces for the expense categories blank so that you can create your own categories. You may not like the ones that John Consumer used.

You'll find the sample budget record in Diagram 17-3. You can make several copies of this diagram—one for each month. Or, if you have many budget categories, you may need to use more than one copy for each month. Remember—it's up to you.

Budgeting Help

In this chapter, we've looked at a way to gain control of your finances. BUT, you MAY have a problem with spending. You probably know if you do, although you may not readily admit it to yourself. If you are a spender, and your bankruptcy hasn't really stopped this, BE CAREFUL!

You might consider seeking out the services of a group or organization that will help you to curb your spending habits. One such organization is Debtor's Anonymous. Debtor's Anonymous provides a 12-step program similar to Alcoholic's Anonymous. They hold meetings nationwide. To attend a meeting, consult your local directory assistance or send a self-addressed stamped envelope to:

Debtor's Anonymous
General Services Board
P.O. Box 20322
New York, NY 10025
(212) 642-8222

Another organization that you may want to consider is the Consumer Credit Counseling Service, or CCCS. The CCCS is a non-profit organization that will help you in budgeting, and in negotiating with your creditors if you're having financial problems.

However, you should probably know that CCCS is organized and sponsored by ... major creditors. Therefore they might tell you to pay all of your debts to all of your creditors—even if that may not be the best option for you. Take that into consideration before you accept their help. You can contact them at:

8701 Georgia Avenue
Suite 507
Silver Springs, MD 20910
(800) 388-2227

Final Words

We've come a long way together and accomplished a great deal! I hope that our journey has been both educational and rewarding for you, and that this book has provided not only knowledge, but inspiration as well. And if you can take only one piece of advice away from this experience, let it be this. You are not a failure for having experienced the protection of bankruptcy. If anything, you are probably much wiser! GOOD LUCK!

Diagram 17-1
[Sample Monthly Expenses Report]

Monthly Expenses Report for March 1993					
Week	1	2	3	4	Total
Rent	710.00	0.00	0.00	0.00	710.00
Groceries	65.72	35.28	27.35	75.89	204.24
Eating Out	37.00	15.00	0.00	52.78	104.78
Entertainment	0.00	22.72	15.00	0.00	37.72
Magazines	7.92	0.00	0.00	5.76	13.68
Gasoline	16.00	15.75	18.00	16.00	65.75
Taxi	0.00	0.00	0.00	17.00	17.00
Tolls	1.50	3.50	3.00	2.50	10.50
Electric	0.00	0.00	0.00	125.00	125.00
Phone	0.00	78.94	0.00	0.00	78.94
Books	0.00	0.00	0.00	18.00	18.00
Clothes	22.57	0.00	0.00	35.75	58.32
Medical	0.00	0.00	0.00	25.00	25.00
Totals	860.71	171.19	63.35	373.68	1468.93

Diagram 17-2
[Sample Budget]

Budget for April 1993							
Week	1	2	3	4	Actual	Goal	+ or -
Rent						710.00	
Groceries						204.24	
Eating Out						104.78	
Entertainment						37.72	
Magazines						13.68	
Gasoline						65.75	
Taxi						17.00	
Tolls						10.50	
Electric						100.00	
Phone						78.94	
Books						18.00	
Clothes						58.32	
Medical						25.00	
Totals						1443.93	

Diagram 17-3
[Budget]

Budget for ____________ 199_							
Week	1	2	3	4	Actual	Goal	+ or -
Totals							

Bankruptcy Courts

State	Telephone	Address
Alabama	(205) 237-5631	12th & Noble Streets, Anniston, AL 36201
	(205) 731-1615	1800 5th Ave., North, Birmingham, AL 35203
	(205) 353-2817	P.O. Box 1289, Decatur, AL 35602
	(205) 441-5391	201 St. Louis Street, Mobile, AL 36602
	(205) 223-7250	P.O. Box 1248, Montgomery, AL 36102
	(205) 752-0426	P.O. Box 3226, Tuscaloosa, AL 35403
Alaska	(907) 271-2655	Federal Building, 605 W. 4th Ave., Suite 138, Anchorage, AK 99501
Arizona	(602) 514-7321	230 North First Ave., 5th Floor, Phoenix, AZ 85025
	(602) 670-6304	110 S. Church St., Suite 8112, Tucson, AZ 85701
Arkansas	(501) 324-6357	P.O. Drawer 2381, Little Rock, AR 72203-2381
California	(209) 487-5217	5301 Federal Building, 1130 O St., Fresno, CA 93721
	(213) 894-3118	906 U.S. Courthouse, 312 N. Spring St., Los Angeles, CA 90012
	(209) 521-5160	P.O. Box 5276, Modesto, CA 95352
	(510) 273-7212	P.O. Box 214, 1300 Clay St., Room 300, Oakland, CA 94612
	(916) 551-2662	8308 U.S. Courthouse, 650 Capitol Mall, Sacramento, CA 95814
	(714) 383-5721	699 N. Arrowhead Ave., Room 105, San Bernardino, CA 92401
	(619) 557-5620	5-N-26 U.S. Courthouse, 940 Front St., San Diego, CA 92189
	(415) 556-2250	235 Pine, 19th Floor, San Francisco, CA 94104
	(408) 291-7286	280 South First St., Room 3035, San Jose, CA 95113
	(714) 836-2993	P.O. Box 12600, Santa Ana, CA 92712
	(707) 525-8520	99 South E. Street, Santa Rosa, CA 95404
Colorado	(303) 844-4045	U.S. Custom House, 721 19th Street, Room 115, Denver, CO 80202-2508
Connecticut	(203) 579-5808	U.S. Courthouse, 915 Lafayette Blvd., Bridgeport, CT 06604
	(203) 240-3675	712 U.S. Courthouse, 450 Main St., Hartford, CT 06103

State	Telephone	Address
Delaware	(302) 573-6174	Lockbox 38, 844 King St., Federal Building, Wilmington, DE 19801
District of Columbia	(202) 273-0992	4400 U.S. Courthouse, 3rd & Constitution Aves., NW, Washington, DC 20001
Florida	(305) 356-7224	299 E. Broward Blvd., Room 206A, Ft. Lauderdale, FL 33301
	(904) 232-2827	P.O. Box 559, Jacksonville, FL 32201
	(305) 536-5216	1401 Federal Building, 51 SW First Ave. Suite 1517, Miami, FL 33130
	(407) 648-6365	135 W. Central Blvd., Suite #950, Orlando, FL 32801
	(904) 435-8475	220 W. Garden St., Pensacola, FL 32501
	(904) 681-7500	227 N. Bronough St., Room 3120, Tallahassee, FL 32301
	(813) 225-7068	4921 Memorial Highway, Room 200, Tampa, FL 33634
	(407) 655-6774	(Direct Inquiries to the Miami Office)
Georgia	(404) 331-5435	1340 R.B. Russell Building, 75 Spring St., SW, Atlanta, GA, 30303
	(706) 649-7837	P.O. Box 2147, Columbus, GA 31902
	(912) 752-3506	P.O. Box 1957, Macon, GA 31202-1957
	(404) 251-5583	P.O. Box 2328, Newnan, GA 30264
	(912) 652-4100	P.O. Box 8347, Savannah, GA 31412
Hawaii	(808) 541-1791	P.O. Box 50121, New Federal Building, Honolulu, HI 96850
Idaho	(208) 334-9337	550 W. Fort St., Box 042, Boise, ID 83724
Illinois	(312) 435-5587	U.S. Courthouse, 219 S. Dearborn St., Chicago, IL 60604
	(217) 431-4820	P.O. Box 657, Danville, IL 61834-0657
	(618) 482-9400	750 Missouri Ave., East St. Louis, IL 62201
	(309) 671-7035	156 Federal Building, 100 NE Monroe St., Peoria, IL 61602
	(815) 987-4350	211 S. Court St., Rockford, IL 61101
	(217) 492-4550	P.O. Box 2438, 226 U.S. Courthouse, 600 E. Monroe St., Springfield, IL 62705
Indiana	(812) 465-6440	352 Federal Building, Evansville, IN 47708
	(219) 420-5100	Federal Building, Room 1188, 1300 S. Harrison St., Ft. Wayne, IN 46802
	(219) 881-3335	610 Connecticut St., Gary, IN 46402
	(317) 226-6710	123 U.S. Courthouse, 46 E. Ohio St., Indianapolis, IN 46204
	(812) 948-5254	121 W. Spring St., New Albany, IN 47150
	(219) 236-8247	224 U.S. Courthouse, 204 S. Main St., South Bend, IN 46601-2196
	(812) 238-1550	203 Post Office Building, 30N. 7th St., Terre Haute, IN 47808

State	Telephone	Address
Iowa	(319) 362-9696	P.O. Box 74890, Cedar Rapids, IA 52407
	(515) 284-6230	P.O. Box 9264, Des Moines, IA 50306
	(712) 252-3757	U.S. Courthouse, 320 6th St., Room 117, Sioux City, IA 51101
Kansas	(913) 236-3732	155 Federal Building, L812 N. 7th St., Kansas City, KS 66101
	(913) 295-2750	444 SE Quincy St., Room 240, Topeka, KS 66683
	(316) 269-6486	167 U.S. Courthouse, 401 N. Market St., Wichita, KS 67202
Kentucky	(606) 233-2608	P.O. Box 1111, Lexington, KY 40588
	(502) 582-5145	412-C G. Snyder Courthouse and Customs House, 601 W. Broadway, Louisville, KY 40202
Louisiana	(318) 473-7387	300 Jackson St., Alexandria, LA 71301
	(504) 389-0211	412 N. 4th St., Room 301, Baton Rouge, LA 70802
	(504) 589-6506	501 Magazine St., New Orleans, LA 70130
	(318) 948-3451	P.O. Box J, Opelousas, LA 70571
	(318) 676-4267	500 Fannin St., Room 4-B18, Shreveport, LA 71101
Maine	(207) 945-0348	P.O. Box 1109, Bangor, ME 04402-1109
	(207) 780-3482	P.O. Box 48, Portland, ME 04112
Maryland	(410) 962-2688	U.S. Courthouse, 101 W. Lombard St., Baltimore, MD 21201
	(301) 443-7010	451 Hungerford Dr., Rockville, MD 20850
Massachusetts	(617) 565-6080	Boston Federal Office Building, 1101 Causeway St., Boston, MA 02222-1074
	(508) 793-0542	10 Mechanic St., Worcester, MA 01608
Michigan	(517) 892-1506	P.O. Box X911, Bay City, MI 48707
	(313) 226-7064	231 W. Lafayette, Detroit, MI 48226
	(313) 766-5050	600 Chuch St., Flint, MI 48502
	(616) 456-2693	P.O. Box 3310, Grand Rapids, MI 49501
	(906) 226-2117	P.O. Box 909, Marquette, MI 49855
Minnesota	(218) 720-5253	416 U.S. Courthouse, 515 W. 1st St., Duluth, MN 55802
	(218) 739-4671	118 S. Mills St., Fergus Falls, MN 56537
	(612) 348-1855	600 Towle Building, 330 Second Ave., South, Minneapolis, MN 55401
	(612) 290-3184	200 U.S. Federal Building, 316 N. Robert St., St. Paul, MN 55101

State	Telephone	Address
Mississippi	(601) 369-2596	P.O. Drawer 867, Arberdeen, MS 39730-0867
	(601) 432-5542	725 Washington Loop, Room 117, Biloxi, MS 39530-2264
	(601) 965-5301	P.O. Drawer 2448, Jackson, MS 39225-2448
Missouri	(816) 426-3321	U.S. Courthouse, 811 Grand Ave., Kansas City, MO 64106
	(314) 539-2222	702 U.S. Courthouse, 1114 Market St., St. Louis, MO 63101
Montana	(406) 782-3354	273 Federal Building, 400 N. Main St., Butte, MT 59701
Nebraska	(402) 221-4687	P.O. Box 428 Downtown Sta., Omaha, NB 68101
	(402) 437-5100	460 Federal Building, 100 Centennial Mall N., Lincoln, NB 68508
Nevada	(702) 388-6257	300 Las Vegas Blvd. South, Las Vegas, NV 89101
	(702) 784-5559	4005 Federal Building & Courthouse, 300 Booth St., Reno, NV 89509
New Hampshire	(603) 666-7532	275 Chestnut St., Room 404, Manchester, NH 03101
New Jersey	(609) 757-5023	15 N. 7th St., Camden, NJ 08102
	(201) 645-2630	970 Broad St., Newark, NJ 07102
	(609) 989-2126	U.S. Post Office & Courthouse, 402 E. State St., Trenton, NJ 08607
New Mexico	(505) 766-2051	P.O. Box 546, 9th Floor, 500 Gold Ave. SW, Albuquerque, NM 87103-0546
New York	(518) 472-4226	P.O. Box 398, Albany, NY 12201-0398
	(718) 330-2188	75 Clinton St., Brooklyn, NY 11201
	(716) 846-4130	310 U.S. Courthouse, 68 Court St., Buffalo, NY 14202
	(516) 361-8601	601 Veteran's Memorial Hwy., Hauppauge, NY 11788
	(212) 668-2867	1 Bowling Green, New York, NY 10004-1408
	(914) 452-4200	176 Church St., Poughkeepsie, NY 12601
	(716) 263-3148	212 U.S. Courthouse, 100 State St., Rochester, NY 14614
	(315) 793-8101	311 U.S. Courthouse, Room 230, North Broad Street, Utica, NY 13501
	(516) 832-8801	1635 Privado Rd., Westbury, NY 11590
	(914) 682-6117	101 E. Post Rd., White Plains, NY 10601
North Carolina	(704) 344-6103	401 W. Trade St., Charlotte, NC 28202
	(919) 333-5647	P.O. Box 26100, Greensboro, NC 27420-6100
	(919) 237-0248	P.O. Drawer 2807, Wilson, NC 27894-2807

State	Telephone	Address
North Dakota	(701) 239-5129	P.O. Box 1110, Fargo, ND 58107
Ohio	(216) 375-5840	455 Federal Building, 2 S. Main St., Akron, OH 44308
	(216) 489-4426	201 Cleveland Ave. SW, Canton, OH 44702
	(513) 684-2572	735 U.S. Courthouse, 100 E. 5th St., Cincinnati, OH 45202
	(216) 522-7555	419 U.S. Courthouse, 201 Superior Ave., Cleveland, OH 44114
	(614) 469-2087	124 U.S. Courthouse, 85 Marconi Blvd., Columbus, OH 43215
	(513) 225-2516	705 Federal Building & U.S. Courthouse, 200 W. 2nd St., Dayton, OH 45402
	(419) 259-6440	411 U.S. Courthouse, 1716 Spielbusch Ave., Toledo, OH 43624
	(216) 746-7702	P.O. Box 147, U.S. Post Office Building, Youngstown, OH 44501
Oklahoma	(405) 231-5143	215 D.A. McGee Ave., Oklahoma City, OK 73102
	(918) 758-0127	P.O. Box 1347, Okmulgee, OK 74447
	(918) 581-7181	320 Grantson Building, 111 W. 5th St., Tulsa, OK 74103
Oregon	(503) 687-4020	125 E. 8th St.., Eugene, OR 97401
	(503) 326-2231	1001 SW 5th Ave., 9th Floor, Portland, OR 97204
Pennsylvania	(814) 453-7580	P.O. Box 1755, Eerie, PA 16507
	(717) 782-2260	P.O. Box 908, Harrisburg, PA 17108
	(215) 597-1644	3726 U.S. Courthouse, 601 Market St., Philadelphia, PA 19106
	(412) 644-2700	1602 Federal Building, 1000 Liberty Ave., Pittsburgh, PA 15222
	(215) 320-5255	4104 E. Shore Office Building, 45 S. Front St., Reading, PA 19602
	(717) 826-6450	217 Federal Building, 197 S. Main St., Wilkes-Barre, PA 18701
Rhode Island	(401) 528-4477	380 Westminster Mall,6th Floor, Providence, RI 02903
South Carolina	(803) 765-5436	P.O. Box 1448, Columbia, SC 29202
South Dakota	(605) 330-4541	P.O. Box 5060, Sioux Falls, SD 57117-5060
Tennessee	(615) 752-5163	31 East 11th Street, Chattanooga, TN 37402
	(901) 424-9751	P.O. Box 1527, Jackson, TN 38302
	(901) 544-3202	200 Jefferson Ave., Suite 413, Memphis, TN 38103
	(615) 736-5590	207 Customs House, 701 Broadway, Nashville, TN 37203

State	Telephone	Address
Texas	(512) 482-5237	816 Congress, First City Centre, Room 1420, Austin, TX 78701
	(409) 839-2617	350 Magnolia, Room 117, Beaumont, TX 77701
	(512) 888-3483	615 Leopard Street, Room 113, Corpus Christi, TX 78476
	(214) 767-0814	14-A-7 U.S. Courthouse, 1100 Commerce St., Dallas, TX 75242
	(512) 775-2021	111 E. Broadway, Room L-100, Del Rio, TX 78840
	(915) 534-6730	511 E. San Antonio St., Room 101, El Paso, TX 79901
	(817) 334-3802	501 W. 10th Street, 310 U.S. Courthouse, Fort Worth, TX 76102
	(713) 250-5150	U.S. Courthouse, 515 Rusk Ave., Houston, TX 77002
	(806) 743-7336	102 Federal Building, 1205 Texas Ave., Lubbock, TX 79401-4002
	(915) 683-2001	P.O. Box 10708, Midland, TX 79702
	(915) 445-4228	P.O. Box 191, Pecos, TX 79772
	(512) 229-6720	P.O. Box 1439, San Antonio, TX 78295
	(903) 592-1212	211 W. Ferguson St., 4th Floor, Tyler, TX 75702
	(817) 756-0307	P.O. Box 608, Waco, TX 76703
	(817) 767-1902	P.O. Box 1234, Wichita Falls, TX 76307
Utah	(801) 524-5157	350 S. Main St., Salt Lake City, UT 84101
Vermont	(802) 773-0219	P.O. Box 6648, Rutland, VT 05702-6648
Virginia	(703) 557-1716	P.O. Box 19247, Alexandria, VA 22320
	(703) 434-8327	P.O. Box 1326, Harrisonburg, VA 22801
	(804) 845-1037	P.O. Box 6400, Lynchburg, VA 24505
	(804) 247-0196	P.O. Box 497, Newport News, VA 23607
	(804) 441-6651	P.O. Box 1938, Norfolk, VA 23501
	(804) 771-2878	P.O. Box 676, Richmond, VA 23206
	(703) 982-6391	P.O. Box 2390, Roanoke, VA 24010
Washington	(206) 553-7545	315 Park Place Building, 1200 6th Ave., Seattle, WA 98101
	(509) 353-2404	P.O. Box 2164, Spokane, WA 99210
	(206) 593-6310	1717 Pacific Ave., Suite #2100, Tacoma, WA 98402
West Virginia	(304) 233-1655	P.O. Box 70, Wheeling, WV 26003
Wisconsin	(715) 839-2980	P.O. Box 5009, Eau Claire, WI 54702-5009
	(608) 264-5178	P.O. Box 548, Madison, WI 53701-0548
	(414) 297-3293	517 E. Wisconsin Ave., Room 126, Milwaukee, WI 53202
Wyoming	(307) 261-5440	111 S. Wolcott St., Room 101, Casper, WY 82601
	(307) 772-2191	P.O. Box 1107, Cheyenne, WY 82003

State Consumer Protection Agencies

State	Telephone	Address
Alabama	(205) 242-7334 (800) 392-5658	Consumer Protection Division, Office of Attorney General, 11 South Union St., Montgomery, AL 36130
Arizona	(602) 542-3702 (800) 352-8431	Complaint Intake Center, Office of Attorney General, 1275 West Washington St., Phoenix, AZ 85007
Arkansas	(501) 682-2341 (800) 482-8982	Advocacy Division of Attorney General's Office, 200 Tower Bldg., 323 Center St., Little Rock, AR 72201
California	(916) 445-1254 (800) 344-9940	Department of Consumer Affairs, Consumer Assistance Office, 1020 N. St., Rm. 501, Sacramento, CA 95814
Colorado	(303) 620-4500 (800) 332-2071	Consumer Protection Unit, Office of the Attorney General, 110 16th St., 10th Fl., Denver, CO 80202
Connecticut	(203) 566-4999 (800) 842-2649	Department of Consumer Protection, State Office Bldg., 165 Capitol Ave., Hartford, CT 06106
Delaware	(302) 577-3250	Division of Consumer Affairs, 820 North French St., Delaware State Office Bldg., 4th Fl., Wilmington, DE 19801
District of Columbia	(202) 727-7000	Department of Consumer and Regulatory Affairs, 614 H. St., NW, Rm. 108, Washington, DC 20001
Florida	(904) 488-2226 (800) 342-2176 (800) 327-3382	Division of Consumer Services, Dept. of Agriculture and Consumer Services, 218 Mayo Bldg., Tallahassee, FL 32399
Georgia	(404) 651-8600 (404) 656-3790 (800) 869-1123	Governor's Office of Consumer Affairs, 2 Martin Luther King Dr., SE, Room 356, East Tower, Atlanta, GA 30334
Hawaii	(808) 586-2630	Office of Consumer Protection, Dept. of Commerce and Consumer Affairs, 828 Fort Street Mall, Room 600B, Honolulu, HI 96813

State	Telephone	Address
Idaho	(208) 334-3313 (800) 432-3545	Idaho Department of Finance, Statehouse, Boise, ID 83720-2700
Illinois	(217) 782-9011 (800) 252-8666	Consumer Protection Division, Office of Attorney General, 500 South 2nd St., Springfield, IL 62706
Indiana	(317) 232-6330 (800) 382-5516	Consumer Protection Division, Office of Attorney General, 219 State House, Indianapolis, IN 46204
Iowa	(515) 281-5926	Consumer Protection Division, Office of Attorney General, 1300 East Walnut, 2nd Fl., Des Moines, IA 50319
Kansas	(913) 296-3751 (800) 432-2310	Consumer Protection Division, Office of Attorney General, 301 W. 10th, Judicial Center, Topeka, KS 66612
Kentucky	(502) 564-2200 (800) 432-9257	Consumer Protection Division, Office of Attorney General, 209 St. Clair St., Frankfort, KY 40601-1875
Louisiana	(504) 342-7373	Consumer Protection Section, Office of Attorney General, P.O. Box 94005, Baton Rouge, LA 70804-9005
Maine	(207) 582-8718 (800) 332-8529	Bureau of Consumer Credit Protection, State House, Station No. 35, Augusta, ME 04333-0035
Maryland	(301) 528-8662 (800) 969-5766	Consumer Protection Division, Office of Attorney General, 200 St. Paul Pl., Baltimore, MD 21202-2022
Massachusetts	(617) 727-8400	Consumer Protection Division, Dept. of Attorney General, 131 Tremont St., Boston, MA 02111
Michigan	(517) 373-1140	Consumer Protection Division, Office of Attorney General, P.O. Box 30212, Lansing, MI 48909
Minnesota	(612) 296-2331	Office of Consumer Services, Office of Attorney General, 117 University Ave., Rm. 124, St. Paul, MN 55155
Mississippi	(601) 354-6018	Consumer Protection Division, Office of Attorney General, P.O. Box 22947, Jackson, MS 39225-2947

State	Telephone	Address
Missouri	(314) 751-3321 (800) 392-8222	Consumer Protection Division, Office of Attorney General, P.O. Box 899, Jefferson City, MO 65102
Montana	(406) 444-4312	Consumer Affairs Unit, Dept. of Commerce, 1424 9th Ave., Helena, MT 59620
Nebraska	(402) 471-2682	Consumer Protection Division, Dept. of Justice, 2115 State Capitol, P.O. Box 98920, Lincoln, NB 68509
Nevada	(415) 744-7920 San Francisco FTC	Nevada does NOT regulate credit bureaus. Send any complaints to the FTC at: Federal Trade Commission, P.O. Box 36005, 450 Golden Gate, San Francisco, CA 94102
New Hampshire	(603) 271-3641	Consumer Protection and Antitrust Division, Office of Attorney General, 208 State House Annex, Concord, NH 03301
New Jersey	(201) 504-6200	Office of Consumer Protection, 124 Halsey St., Newark, NJ 07102
New Mexico	(505) 827-6060 (800) 678-1508	Attorney General of New Mexico, P.O. Drawer 1508, Santa Fe, NM 87504
New York	(518) 474-8583	Consumer Protection Board, 99 Washington Ave., Albany, NY 12210-2891
North Carolina	(919) 733-7741	Consumer Protection Division, Office of Attorney General, Dept. of Justice, P.O. Box 629, Raleigh, NC 27602
North Dakota	(701) 224-2253	Department of Banking and Financial Institutions, 600 East Blvd. Ave., Bismark, ND 58505-0080
Ohio	(614) 466-4986 (800) 282-0515	Consumer Protection Division, Office of Attorney General, 30 East Broad St., 25th Floor, Columbus, OH 43266-0410
Oklahoma	(214) 767-7050 Dallas FTC	Oklahoma does NOT regulate credit bureaus. To complain, write: Federal Trade Commission, Dallas, TX 75247
Oregon	(503) 378-4320	Financial Fraud Section, Dept. of Justice, Justice Bldg., Salem, OR 97310
Pennsylvania	(717) 787-9707 (800) 441-2555	Bureau of Consumer Protection, Office of Attorney General, Strawberry Sq., 14th Fl., Harrisburg, PA 17120

State	Telephone	Address
Rhode Island	(401) 277-2104 (800) 852-7776	Consumer Protection Division, Dept. of Attorney General, 72 Pine St., Providence, RI 02903
South Carolina	(803) 734-9452 (800) 922-1594	Dept. of Consumer Affairs, P.O. Box 5757, Columbia, SC 29250-5757
South Dakota	(605) 773-4400	Division of Consumer Affairs, Office of Attorney General, 500 E. Capitol, State Capitol Bldg., Pierre, SD 57501-5070
Tennessee	(615) 741-4737 (800) 342-8385	Division of Consumer Affairs, 500 James Robertson Pkwy., 5th Fl., Nashville, TN 37243-0600
Texas	(512) 463-2070	Consumer Protection Division, Office of Attorney General, P.O. Box 12548, Capitol Station, Austin, TX 78711
Utah	(801) 530-6601	Division of Consumer Protection, Dept. of Business Regulation, 160 East 3rd South, P.O. Box 45802, Salt Lake City, UT 84145-0802
Vermont	(802) 656-3183 (800) 649-2424	Consumer Assistance, Office of Attorney General, Terrill Hall, University of Vermont, Burlington, VT 05405
Virginia	(804) 786-2042	Office of Consumer Affairs, Dept. of Agriculture and Consumer Services, Rm. 101 Washington Bldg., 1100 Bank St., Richmond, VA 23219
Washington	(206) 464-6684 (800) 551-4636	Consumer Protection Division, Office of Attorney General, 900 4th Ave., Room 2000, Seattle, WA 98164
West Virginia	(304) 348-8986 (800) 368-8808	Consumer Protection Division, Office of Attorney General, 812 Quarrier St., 6th Fl., Charleston, WV 25301
Wisconsin	(608) 266-9836 (800) 422-7128	Division of Trade and Consumer Protection, Dept. of Agriculture, Trade, and Consumer Protection, 801 West Badger Rd., P.O. Box 8911, Madison, WI 53708
Wyoming	(307) 777-7797	Division of Banking, Herschler Building, 3rd Floor East, Cheyenne, WY 82002

Banks Offering Secured Bankcards

Bank	Telephone	Address
American Pacific Bank	(800) 879-8757 (800) 879-8745	P.O. Box 19360 A Portland, OR 97280-9360
Bank of Hoven	(800) 777-7735	Credit Card Division, P.O. Box 9068, Van Nuys, CA 91499-4009
Bank One, Lafayette, NA	(800) 395-2556 (800) 395-2555	Credit Card Services, P.O. Box 450, Lafayette, IN 47902-0450
Central National Bank	(217) 234-6434	Broadway & Charleston Avenue, Mattoon, IL 61938
Citibank, South Dakota, NA	(800) 743-1332	Treasury Dept. 1247, P.O. Box 6218, Sioux Falls, SD 57117-9783
Community Bank of Parker	(800) 770-8472	Spirit VISA, 19590 East Main Street, Parker, CO 80134-9900
Dryfus Thrift & Commerce	(800) 727-3348	P.O. Box 6003, Garden City, NY 11530-9841
Farrington Bank	(609) 488-6206	U.S. Liberty, Inc., P.O. Box 3320, Cherry Hill, NJ 08034-9440
Fifth Thrid Bank	(800) 972-3030	38 Fountain Square Plaza, Cincinnati, OH 45263
First Consumers National Bank	(800) 876-3262	P.O. Box 2088, Portland, OR 97208-9766

Bank	Telephone	Address
First Interstate Bank of South Dakota	(800) 825-1158 (708) 515-0817	Centennial Bancard, 125 Armstrong Road, Des Moines, IL 60019-9302
First Interstate Bank of South Dakota	(800) 825-8472 (605) 330-8686	United National Processing Center, 4300 S. Louise Ave., Sioux Falls, SD 57106-9912
First National Bank in Brookings	(605) 692-2680	700 22nd Avenue South, P.O. Box 784, Brookings, SD 57006-2680
First National Bank of Marin	(714) 492-2621	The Bankcard Service Center, P.O. Box 3696, San Clemente, CA 92674
First State Bank	(302) 322-4305	P.O. Box 15414, Wilmington, DE 19885-9394
Key Federal Savings Bank	(800) 228-2230 (301) 939-0016	626 Revolution Street, P.O. Box 6057, Havre de Grace, MD 21078
New Era Bank	(908) 937-4600	New Era Credit Card Center, 675 Franklin Boulevard, P.O. Box 1369, Somerset, NJ 08875
Signet Bank	(800) 333-7116	Card Center, P.O. Box C32131, Richmond, VA 23286-8873
Texas Bank	(800) 451-0273	1845 Precinct Line Road, Suite 100, Hurst, TX 76054

Appendix 4

Restrictions on Credit Repair Companies

I. Sample Credit Repair Law

PART III CREDIT SERVICE ORGANIZATIONS

817.7001 Definitions

As used in this part:

(1) "Buyer" means any individual who is solicited to purchase, or who purchases, the services of a credit service organization.

(2)(a) " Credit service organization" means any person who, with respect to the extension of credit by others, sells, provides, performs, or represents that he or she can or will sell, provide, or perform, in return for the payment of money or other valuable consideration, any of the following services:

1. Improving a buyer's credit record, history, or rating;

2. Obtaining an extension of credit for a buyer; or

3. Providing advice or assistance to a buyer with regard to the services described in either subparagraph 1. or subparagraph 2.

(b) " Credit service organization" does not include:

1. Any person authorized to make loans or extensions of credit under the laws of this state or the United States who is subject to regulation and supervision by this state or the United States or a lender approved by the United States Secretary of Housing and Urban Development for participation in any mortgage insurance program under the National Housing Act;

2. Any bank, savings bank, or savings and loan association whose deposits or accounts are eligible for insurance by the Federal Deposit Insurance Corporation or the Federal Savings and Loan Insurance Corporation, or a subsidiary of such bank, savings bank, or savings and loan association;

3. Any credit union, federal credit union, or out-of-state credit union doing business in this state;

4. Any nonprofit organization exempt from taxation under section 501(c)(3) of the Internal Revenue Code;

5. Any person licensed as a real estate broker by this state if the person is acting within the course and scope of that license;

6. Any person collecting consumer claims pursuant to s. 559.72;

7. Any person licensed to practice law in this state if the person renders services within the course and scope of his or her practice as an attorney and does not engage in the credit service business on a regular and continuing basis;

8. Any broker-dealer registered with the Securities and Exchange Commission or the Commodity Futures Trading Commission if the broker-dealer is acting within the course and scope of that regulation; or

9. Any consumer reporting agency as defined in the Federal Fair Credit Reporting Act, 15 U.S.C. ss. 1681 through 1681t.

(3) "Extension of credit" means the right to defer payment of debt or to incur debt and defer its payment offered or granted primarily for personal, family, or household purposes.

817.7005 Prohibited acts

A credit service organization, its salespersons, agents, and representatives, and independent contractors who sell or attempt to sell the services of a credit service organization shall not do any of the following:

(1) Charge or receive any money or other valuable consideration prior to full and complete performance of the services the credit service organization has agreed to perform for the buyer, unless the credit service organization has obtained a surety bond of $ 10,000 issued by a surety company admitted to do business in this state and has established a trust account at a federally insured bank or savings and loan association located in this state; however, where a credit service organization has obtained a surety bond and establisheda trust account as provided herein, the credit service organization may charge or receive money or other valuable consideration prior to full and complete performance of the services it has agreed to perform for the buyer but shall deposit all money or other valuable consideration received in its trust account until the full and complete performance of the services it has agreed to perform for the buyer;

(2) Charge or receive any money or other valuable consideration solely for referral of the buyer to a retail seller or to any other credit grantor, who will or may extend credit to the buyer if the credit that is or will be extended to the buyer is upon substantially the same terms as those available to the general public;

(3) Make, or counsel or advise any buyer to make, any statement that is false or misleading or that should be known by the exercise of reasonable care to be false or misleading, or omit any material fact to a consumer reporting agency or to any person who has extended credit to a buyer or to whom a buyer is applying for an extension of credit with respect to a buyer's credit worthiness, credit standing, or credit capacity; or

(4) Make or use any false or misleading representations or omit any material fact in the offer or sale of the services of a credit service organization or engage, directly or indirectly, in any act, practice, or course of business that operates or would operate as fraud or deception upon any person in connection with the offer or sale of the services of a credit service organization, notwithstanding the absence of reliance by the buyer.

817.701 Surety bonds; exemption

The requirement to obtain a surety bond and establish a trust account as provided in s. 817.7005(1) shall be waived for any salesperson, agent, or representative of a credit service organization where the credit service organization obtains such surety bond and establishes such trust account.

817.702 Statement to buyer

Upon execution of the contract as provided in s. 817.704 or agreement between the buyer and a credit service organization and before the receipt by the credit service organization of any money or other valuable consideration, whichever occurs first, the credit service organization shall provide the buyer with a statement, in writing, containing all the information required by s. 817.703. The credit service organization shall maintain on file for a period of 5 years an exact copy of the statement, personally signed by the buyer, acknowledging receipt of a copy of the statement.

817.703 Information statement

The information statement required under s. 817.702 shall include all of the following:

(1)(a) A complete and accurate statement of the buyer's right to review any file on the buyer maintained by any consumer reporting agency, as provided under the Federal Fair Credit Reporting Act, 15 U.S.C. ss. 1681 through 1681t;

(b) A statement that the buyer may review his or her consumer reporting agency file at no charge if a request is made to the consumer reporting agency within 30 days after receiving notice that credit has been denied; and

(c) The approximate price the buyer will be charged by the consumer reporting agency to review his or her consumer reporting agency file.

(2) A complete and accurate statement of the buyer's right to dispute directly with a consumer reporting agency the completeness or accuracy of any item contained in any file on the buyer maintained by the consumer reporting agency.

(3) A statement that accurate information cannot be permanently removed from the file of a consumer reporting agency.

(4) A complete and detailed description of the service to be performed by the credit service organization for the buyer and the total amount the buyer will have to pay, or become obligated to pay, for the services.

(5) A statement notifying the buyer of his right to proceed against the bond or trust account required under s. 817.7005.

(6) The name and address of the surety company which issued the bond, or the name and address of the depository and the trustee and the account number of the trust account.

817.704 Provisions of contract

(1) Each contract between the buyer and a credit service organization for the purchase of the services of the credit service organization shall be in writing, dated, signed by the buyer, and shall include all of the following:

(a) A conspicuous statement in boldfaced type, in immediate proximity to the space reserved for the signature of the buyer, as follows: "You, the buyer, may cancel this contract at any time prior to midnight of the fifth day after the date of the transaction. See the attached notice of cancellation form for an explanation of this right";

(b) The terms and conditions of payment, including the total of all payments to be made by the buyer, specifying the amount of the payments to be made to the credit service organization or to some other person;

(c) A full and detailed description of the services to be performed by the credit service organization for the buyer, including all guarantees and all promises of full or partial refunds, and the estimated date by which the services are to be performed or the estimated length of time for performing the services; and

(d) The credit service organization's principal business address and the name and address of its agent in the state authorized to receive service of process.

(2) The contract shall be accompanied by a complete form in duplicate, captioned "Notice of Cancellation," that shall be attached to the contract, be easily detachable, and contain in boldfaced type the following statement written in the same language used in the contract:

NOTICE OF CANCELLATION

You may cancel this contract, without any penalty or obligation, within 5 days from the date the contract is signed.

If you cancel any payment made by you under this contract, it will be returned within 10 days following receipt by the credit service organization of your cancellation notice.

To cancel this contract, mail or deliver a signed dated copy of this cancellation notice, or any other written notice to:
—(name of credit service organization) — at
—(address of credit service organization) —,
—(place of business)— not later than midnight
—(date)—.
I hereby cancel this transaction —(date)—.
—(purchaser's signature)—.

The credit service organization shall give to the buyer a copy of the completed contract and all other documents the credit service organization requires the buyer to sign at the time they are signed.

817.705 Waivers; burden of proof; penalties

(1) Any waiver by a buyer of any part of this part is void. Any attempt by a credit service organization to have a buyer waive rights given by this part is a violation of this part.

(2) In any proceeding involving this part, the burden of proving an exemption or an exception from a definition is upon the person claiming it.

(3) Any person who violates this part is guilty of a felony of the third degree, punishable as provided in s. 775.082, s. 775.083, or s. 775.084.

(4) This section does not prohibit the enforcement by any person of any right provided by this or any other law.

817.706 Actions for damages

(1) Any buyer injured by a violation of this part may bring an action for recovery of damages. Judgment shall be entered for actual damages, but in no case less than the amount paid by the buyer to the credit service organization, plus reasonable attorney's fees and costs. An award may also be entered for punitive damages.

(2) Any buyer injured by a violation of this part may bring an action against the surety bond or trust account of the credit service organization.

(3) The remedies provided under this part are in addition to any other procedures or remedies for any violation or conduct provided for in any other law.

II. State Laws

State	Code Section	Comments
Arizona	44-1701 - 1711	Similar to Appendix. Bond ranges from $5,000 to $25,000. Buyer has three days to cancel contract.
Arkansas	4-91-101 - 109	Similar to Appendix.
California	1789.10 - 23	Similar to Appendix. Bond ranges from $5,000 to $25,000.
Colorado	12-14.5-101 - 113	Similar to Appendix.
Connecticut	36-4351	Only requires informational statement.
Delaware	6 Del. Code 2401 - 2414	Similar to Appendix. Bond is $15,000. Buyer has three days to cancel contract.
District of Columbia	28-3904, 28-4601 - 4608	Similar to Appendix. Bond is $25,000.
Florida	817.7001, .7005, .701 - .706	See Appendix.
Georgia	16-9-59	Credit Repair Services Organizations are prohibited.
Hawaii	481B-12	Prohibits Credit Repair Organizations from seeking fees based on false representations.
Illinois	121 1/2 2101 - 2116	Similar to Appendix. Requires $100,000 bond. Buyer has three days to cancel contract.
Indiana	24-5-15-1 - 11	Similar to Appendix. Buyer has three days to cancel contract.
Iowa	533C.1 - 14	Similar to Appendix. Buyer has three days to cancel contract.
Louisiana	9:3573.1 - 8	Similar to Appendix.

State	Code Section	Comments
Maine	10-101, 102, 201, 202, 301 - 305, 401	Similar to Appendix. No cancellation period.
Maryland	14-1901 - 1916	Similar to Appendix. Buyer has three days to cancel contract.
Massachusetts	93-68A - D	Similar to Appendix. Buyer has three days to cancel contract.
Michigan	445.1701 - 1708	Similar to Appendix. Owner must have $50,000 net worth.
Minnesota	332.52 - .60	Similar to Appendix.
Missouri	407.635 - .644	Similar to Appendix. Buyer has three days to cancel contract.
Nevada	598.281 - .289	Similar to Appendix.
New Hampshire	359-D:1 - 11	Similar to Appendix.
New York	GBL 458-a - k	Similar to Appendix. Buyer has three days to cancel contract.
North Carolina	66-220 - 226	Similar to Appendix, but company cannot accept any compensation until all services rendered. Buyer has three days to cancel contract.
Oklahoma	24-131 - 147	Similar to Appendix.
Tennessee	47-18-1001 - 1011	Similar to Appendix, but company cannot accept any compensation until all services rendered. Buyer has three days to cancel contract.
Texas	Bus. & Comm. 18.01 - .15	Similar to Appendix. Buyer has three days to cancel contract.
Utah	13-21-2 - 9	Similar to Appendix.
Virginia	59.1-335.1 - .12	Similar to Appendix, but company cannot accept any compensation until all services rendered. Buyer has three days to cancel contract.
Washington	19.134.010 - 134.900	Similar to Appendix.
West Virginia	46A-6C-1 - 12	Similar to Appendix. Buyer has three days to cancel contract.

Appendix 5

Additional Resources

Emotional Recovery

Books

Couples and Money by Victoria Felton-Collins, Bantam Books, 1990. $17.95.

Living Though Personal Crisis by Ann Kaiser Stearns, Ballentine Books, 1984. $19.95.

Who Do You Think You Are? How to Build Self-Esteem by Joel Wells, The Thomas More Press, 1989. $7.95.

Credit, Credit Reports and Credit Repair

Books

Credit Approved: How to Establish Credit When You Have No Credit History, How to Regain Credit When You Have a Bad Credit History by Kevin Pilot, Bob Adams, Inc., 1992. $5.95.

Credit Card Secrets You Will Surely Profit From by Howard Strong, Boswell Corporation, 1989. $29.95.

Credit Improvement Handbook by James L. Brandy and Robert A. Freiheit, Coastline Associated Enterprises, 1986. $6.95.

Credit Secrets: How to Erase Bad Credit by Bob Hammond, Paladin Press, 1989. $12.

The Credit Power Handbook for American Consumers by Daniel K. Berman, CreditPower Publishing Company, 1989. $14.95.

Fresh Start by John Ventura, Dearborn Financial Publishing, Inc., 1992. $17.95.

How to Borrow Money and Use Credit by Martin Weiss, Houghton Mifflin Company, 1990. $4.95.

How to Erase Bad Credit: A Manual for the Credit Impaired by Stanley R. Stern, Esq., D. Waldman, 1990. $9.95.

How to Use Credit and Credit Cards by Arnold Corrigan and Phyllis C. Kaufman, Longmeadow Press, 1986. $3.95.

Pearl Polto's Easy Guide to Good Credit by Pearl B. Polto with Bob Oskam, The Berkley Publishing Group, 1990. $6.95

Your Credit: A Complete Guide by Emily Card, Ph.D., J.D., American Association of Retired Persons, 1989. Free. To order, write: AARP, 601 E. St., N.W., Washington, D.C. 20049.

Brochures and Handbooks

From BankCard Holders of America (To order, see the address and telephone number in "Organizations" below.)

Consumer Credit Rights, 1990. $1.

Credit Check-up Kit, 1990. $2.

Credit Secrets Manual, 1990. $1.

How to Choose a Credit Card, 1990. $1.

How to Re-establish Good Credit, 1990. $1.

Secured Credit Cards: Selecting the Best One For You, 1990. $1.

Understanding Credit Bureaus, 1990. $1.

From the Federal Trade Commission (To order, write: FTC, Public Reference, Washington, DC 20580.):

Avoiding Credit Scams.

Building a Better Credit Record: What To Do, What To Avoid. .50.

Buying and Borrowing: Cash in on the Facts. .50.

Cosigning a Loan.

Credit Repair Schemes, 1991. $1.

Fair Credit Reporting.

Fair Credit Reporting Act.

Fix Your Own Credit Problems and Save Money.

Scoring For Credit.

Solving Credit Problems.

From the Federal Reserve (To order, write: Board of Governors, Federal Reserve System, Publications Services, MS-138, Washington, DC 20551.):

Consumer Handbook to Credit Protection Laws, 1989.

From RAM Research Corporation (To order, see the address and telephone number in the "Organizations" section below.):

Cardsearch 92, 1992. This publication lists thousands of secured and unsecured bank credit cards available in the U.S. It covers interest rates, annual fees, grace periods, cash advance fees, etc. Also offers practical credit tips. $35.

CardTrak. A monthly publication that provides up-to-date information on credit trends and secured and unsecured credit cards. $28 for six months. $50 for one year.

Secured Credit Card Report. A special report on how and where to locate secured bank credit cards. Also includes practical information on establishing and rebuilding credit. $10.

Organizations

BankCard Holders of America
560 Herndon Pkwy., Suite 120
Herndon, VA 22070
(800) 638-6407

Consumer Fresh Start Association
217 N. Church
Princeton, IL 61356
(815) 875-4078

RAM Research Corporation
Box 1700, Frederick, MD
21702
(301) 695-4660

Vehicle Financing and Renting

Brochures and Handbooks

From BankCard Holders of America (To order, write: BankCard Holders of America, 560 Herndon Pkwy., Suite 120, Herndon, VA 22070.):

Your Next Car: Leasing Vs. Buying. What's Best For Consumers, 1990. $1.

From the Federal Trade Commission (To order, write: FTC, Public Reference, Washington, DC 20580.):

A Consumer Guide to Vehicle Leasing, 1989. .50.

Buying a Used Car, 1989.

Car Rental Guide, 1989.

New Car Buying Guide, 1988.

Vehicle Repossession.

Home Financing

Books

Buy Your First Home Now: A Practical Guide to Better Deals, Cheaper Mortgages, and Bigger Tax Breaks for the First-Time Home Buyer by Peter G. Miller, Harper Perennial, 1990. $8.95.

How to Buy Your Own Home in 90 Days: A 10-Step Plan For Finding and Buying a House in Today's Market by Marc Stephen Garrison, Doubleday, 1989. $12.95.

The Common Sense Mortgage: How to Cut the Cost of Home Ownership by $100,000 or More by Peter G. Miller, Harper and Row, 1987.

Brochures and Handbooks

From the Federal Reserve Board (To order, write: Board of Governors, Federal Reserve System, Publications Services, MS-138, Washington, DC 20551.):

A Consumer's Guide to Mortgage Refinancing, 1988.

Consumer Handbook on Adjustable Rate Mortgages, 1984.

From the U.S. Department of Housing and Urban Development:

A Home of Your Own, 1990.

Wise Homebuying, 1987.

From the Federal Trade Commission (To order, write: FTC, Public Reference, Washington, DC 20580.):

Getting a Loan, Your Home as Security, 1984.

Home Financing Primer, 1990.

The Mortgage Money Guide, 1986.

Refinancing Your Home.

Second Mortgage Financing.

From the Veteran's Administration:

Federal Benefits for Veterans and Dependents, 1990.

From the BankCard Holders of America (To order, write: BankCard Holders of America, 560 Herndon Pkwy., Suite 120, Herndon, VA 22070.):

Credit Repair Clinics: Consumers Beware. $1.

Debt Management

Books

Conquer Your Debt by William Kent Brunette, Prentice Hall Press, 1990. $9.95.

How to Get Out of Debt by Michael C. Thomsett, Dow Jones-Irwin, 1990. $10.95.

How to Get Out of Debt, Stay Out of Debt & Live Prosperously by Jerrold Mundis, Bantam Books, 1988. $4.95.

Money Troubles: Legal Strategies to Cope With Your Debts by Robin Leonard, Nolo Press, 1991. $16.95.

Brochures and Handbooks

From BankCard Holders of America (To order, write: BankCard Holders of America, 560 Herndon Pkwy., Suite 120, Herndon, VA 22070.):

Getting Out of Debt, 1990. $1.

Managing Family Debt, 1990. $1.

Organizations

Consumer Credit Counseling (CCCS)
8701 Georgia Avenue, Suite 507
Silver Spring, MD 20910
(800) 388-2227

Debtors Anonymous
General Service Board
P.O. Box 20322
New York, NY 10025-9992

The Family Service Association of America
333 Seventh Avenue, 3rd Floor
New York, NY 10001
(212) 967-2740

Index

D

E

F

G

H

I

J

L

M

N

O

P

Q

R

S

T

U

V

W

Order Form

Did you borrow this book? If so, why not order your own copy? Then, you can highlight, underline, and use ***Life After Bankruptcy*** however you please.

Telephone Orders: Call Toll Free: 1(800) SO RIGHT (767-4448)

Postal Orders: Practical Publications, Inc., P.O. Box 1244, Tallahassee, FL 32302
(904) 877-2095

Make checks or money orders payable in U.S. funds to Practical Publications, Inc.

Qty.	Name of Book	Price Each	in FL 7% tax	Shipping	Total
___	***Life After Bankruptcy***	**$19.95**	____ **($1.40)**	**$3.00**	____

Please expedite my order for Charles Price's book:

☐ I have enclosed a check or money order for $_______

☐ Charge the total amount to: ☐ VISA ☐ MasterCard

Card number: ____ ____ ____ ____
Expiration date: ____/____
Phone Number: (_____)_____ - _______
Name on Card: ______________________________

Please print your complete mailing address below:

Name: ______________________________

Company Name: ______________________________

Address: ______________________________

City, State, Zip: ______________________________